FRANCIS
CHICHESTER

FRONTISPIECE : *Portrait by Sheila Chichester*

SHEILA CHICHESTER

ANITA LESLIE

Francis Chichester

HUTCHINSON OF LONDON
WITH
HODDER & STOUGHTON

Hutchinson & Co (Publishers) Ltd
3 Fitzroy Square, London W1P 6JD

London Melbourne Sydney Auckland
Wellington Johannesburg Cape Town
and agencies throughout the world

and Hodder & Stoughton Ltd, St Paul's House
Warwick Lane, London EC4P 4AH

First published 1975
© Anita Leslie 1975

Set in Monotype Baskerville

Printed in Great Britain by The Anchor Press Ltd
and bound by Wm Brendon & Son Ltd
both of Tiptree, Essex

ISBN 0 340 18316 0

*For Francis
and
Sheila and Giles*

Acknowledgements

The author extends thanks to all those who have contributed stories and reminiscences concerning Francis Chichester. Mr and Mrs Charles Chichester of Hall, Bishop's Tawton, Group Captain Patrick Chichester, Mr Geoffrey Goodwin and Mr William Wilkey, M.B.E., have been of particular assistance in describing his youth, and Colonel and Mrs G. S. Incledon-Webber of Buckland House, Braunton, and Mr W. M. Lines, C.B.E., and Mrs Lines of The Old Rectory, Shirwell, have showed their houses which form a background to the text.

Sincere thanks are also due to Sir Peter Bristow, Q.C., Mrs Clare Crowhurst, Dr Gordon Latto, Sir Alec Rose and Commander Oliver Stoney for permission to quote from their letters; and to Murray Sayle and the *Sunday Times* for permission to quote from an article.

Gratitude must also be expressed to the following who knew Francis Chichester and have lit up new aspects of his extraordinary personality – Wing Commander E. W. Anderson, Mr John Anderson, Mrs Louise Balfour, Mr Christopher Brasher, Miss Monica Cooper, Commander Erroll Bruce, Lady Dulverton, Mr George Greenfield, Colonel H. A. G. Hasler, Mr and Mrs Tim Heywood, Mr Michael Richey, the Lady Rotherwick, Sir Michael Rowe, Q.C., Lieutenant-Colonel Jack Odling-Smee, Mr Nigel Tangye.

Finally special acknowledgement must be made to Mr Philip Bates for clarifying the tragic circumstances pertaining to the sinking of the *Lefteria*.

Contents

Illustrations

1. Childhood

Beautiful as a medieval tapestry with its steep wooded hills and almost hidden winding rivers, the countryside of North Devon has remained curiously separate from the rest of England. Throughout many centuries, in scattered villages and remote manor houses, a people grew up who tended to regard intruders from the other counties with suspicion. North Devon stoutly preferred to remain a world of its own, cut off, impenetrable, hostile to newcomers, and indeed to new ideas. It became the habit of small merchants quietly to shoulder out 'foreign settlers' from Gloucestershire or Somerset, while the gentry stuck firmly to their land, never gambling, never selling, and often intermarrying so that many families seem to bear North Devon names repeated again and again in their carefully kept pedigrees.

In this fair green fastness, swept to the north by the Atlantic and guarded to the south by a great emptiness of moors, the Chichesters during six hundred years developed into a powerful tribe. Having proved their worth by the sword, in a past when only the sword could prove it, they had multiplied and spread into a top-crust landed gentry of very particular character.

The first Chichester to settle in Devon came there in 1385, when he married Thomasine Raleigh, heiress of all the land around Barnstaple. They prospered and they bred. A hundred and fifty years later, in 1537, it was recorded of their descendant, Sir John Chichester, High Sheriff of the County: 'This worthy knight was of great reputation for his many virtues but much more favoured for his issue; he had seven sons whereof four were knights, one created a baron and one a viscount, and nine daughters all married to the chiefest families in the county.' Four hundred years later found six great Chichester families each centred in a huge house surrounded by park and owning five to ten thousand acres of land. Youlston

Park and Arlington Court with adjoining walls each held a Chichester baronet; Hall and Eggerford and Calverleigh (the Catholic line) lay a few miles away. The Widdeworthy branch emigrated to Virginia in 1701.

Each village church testified in stern, unflamboyant stone memorials the dates and virtues of Chichesters and their spouses. One might have envisaged lives of bliss in a paradise where lawns and gardens made a setting for the ladies, and salmon rivers and fox-hunting for the men, but perusal of family histories reveals a cooling repetition of events; no Chichester ever seems to marry a girl less than twenty years younger than himself and she nearly always dies after the fourteenth child! Then he re-marries a widow (some of the luckier ladies lost their spouses early) and this choice would be dictated by the shooting and fishing she could provide on the deceased husband's estate. Some of the daughters married titled gentlemen, the rest had to remain at home busying themselves with household chores in the eighteenth century and good works in the nineteenth. What girls endured in this man-run world is depicted by the story of Mr Chichester of Hall who reached the age of forty-five as a sought-after bachelor. Then in 1740 he spied a pretty girl in Barnstaple, made enquiries and learned she was one of the eleven Miss Webbers of Bucklands – an estate a few miles away. He wrote to the widowed Mrs Webber concerning his interest and was invited to dinner, but so large and confused proved the family gathering (there were four sons as well) that Mr Chichester admitted bewilderment. It was decided that the daughters should be paraded singly through the drawing-room after the meal ended. Bucklands has a Queen Anne drawing-room with superb plasterwork and two doors. Each girl came in at one door, curtseyed, simpered hopefully at a possible husband and retired through the other door. When the sixth daughter entered Mr Chichester's hesitations ceased: 'You needn't send for any more, Mrs Webber,' announced the manly voice.

That was that. Pretty Henrietta whose deep-set blue eyes look out winningly from her portrait which still hangs at Hall, said good-bye to her ten sisters and considered herself lucky.

Younger sons of the landed gentry were spared the ennui of sitting at home unwanted. If the estate was large enough to allow separate farms to be carved out of it, a cadet might settle near his home and continue to live as a gentleman farmer. If not, he entered the Army, the Navy or the Church. Chichester males had a *raison d'être*. They served England. The memorials in every local church attested their deeds. And Chichesters consistently married Chichesters, preferring to look for wives among fifth and sixth cousins rather than take a chance with some flighty miss from an adjoining county.

This was a tribe which disliked innovation. Until recently, Chichester houses preferred to make their own electric light rather than be linked onto the common grid over the management of which they could have no control. Proud and brave and rigidly faithful to their own code many Chichesters seem more laudable than human.

To concentrate on the great family of Youlston Park, here Sir Arthur Chichester, eighth Baronet, lived in a vast, rambling, rather gloomy house set in a hollow. His wife bore him four daughters and ten sons of which three died in infancy. In 1879 she passed away and in 1881 Sir Arthur took the traditional step. He married the widow of Sir Bruce Chichester of Arlington Park who had died leaving one daughter, Rosalie, a great heiress. It just suited Sir Arthur to ride over to Arlington, four miles away, from Friday to Monday; the shooting and fishing were much better than his own. The new Lady Chichester did not have to change her surname, her title or her residence. She was told to stay put and her second husband would visit her at his pleasure.

Meanwhile, back at Youlston, Sir Arthur decreed that his second daughter, Norah, should consider herself in charge of the house. The other three girls married suitably. Beatrice, the elder, remained a Chichester, for she had been chosen by her very distant cousin, Mr Chichester of Hall, a descendant of Henrietta, whose home was a magnificent manor house built on a hill top on the other side of Barnstaple. Chosen is an exact word in this case, for when Beatrice was christened in Shirwell Church the twenty-two-year-old heir of Hall had attended the family gathering, remarked, 'What a pretty little thing. I should like to marry her,' and waited twenty years to do so.

Of Sir Arthur's surviving sons the eldest was laid in moth balls to inherit the family estates, the second was having a distinguished naval career, another left for California, where he was promptly shot dead, two were being groomed for local squiredom, and Charles, the youngest son but one, was, after gaining his M.A. at Brasenose College, Oxford, installed as Rector of the family church in Shirwell. In 1896 he married Emily Page, a girl who came from quite a different setting – musical and with a modest fortune, she had been brought up in London, not in high society, but in a quiet middle-class way. The hearty, arrogant, self-opinionated, conceited Chichesters must have filled her with awe, for it was in those days considered very grand indeed to belong to an ancient county family and have a coat of arms unaltered for six hundred years. Emily's white wedding gown and the pale rose satin dress in which she was presented at court are now on display at Arlington Court. One can see that she was a little woman, and by his photograph one can see the Reverend Charles was large and handsome in a heavy way.

What could a cultivated London girl have made of rural life in North Devon? How lonely she must have been in the rambling old Rectory with its wide Georgian windows looking out on so many beautiful views. Green hills, deep valleys, rivers and woods – all these lay around Mrs Chichester, but the impression she has left on those who knew her is one of sadness. Whatever her musical talent as a young girl, she became withdrawn. It was not enough to play the piano, and to accompany her husband on the five-minute walk to the old stone church below the Rectory, and to go for calls in the pony trap.

In 1897 she bore a son James, who was naturally christened in that ancient stone font where generations of Chichester babies had been held. Then, four years later, on 17 September 1901, the Rector called Wilkey, his gardener-groom, to harness up and drive the trap fast to Barnstaple to fetch a doctor. That evening a second son was born and named Francis. He was, of course, christened in the same ancient font.

The Rectory nurseries overlooked the green, steeply sloped hills around Shirwell and the first world of which Francis grew conscious was that of the spacious servants' wing with its shining stone-paved floors and the cosy kitchen which looked onto a little cobbled yard. Here old Wilkey, who cleaned the boots and polished the trap and fed the horse, would become his first friend and Wilkey's son Bill his first playmate.

From the very start Francis did not behave as a Chichester should. He was high-strung and prone to tantrums, while James, his elder brother, remained stolid and submissive. Downstairs in the kitchen little Bill Wilkey would listen awestruck to the shrill screams of Master Francis. An indignant baby eagle seemed to have hatched out in this nest of pious rooks. As the Reverend Charles had no idea that a child could be taught anything except by chastisement, the tiny boy knew a fair amount of unhappiness. When Michael Cardus, the son of the Rector at Arlington, came to play at Shirwell, he was aghast at the manner in which Francis was beaten for small offences.

Maybe the Rector suffered from a certain frustration at being merely the *ninth* son of a sporting baronet. Certainly he must have suffered certain inhibitions due to the creed he dinned into the villagers. 'Sex was wrong, except for the purpose of procreation.' Strange indeed the religion which can decree that the joys of sex have been invented by the Devil, the pangs of childbirth by God!

Mrs Chichester, growing ever quieter, remained what Bill Wilkey, who watched the scene at close quarters, would later describe as 'a dutiful wife', living obediently in a house where the emotional atmosphere could be likened to a 'refrigerator'. Apparently no affectionate utterances ever passed between the Rector and his wife, their mode of addressing each other remaining absolutely formal. At long intervals Mrs Chichester produced a child. Two little sisters were born several years after Francis. They were too young to be playmates and he never got on with his brother James, so that naturally he turned to jolly old Wilkey with his marvellous gift for telling stories in the slurred Devon accent, and then to Wilkey's son Bill, just a year older than himself.

Beyond the garden, the village and the fourteenth-century church, lay a paradise of wild hills. Francis soon grew to prefer outdoors to indoors. Within those high-ceilinged well-proportioned rooms of Shirwell Rectory lay a cold, penetrating Calvinistic mist. It was so easy to sin in that house, or even in the garden by plucking a wrong flower. When a first cousin of his own age, Patrick Chichester, came to stay the child happened to exclaim at table, 'Good Lord no –'. There was an ominous silence; then his uncle, the Rector, rounded on the quailing child: did Patrick realize that he had taken the name of the Lord his God in vain?

Patrick remembered this terrifying encounter to the end of his days – the piercing blue stare of Uncle Charles always sent chills up his spine.

If his mother loved him Francis had to guess at her feeling. As for the Rector, he made it clear that Francis was the *least favourite* of his four children. Yet this clergyman held the respect and admiration of the countryside. He had been bred and trained to command. Had he entered the Navy where his elder brother Edward was in the process of becoming an admiral, he might have attained distinction. For, though a martinet, he was just. Small boys who failed to touch their caps when he strode through the village would be caught by the ear and marched straight to their homes for punishment. But when misfortune overtook anyone in his parish the Rector's trap stood at the door, presents of food and silver half-crowns would be left along with biblical admonitions. In his way, his hard horrible way, the Rector strove to do right. He could punish himself for the sake of justice. On one occasion when he reprimanded a drunken villager the man retorted that it was all very well for the likes of him who could keep 'wine on the table at every meal' in his own home, whereas the poor could only afford the pub. Reverend Charles felt this illogical reprimand deeply. He liked his wine, but from that day forth he refused to touch it. Mealtimes grew yet grimmer.

From the very start Francis was sensitive to his own situation; he realized that he was the least-liked child in that strictly disciplined circle. So he turned elsewhere for friendship. He turned to old Wilkey, who, while driving him to infant school in Barnstaple, would recount wonderful Devon stories as the horse plodded uphill, and sometimes take him marketing or to the Fair where he saw a wonder world of swings and stalls and laughter. And naturally he turned to Bill Wilkey, a year older than himself. 'Master Francis' he had to be called, but this put no barrier between two high-spirited boys. Bill quailed like everyone else when the Rector looked his way, but he had his own home in the village to return to where smiling faces and affectionate demonstration existed. He and Francis began to explore the magic world that lay beyond the hillside village – woods and twisting streams offered a wonderland where otters, badgers and foxes abounded. Lessons done, they would roam as far afield as their legs could take them. It was a great thing to 'keep out of the way'.

Once or twice in all the long years of childhood Francis would recall a moment when his father approached a friendly gesture but it never quite came off. The mirage of possible communication occasionally flickered up during long walks. It was as if the open air and sunlight softened the veneer of a man sternly intent on repressing his own desires and emotions. There was one afternoon in particular. The Rector had spied a water-wagtail's nest built over the side of a bridge and he wanted to hold Francis upside-down by the ankles to remove an egg for his collection. But his son recoiled and would not be lifted. Such an expression of disappointment crossed the usually impassive grown-up face that years later Francis would surmise: 'If he minded missing the egg so much maybe he was human after all.' But at home the Reverend Charles dropped human tendencies and never ceased to disapprove, to snub, to chastise and to squash every outburst of enthusiasm. Even cousins who only saw him on occasional visits felt fearful and called Uncle Charles 'a most formidable man'.

Francis was, of course, aware of his numerous other relations; several Chichester uncles had married and were producing offspring, so there was an immense encirclement of cousins throughout the countryside. His four aunts had all married and he never forgot the first occasion on which, as a very small boy, he faced them all together in one room. This meeting took place in Aunt Norah's house in Barnstaple. The four large women, all with particularly enormous behinds about which they were prone to chaff each other, were seated – a terrifying array, in crackling bombasine – and little Francis had to greet each one in turn. Aunt Geraldine, who had no children of her own, took a liking to him and Francis, craving any manifestation of affection or attention, quickly responded. Aunt Beatrice, the eldest of this party, had been the baby selected as his bride by Mr Chichester of Hall at her christening. She might have done better as a parson's wife, for she took to church-going in a big way and insisted on attending three services on Sunday. In the morning she would proceed to Bishop's Tawton, four miles away, by carriage. In the afternoon she walked down the steep green field which sloped from the manor of Hall to the small stone church she had had built. Here she could see that the estate workers, tenants and domestics were in attendance, also local small farmers who wished to please. More important still, she could read the sermons in advance and dictate that which was to her liking. The next-best thing to making a sermon is correcting one and hearing it spoken. Then, refusing to disturb again the coachmen on the Sabbath, Mrs Chichester of Hall would stoutly walk all the way to Bishop's Tawton for evening service. Legend has it that no storm or snowdrift could deter her, and when a lady showed such fortitude of course the men of her family could hardly remain idling by the fireside. 'The time might come when I shall not be able for it,' she replied to remonstrances about the necessity for *three* services each Sunday. Mr Chichester, being her senior by twenty years, did not take kindly to so many hours in the pew. One dark afternoon while he was descending the steep hill from Hall he slipped in the mud and was heard by those seeking to clean his coat loudly invoking his Maker to allow 'the Devil to carry away Beatrice's church'.

After her spouse's death, Mrs Chichester wore widow's weeds for forty years, copying the same unbecoming bonnet worn by Queen Victoria. Photographs, in fact, reveal her looking like a bigger, fatter model of her monarch. When not attending to church affairs she kept busy with good works amidst the deferential but adoring peasantry. Embroidery also helped to while away the hours and the exquisite crocheted bedspreads made by Beatrice Chichester still cover the big beds at Hall.

The aunt whom Francis saw most of was Norah because she lived in Barnstaple. While her father was alive Norah had not been allowed

to marry. Sir Arthur decreed that his youngest daughter should stay
with *him* even after his own wedding to the widowed Lady Chichester
of Arlington. For many years Norah only glimpsed her beau, Dr
Manning, when he visited Youlston to attend someone's complaint.
Her secret feelings were spied and frowned on. At that time the
county families did not allow their daughters to marry doctors; that
profession had not yet become smart. The local clergymen would
often be invited to lunch, the doctor never. The taboo might have
stemmed from fear that 'shop' might creep into the conversation.
Gentlefolk could talk about religion but not about physical organs.
A doctor knew embarrassing things about the *insides*. So Dr Manning
had to woo by stealth and it was not until Sir Arthur died that Norah
dared to marry. She was by then forty-seven and grown extremely
stout. Dr Manning, a dapper little man of considerable charm, loved
her dearly, but insisted that she must do something about her figure.
Norah promised to start wearing stays and on her wedding day in
1898 she could hardly breathe for tight-lacing. But it was once and
once only. Chichesters did not like being tidied up. For the rest of
his life Dr Manning had to put up with things as they were.

These were Francis's nearer relations. A more fascinating, if tragic,
connection was Miss Rosalie Chichester, the heiress of Arlington.
Born in 1865 she had been the only child of the last Baronet of this
line. As a girl she had known joyous travel on her father's yacht and
her home was the scene of constant balls and entertainments. Then
he died leaving his country-bred daughter in the power of a stupid,
extremely selfish mother. Rosalie was never told that she owned her
beautiful home with its wide parks and magical woods. When her
mother remarried and fell completely under the influence of the
dominating Sir Arthur it may well have seemed to them *both* that
Rosalie ought to be well hidden from fortune hunters. Whether her
stepfather insisted, or advised this, the fact remains that this girl was
never allowed to talk to young men at balls and her nitwit mother
displayed surprising ingenuity in keeping her a prisoner in Arlington
Court. If ever she spied Rosalie talking animatedly to a male, she
would walk up and pinch her. Then Lady Chichester would be seen
driving her daughter home in the carriage.

It was, of course, pleasant for Lady Chichester to remain chate-
laine of Arlington and Sir Arthur preferred the sport in Rosalie's
demesne. Had she married, another man would be in charge. So the
years passed and Rosalie rode plump and beloved ponies through
her own woods without understanding they were hers, and talked
with the employees without knowing she was their mistress. Local

people must have been puzzled at the seclusion obviously forced on this gentle attractive girl but no one of legal turn of mind ever impressed on her that *she* owned five thousand acres of good rich farming land as well as her walled paradise prison.

When Francis knew Miss Chichester she had reached her late forties and was free. Sir Arthur (her stepfather, and also Francis's grandfather) had died in 1898 and Lady Chichester in 1905. But the pressure imposed during all the years of youth had rendered Miss Rosalie, who was adored throughout the countryside, incapable of readjusting herself to the idea of marriage. By the time she realized what she had inherited she was in truth wedded to Arlington – the bride of her own estate. Yet she radiated wistful tenderness – the faded photographs of her as a slim-waisted girl with her pony, or in court-gown before being presented at one of Queen Victoria's drawing-rooms (these took place in the afternoon but necessitated full evening dress), evoke a feeling of wasted potentiality. Here was a girl who, had she dared, could happily have become wife and mother. Now she collected china and paper weights and cared greatly for animals. Her kind nature and her perspicacity led her to become one of the first resolute protectors of wild life. Miss Chichester would not allow hunting within her walls – the steep, jungly valleys of her demesne led to a heronry and a sanctuary for wild fowl. Foxes, otters and badgers she specially loved, keeping her woods as their paradise. And she could be kind to a little boy.

Francis would always work for a smile. Under his father's eye he fidgeted rebelliously, with Wilkey he became obedient and eager to please, and with Aunt Rosalie he responded like a petted animal.

For the first seven years of his life, therefore, Francis could always escape from the harshness of his home into a miraculous unspoiled countryside; he had friends in the village and in farms beyond and the wonders of Barnstaple town life were amusingly revealed. The cousin he would care for most was Angela, the pretty daughter of his uncle Orlando Chichester who lived in Shirwell House set in its own wooded estate near the village. Lessons did not seem over-onerous in the local school and every moment he was free he and Bill Wilkey spent far from grown-up eyes joyously exploring the wilderness which lay beyond the Rectory garden.

2. Boyhood

In Francis's seventh year a terrible blow fell. According to English upper-class tradition this was the age at which to separate a small boy from all to which he had grown accustomed and send him to boarding school. Brother James had already spent four years at a 'prep school' at Ellerslie, seven miles away, and now it was decided to uproot Francis. His parents drove him off in the family buggy and after two hours he was suddenly left alone to adjust as best he could to a terrifying new existence. The imaginative Francis had learned the mystic joy of being alone with nature; this was now denied him. He had found a stalwart friend to fight and climb and romp with, but Bill Wilkey did not belong to the boarding-school class! The bleak stone school filled him with dismay. James, a senior boy, showed no inclination to help, in fact he immediately led his brother into trouble. At the start of his first term Francis, who was very lively and eager for fun, tried to make friends and join in whatever came his way. Unfortunately he noticed some bigger boys having a game in which they tried to prevent each other climbing into the wash-house. Francis watched them with childish excitement. Then, seeing his brother pushing through a window, he lost his head, thoughtlessly picked up a handful of sand from a fire bucket and threw it. Some grit went into his brother's eye and had to be washed out. As a punishment for this foolish, impetuous act, Francis was put 'into Coventry' for three weeks. During all this period – such a vital one for a little chap at a new school – no boy addressed a single word to him. For a seven-year-old this was a searing wound – Francis never forgot it. He felt that he had been sent to a prison where even friends were denied him. His spirit rose rebelliously but he was so small against the world – and so alone.

From the very beginning the headmaster – one of those numerous sadists who cunningly found their métier in expensive, unsupervised boys' schools – took a dislike to him. Maybe he spotted the unusual in Francis. This boy had an independence of spirit, and a capacity for joy which evidently aroused the older man's perverted inclinations. During his first term Francis was seven times sent up to wait beside his dormitory bed until this big powerful man went up to beat him on the bare bottom with a cane. The child found that he could not stop himself from trembling while he waited for the headmaster's step. Outside the windows of the dormitory were creeping vines with sparrows flitting in them and this picture remained imprinted on his mind as a visual evocation of misery. The headmaster was odd. Sometimes he would order the boys to strip off and bend over and then he would not beat them, merely enjoying apparently their trepidation.

Luckily for him, Francis kept getting ill in this establishment and this proved such a nuisance to his parents that after two years they removed him. His character had changed, however. He had been unable to make friends at this school and he had none at home except Bill Wilkey to whom it was difficult to speak of the misery and degradation imposed on him. Bill had his own troubles, but these were ordinary boyhood woes. Francis suffered even more from the prisonlike *atmosphere* of institutions than from rough handling. Later he recalled this: 'I gradually drifted into the habit of setting off on my own into an escape world of excitement and adventure.'

By the age of nine Francis was different from other boys in that he craved beauty and contact with nature in a way that was far beyond their ordinary inclinations.

His parents, perturbed at his wan appearance, chose the next school for health reasons. It lay in bracing sea air near Bournemouth and proved an altogether happier establishment. The resilient nine-year-old immediately explored his new environment, and the sandy wasteland set with perfumed pine trees delighted him. Given the slightest chance Francis would find elation. On summer mornings the boys climbed down to bathe in the sea through a chink in the cliff. Scrambling down, Francis, who had obtained a fair grounding in natural history at home, would find puss moth caterpillars on the silvery undersides of leaves. Sometimes he brought back their eggs to rear through cocoondom.

Aged eight to thirteen, the boys in a segregated boys' school might themselves be likened to chrysalises emerging from one stage to another. But it was not the policy of grown-ups to make any attempt to help them understand themselves. Ominous warnings were occasionally delivered in a specially gloomy tone but there was never any explanation as to precisely what boys must beware of.

Suddenly, a mysterious drama swept through the school. Most of the boys, having no idea of the implication, were utterly bewildered. They had all taken to creeping into each other's beds after 'Lights Out', when talking was forbidden, to whisper yarns. One night the authorities pounced, pulled off blankets and found their suspicions justified – the boys rushed guiltily back to their own beds. Each boy was questioned alone for weeks, but as none of them had heard of homosexuality, and it was financially inexpedient to expel the entire school, the headmaster finally decided merely to flog everyone and issue dire if incomprehensible warnings. The whole affair was more puzzling than traumatic.

Francis changed considerably during his years at Bournemouth. The most sensitive and vulnerable of small boys, he hardened into a rather beastly tough and eventually became head of the school. Then he could threaten and bully the boys competing in school sports – 'You have *got* to win – or else! . . .'

On one occasion, which he would deeply regret later, he seized the opportunity of ragging a pathetic new master obviously unable to control his charges during a Sunday walk. Francis, who was no longer the dear little boy who had crept through the woods to visit Miss Rosalie at Arlington, immediately recognized weakness. Running up from behind, he tipped the young man's bowler over his eyes. When the baited master lashed out with his stick he hit the wrong boy, and that of course caused laughter. By chance, a cousin saw the episode, called Francis over and severely told him off. Francis never forgot his sense of shame when he realized that he, who had suffered much from bullying, had turned bully at the first opportunity.

The holidays back in Devon remained bliss. Boys were allowed complete freedom in the countryside and Francis bicycled for miles. sometimes lying under a haystack listening to nightingales singing in the surrounding bushes. One spring day when he was eleven he set off to a favourite haunt in the woods at Arlington. He was running down its lush, sheltered valley when he saw a snake twisting through the undergrowth. He caught it by the tail, tied it up in his handkerchief and set off for home three miles away. Half-way back he caught a beetle to feed to his snake. But it paid no attention to the proffered meal and when the beetle touched its mouth it coiled up and hissed, striking Francis in a finger which immediately swelled tight and turned blue. After dancing with pain, he tied up the snake once again in his handkerchief and continued his way home, running and walking alternately. Once, as his whole arm stiffened, he knelt down in the spring sunshine and prayed not to die. He had reached a road quite close to Shirwell when he met a farmer on horseback. Francis told him the story and showed him the snake, which, to his sorrow, the man, recognizing it as an adder, promptly killed with his heel. On reaching the Rectory he found his father and recounted his trouble. 'What a thing to do, bringing the snake home! Why it might have bitten your sister,' roared the Reverend Charles. 'Get out your bicycle at once and go to the Infirmary in Barnstaple.' With his hand aching Francis pedalled the four and a half miles up and down steep hills until he reached the town. Then all grew blurred and he lost his way. Strangers guided him to the Infirmary and he found himself in the waiting-room. No sooner had he related his experience than he was led off and chloroformed while the finger was sliced open. An hour later his father arrived and Francis hazily overheard the conference concerning antidotes. If the dead snake could be found its own poison could be injected, otherwise they must await stuff from London. Actually the doctors did not know if he would survive. Later Francis rather liked reading of his adder-encounter in the local paper, but he kept thinking of this father's exclamation, 'Your *sister* might have got bitten!' It was time to accept the fact that he was the least favourite child, and yet he fought against that acceptance. This boy, who did such troublesome things, longed to be everyone's darling.

The 1914 war had broken out before Francis left his Bournemouth preparatory school to go to Marlborough, one of England's most famous colleges. No one can clearly describe a school who has not been there and the comments made by different boys vary enormously, so comment on the following four years is best made by Francis, who summed up his college thus:

... the iron discipline was prisonlike; and the food, no doubt made worse by the war, was terrible. The diet was 150 years out of date ... we felt half-starved and would have eaten anything. This feeling of starvation was certainly due to vitamin deficiency. From one term to the next we never had any fresh fruit or uncooked salad, or vegetables. There was no excuse for this because we could easily have grown these things ourselves in the college meadows ... it is no wonder that we had a general outbreak of boils at one time.

Marlborough Downs are exceptionally cold. ... There was some heating in the form rooms, but none in the dormitories. The huge upper school room where 200 senior boys lived during the day, when they weren't in actual classes, had only two open fires. Only the biggest boys were allowed to warm themselves at these fires. I decided that the occasional periods of warm-up available during the day only made one suffer more, so I wore nothing but a cotton shirt under my coat, discarded my waistcoat, and slept under a sheet only at night . . .

Most of the discipline was in the hands of the senior boys. Their sole form of punishment was beating, and this was so copiously applied for any infringement of an extensive and complicated social code, that it amounted to licensed bullying. At certain stages of their career, boys could fasten one button of their coats, put one hand in a trouser pocket, and things of that sort . . . Marlborough was a better place in the summer term. Cricket was not compulsory and one was allowed to go off on one's own . . . On a fine sunny day, bicycling along the hot dusty road, army lorries would be passing in a steady procession. Sometimes I would find a nice patch in a wood, and lie there for an hour or two under the trees, reading or watching the birds. Sometimes I would lie on the banks of a river watching the fish. These periods of comparative freedom were a great joy.

Francis Chichester was a very famous man when he looked back on the famous college which had harboured him from the ages of thirteen to seventeen.

There was something mean and niggardly about our existence at Marlborough; we seemed to be mentally, morally and physically constipated. The whole emphasis was on what you must *not* do, and I consider that I am only now beginning to shake off the deeply-rooted inhibition which had gripped me by the time I left. One instance of the effect of this is that until recently I would shake with fear if I had to get up and speak to more than half a dozen people, because the terror of doing or saying anything which would not be approved of by a mob code was so rooted in me.

There lay indeed a strange streak in the English upper classes, living in the most beautiful country, loving their homes, caring for dogs and horses and wild life, yet during this period when they ran the world's greatest empire, they thought it more important to inculcate ritual beating than to feed their sons properly. They all bred livestock on their country places and they well knew such treatment would not improve young animals.

The public school system could be excellent but it could also become a fetish. Michael Rowe* who shared a study with Francis noticed how bitter Francis became during his last year at Marlborough. He never quite understood the reason, but thought it might have been due to being kept in the Second Rugby XV.

Far more sensitive than the rest of his family and certainly attuned

* Sir Michael Rowe, Q.C.

to some vibrations of the wild earth which eluded his school mates, Francis also knew the burning ambitions of the ordinary schoolboy – he played football hard, longed to get into the First XV. He had always had to wear spectacles, but now his short sight proved an insuperable handicap. He had hoped that frenzied activity on the football field would hide from onlookers the fact that the ball passed so quickly out of his visual range. But he was not selected for the First XV. How he cursed that unfair destiny which gave him, of all people, poor eyes. Turning despondently from the football field he plunged energetically into the Officers' Training Corps. Eventually he went to camp, the youngest of two thousand boys, and found that when wearing two pairs of spectacles he could shoot extremely accurately. This increased his resolution. He would *not* let his eyes get him down.

In the autumn of 1918 Spanish influenza swept through Marlborough College. So many boys were stricken that beds ran out and Francis found himself with a high fever lying with many other boys on mattresses on the floor of the sanatorium. Some of his comrades were desperately ill. A few died. There were no newspapers, and, indeed, none of them could have sat up to read, but everyone heard that the Armistice was about to be signed. They knew what it meant when the roar of cheering crowds came through the window, but Francis was too weak to lift himself on an elbow. This was the end of the war. He resolved it would also be the end of his school life.

As the Christmas holidays approached, Francis, still shaky on his legs, but quite sure what he was about, announced that he would not be returning. Marlborough took the news coolly. If he thought he had learnt enough plenty of others waited to fill his place.

On reaching Shirwell he tried to explain to his father that school had nothing more to give him. He wanted to move on into more interesting spheres. The parson was sore displeased. How dare this tiresome seventeen-year-old announce that he was leaving Marlborough without asking permission. There stood the boy muttering about adventure at the other side of the globe just because he had read a few novels about bush-ranging.

The Rector resolved that there would be no nonsense about 'adventure'. His nephew Patrick had recently been sent to study farming in Devon. Patrick's father was paying handsomely for this instruction but maybe Francis could be apprenticed free. The Chichesters were not short of money but Francis really did not seem worth spending *anything* on. The Reverend Chichester glanced swiftly through the newspapers, saw an advertisement for a boy needed on a farm in Leicestershire, and answered it in his son's name. Before Francis quite realized what was happening he found himself packed off to a distant county where he could learn what hard work really meant, and be paid five shillings a week.

During the following icy months of early spring Francis had to get up in the dark to feed and milk fifteen cows, then he spread manure till dusk, then came more milking and the feeding of calves. The warmth of summer made things pleasanter but by then he had caught ringworm from the calves and damaged his as yet unformed shoulder muscles by carrying heavy sacks. And the sunlit days increased his longing for romantic companionship. During his seven months on this farm his employer only allowed him one day off. On this occasion he was permitted to visit the Leicester Horse Show between morning and evening milkings. This was the way in which non-paying apprentices were treated at the period. Perhaps the farmer noticed that 'the hand' had fallen in love with his pretty daughter. However that may be, he snatched at the opportunity of sacking young Chichester when he did something wrong. And very wrong it was. Having driven the milk churns to the station with an ex-stallion between the shafts, Francis had turned the dray for home, when a man who had also delivered milk by means of a frisky mare suggested they race back. Francis merrily agreed and was scorching along when a back wheel of his dray hit a stone on the footpath. Jehu flew through the air with eleven large milk churns. All landed heavily on the ground while the horse galloped on, smashed two five-bar gates and ended up in the outraged farmer's garden. Francis ran two miles hoping he could catch the runaway and do some quick repairs, but he found his employer waiting in the yard.

Incensed, the hefty farmer pulled Francis into the dining-room, knocked him down and held a chair over his head as if going to bring it down. Francis felt curiously calm, there was absolutely nothing he could do except wait to be killed. Yet he did not think the man would go that far. He felt no panic, only a terrible sadness, when he heard the daughter sobbing in the next room. Then, over-excited by such goings-on, the farm dog joined in the fray and bit his wrist. Suddenly the farmer released him. There would be no question of a tender good-bye.

It was midday before Francis left the farm; he had been working for seven hours, had run two miles fast, had been knocked down, bitten, and turned off without food. Despite his physical fitness, he felt a little dazed. He made the mistake of trying to save money by travelling back to Devon on cross-country trains. Midnight found him pacing the platform of Burton-on-Trent clasping a throbbing wrist and wondering if rabies felt like this. A careful streak existed in Francis. He had prayed to live when the snake bit him and now he looked around for a doctor. Passers-by suggested a surgery. He rang the bell in vain. Then peering through a window he spied several people laughing round a roulette table. The windowpane tap caused consternation. Figures dispersed. Then a door opened and the doctor drew him in, examined the dog bite and dressed it without asking payment. Back at the station Francis tried to rest but two plain-clothes detectives suddenly seized him for questioning. Where had he come from? Frightened of giving away a kindly gambling establish-ment he refused to say. Eventually they let him go and he boarded a train heading south-west. Half unconscious from fatigue, he curled up on a seat and when he awoke the train had passed right through Exeter and was approaching Land's End. Not until the following afternoon did he reach the Rectory and find himself struggling to explain the situation to his father. The Rector listened grimly to his son's faltering account. This was the second time that Francis had reappeared without permission. There would be no welcome, no sympathy, and certainly no allowance. He could not know about that gentle girl, but perhaps the Reverend Charles sensed, like the farmer, that Francis had done the most useless thing a useless young man *could* do. He had fallen in love.

3. Escape

And still the valleys stretched green around Shirwell and the woods tumbling to the edge of hidden salmon rivers turned to gold and then to orange till leafless grey-black patterning covered the slopes. Where earth had been cut by river or plough it showed red and rich, all except the strange cluster of high gravel hills deposited long ago by some glacier – these lay open to the wide sky, treeless downland marked by prehistoric barrows of a forgotten race. Amidst this beauty, Francis fretted. Fond as he was of the old aunts and cousins, the mental pressure of the family blanket weighed on his spirit. The next generation of Chichester males had already flitted off into recognized careers. His father's elder brother, Sir Edward Chichester, ninth Baronet, had died, leaving four sons and six daughters all doing well by conventional standards. The eldest son, after serving in the Navy throughout the war, was now retired as a Commander, and a daughter, Victoria, had married Sir Gilbert Wills,* Director of the British American Tobacco Company. George Chichester's son, Patrick, who was Francis's contemporary, had enjoyed *his* expensive agricultural training. Although now fitted to be a gentleman farmer, he was contemplating the Royal Air Force.

Aunts Norah and Geraldine had no children, but Aunt Beatrice's two Chichester sons were long settled as country gentlemen and Aunt Evelyn's six sons and five daughters had grown up to fit into orthodox moulds, trustworthy and respectable. Chichesters who did not inherit fortunes were expected to marry them. Only Francis did not seem to realize that life is a weighty matter. He kept talking about adventure. His mother seemed not to notice that her son

* Later first Lord Dulverton.

existed – her gaze went right through him, calm, indifferent. He wondered if she had been happy in Shirwell. Indeed, now that he was old enough for such speculation he wondered if she had cared for some other man – some man who addressed words to her that were not purely formal. He overheard old Wilkey calling Mrs Chichester a 'dutiful wife' – whatever that meant. Could it mean her intense interest in whether there was a spot on the white linen cloth of the dining table?

Every Sunday Francis sat beside her in the family pew listening to endless sermons. Did *she* believe all this about retribution? Her face remained expressionless except when the girls clung to her petticoats. He would never understand her. Nor would he really understand any member of his family. How did one become a grown man in this atmosphere? On the other hand, how did one escape?

Francis started answering advertisements in the employment columns. Short sight closed many openings for him; he had made a fine hash of farming, and it was clear that no capital would be available to launch him in business. He had proved himself most ungrateful. His expensive education was now over and funds must cease.

In the Rectory, trite conversation at mealtimes grew ever more insufferable. But he had to eat, and paid work was extremely difficult to find. Francis passed his eighteenth birthday in deep depression. So old. Nothing achieved. Nothing in view either. All through October and November he attempted to discover some job. Of medium height and very strongly built, he was quick on his feet and had exceptionally powerful arms and shoulders – rendered even stronger by seven months of hard labour and carrying heavy sacks.

With the young village carpenter, George Moore, as sparring partner, he practised boxing – the one sport which short sight did not hinder. But no one paid you to be a boxer unless you were very good indeed and the only obvious result of this training was a broken nose. Each night he opened the wide square-paned window of his room and looked wistfully out over the silvered mists. Was this life?

The Rector watched sardonically. He could pride himself on one satisfactory son. James, virtuous and submissive, had gone to Sandhurst. After the Army, banking would be his career. Respectable and safe.

One morning, Francis set off early to ride his bicycle forty-five miles to Exeter and search hard for a job. He was quite a good mechanic, but the dozen or so garages to which he proffered his services had no vacancies. Unemployment was rife; there were many men on the dole. In the evening Francis bicycled wearily home. He felt that his father enjoyed watching his failures.

The Rector was, in fact, slowly turning over possibilities. He had no faith in this son; he had never really liked him, but he did not want to be embarrassed by a dud in public. As the boy had talked of yearnings for adventure at the other side of the world, why not let him have it?

There happened to be a ship refitting in Plymouth prior to sailing for New Zealand. Francis longed to sail on her and the Rector agreed that his son should go out – not as a black sheep, but as a likely farming apprentice. Impoverished younger sons often went to farms and New Zealanders had a term for the practice. It was called 'cadeting' and the youth lived as one of the family. Having left school six months early and been fired from his first farm job, Francis would be sent off with a 'remittance man' aura, but he had one good friend awaiting him. Ned Holmes, a New Zealander whom he had met on various shooting parties, had always promised him a welcome and would find him a job.

Pleased with his son's idea, the Reverend Charles purchased a steerage ticket and told Francis how lucky he was. Francis rejoiced. He bid a warm farewell to the Wilkeys and kissed his young sisters and his cousin Angela. When the moment came to part from his parents there did not seem to be anything to say except 'Good-bye, Mother' and 'Good-bye, sir'. But the Rector was in an affable mood. It was all turning out satisfactorily. He felt generous, and not wanting any son of his to face a new continent entirely destitute, he placed ten gold sovereigns in Francis's hand. 'Oh! thank you – thank you, sir.' The train rolled out of Barnstaple towards Exeter, passing the tiny stations with curious ancient names. Francis did not want to be seen off by any member of his family. He wished to savour to the full the excitement of his going, but James insisted on travelling to Plymouth with him. It was most aggravating, just when Francis wanted to look out of the window, mentally pulling up his roots and indulging in the luxury of a dramatic farewell to his countryside, that this uncongenial brother would keep chatting about the importance of making good.

Before they reached the port James had injured Francis's fragile pride. 'I think I need a revolver,' said Francis. His brother jeered. Francis scowled and placing his gold coins in a money-belt around his waist, resolved to defend them with his fists. It was a relief when the ship sailed and he found himself alone, heading for a new world, far from the oppressive atmosphere of the Rectory. Nor for ten years would he see a member of his family again.

It was December 1919. The war had been over for more than a year and men were settling into new patterns, scattering over the face of the world looking for jobs. Crowded quarters and vile food increased everyone's seasickness, but as the ship left the Bay of Biscay and headed southward, with the winds growing balmy and phosphorescence gleaming in the waves, Francis felt overwhelmed by the romance of the voyage. He had never left England before and the sight of the ship's prow cutting into the waves moved him deeply. He would stand in the bows at night listening to the swish of the water and watching the stars change into their southern patterns. At this stage Francis Chichester was lively enough and agile, but he found it hard to emerge from the shell of his upbringing. Ridicule and punishment had taught him to be nervous of doing wrong. At the slightest rebuff he would retreat into himself and freeze. It was the company of rough, uninhibited men that helped him to find release from self-consciousness and emotional tension. And his prowess as a boxer showed up during matches.

At Durban, one of the trimmers who shifted clinkers in the stoke-holds deserted, leaving the watch one man short. 'George' Chichester promptly volunteered to sign on. He now called himself George, fearing that Francis might be thought cissy. His six mates of the watch were a tough batch of London-Irish, but they treated 'George' as a comrade and he could shovel coal with the best. It was gruelling work and he often felt near the end of his tether, but that harsh farm employment had taught him how to drive himself and he never missed his task in the hot furnaces even when older, stronger men collapsed.

During the stormy weather the watch shovelled ten hours a day – four hours on, eight off, followed by six hours on and six off. After each watch they washed the coal dust from their bodies and stuffed themselves with food. Rations were plentiful but, probably owing to vitamin deficiency, they always felt ravenous and nearly every day a fight occurred over the share-out of food. Sometimes knives were drawn.

On reaching New Zealand, young Chichester proudly drew £9 in wages and a ticket endorsed (unlike his early school reports) with 'Very Good'. He met Ned Holmes and soon found himself posted to a famous sheep station. This family was, however, extremely wealthy and lived in a formal fashion which did not appeal to our hero. Francis discovered that instead of falling into a Wild West setting,

C

he would be expected to dress for dinner. The impression he gave his host-employer was of an 'extremely wild young man'. After three weeks the farm manager sacked him on the grounds that his bad eyes might prevent him spotting ewes cast on their backs at lambing time. But Francis could, through spectacles, see well enough to shoot running rabbits with a rifle. He had specially trained himself to overcome short sight. So maybe the manager was thinking about his young daughter. Reserved as he was, Francis could not control the expression of adulation which crossed his face when looking at a pretty girl. Guileless and ignorant and painfully susceptible to the fair sex, Francis Chichester presented an open book to irritable elders.

He next found employment on a sheep station thirty-eight miles from the nearest township and hoped the job would prove less tame. Here he had to work alone with one Arthur, a riding-shepherd who could control sheepdogs from a mile distant. Francis and Arthur had to cover two thousand acres of steep volcanic hills cut through by bramble-deep gullies. Three thousand sheep and two hundred head of cattle grazed on the blue rock. The entire day was usually spent in the saddle. When the time came for mustering the sheep, both shepherds would start off in early-morning moonlight to drive the herds out of the hills into prepared paddocks where the dogs corralled them with thrilling exactitude. Except for the yearly main-shearing, Arthur and Francis had to undertake every job themselves. They dipped the sheep to kill parasites, castrated young rams and themselves did the 'dagging' which meant a short clip of tail and hind legs with hand shears. As under-shepherd, Francis had to kill and dress the hoggets selected for food. 'I shall never forget,' he would write, 'how my knees trembled when I killed my first sheep and the blood spurted out in beats as I cut its throat. I think that few mature people would eat beef or lamb if they had to kill the animals first.'

Arthur was extremely practical. He washed up after every meal, and insisted on a domestic tidiness unknown to the expensively educated English youth. Once Arthur attempted a holiday off the ranch but he could not bear being away and returned unexpectedly to find his underling had not washed up for six days. Francis felt most contrite under the older man's silent disapproval.

In its way it was a wonderful life, but Francis liked change, and when the visiting owner refused to raise his wages from fifteen to twenty-five shillings a week, he gave notice. The next farm to accept him paid the princely sum of fifty shillings a week. There were eighty horses here and youngsters had to be broken in by just sitting

34

out the bucking. Much of the land had recently been reclaimed from virgin forest. Trunks of great trees, too heavy to drag away, lay on the ground and when mustering cattle the horses would jump these at full gallop. Francis enjoyed everything – the riding, the shearing, working on the sawmill, and after the drab school years of foul food in wartime England, he enjoyed *eating*! Social life began to appear less onerous. Occasionally he asked permission to ride away to a dance. There he would overcome shyness in rhythm. Dancing was like boxing, an activity in which short sight proved no handicap.

Two years passed, and there he was – mahogany brown, hard and fit, able to earn his living, discontented. He had survived many rough adventures, including nearly drowning in a river flood – yet he felt a failure. Long hours alone in the open air stirred up new ambitions. Now he longed to be an author, a great writer in fact. After earning enough money on the farm, Francis installed himself, as he had heard authors do, in a quiet room in the nearby country town. There he sat, pen in hand, conscientiously perusing a book entitled *How to Write Short Stories*, but no masterpieces appeared.

Crestfallen, Francis decided to see more of life before writing about it. He packed his bag and took a steamer from North Island to South Island. After crossing the Southern Alps in a stage coach pulled by five horses, he reached the West Coast and found a job at a bush timber-mill. His fellow-workers proved a dull suspicious lot and as soon as Francis heard rumours of a gold strike he was off with a pack on his back into the virgin forest. They told him a trail had been blazed through dense jungle by hatchet marks on trees every fifty or a hundred yards, but these were often undiscernible. Eventually he found himself in a small creek and realized there were no notched trees in sight. He cast around and for a time mistook a deer track for the trail. Suddenly Francis knew he was lost. For a moment panic paralysed him. He longed to hurry wildly through the bush. The wise thing must be to rest while his senses revived. Forcing himself to remain calm he rolled up in his blanket and deliberately ordered himself to sleep. Dawn found him staring up into branches that blotted out the sky and trying to recollect each yard he had travelled. He now became aware of himself as a living, calculating creature lying alone in a vast rain forest. He carried no compass, but hoping to get a bearing on the sun, he plodded up a steep, moss-covered hill. At the summit he climbed a tree but the leaves were so thick that he could see nothing. Again panic swept over him and again he forced his mind to tick coldly. If he could not find the original stream it would be reasonable to follow any creek leading downwards until it reached the sea. Slowly, carefully, he began to look, then suddenly he recognized a portion of his lost stream. He retraced his trail, always keeping a notch in sight. At the end of a long day Francis reached the log hut, crawled in and slept unquestioned by the other mining prospectors. Next morning when he had sufficiently recovered, he asked naïvely enough how one made a fortune out here. The men, who had been at the game for a lifetime, explained that they had already pegged out six miles of claims by prodding through the moss. It seemed hardly likely that a newcomer, without tools, could follow their claims, much less discover new gold for himself. So it was back to the sawmill, carrying two pieces of quartz in which the glint of gold could be seen under a microscope. It had been an adventure in which he'd had practice in not letting himself die stupidly.

He would now become a coal miner. This was curious work. Instead of being lowered in a cage into the bowels of the earth, these miners had to climb two thousand feet before entering a tunnel in the face of a coal-capped mountain. Francis liked his mates, and they liked him. His very English accent made them laugh and his humour appealed to them. They thought he was a ship's steward who had run away and he didn't seek to dispel this impression. Boxing prowess impressed the miners and they soon elected him to be their middle-weight representative. With sparring partners who treated him as if he were a professional, young 'Chester', as he now called himself for easy pronunciation, travelled to West Coast competitions and enjoyed his own popularity.

When a strike grew imminent, Francis as a member of the miners' trade union stood up to make a speech, but he couldn't resist joking and the meeting broke up in laughter. Although this mountain mining was the hardest work he had ever known, there was always a touch of excitement in entering that cave where a network of tunnels divided the seam into pillars. After each long day the men would walk down the mountain and, muscular as he was, Francis often found his legs trembling with fatigue. It was difficult to pass the shack-pub at the hill's base and a pint of beer tasted incredibly good. Gradually Francis followed the general form; his pint became two pints, then turned into three, four, five sweet pints. After that something jolly usually happened – a fight or a song. Eventually Francis overdid it. He weaved home to fall over into the fire built to heat his bathwater. Another lesson – stop at five pints.

Shirwell village could hardly have recognized the lusty young man who gave himself a twentieth birthday party. Francis invited a few friends to enjoy a ten-gallon keg of beer in his wooden hut. The guests played poker and two-up until a huge miner, subject to delirium tremens, went berserk. To carry him away two men were needed for each leg and two for each arm. Francis observed this display with interest. What forces were latent in a human being! Did one have to be mad to have that strength? Could he himself not discover the trick – if only he could find the right way to apply his willpower he could do *anything*, literally *anything*.

The other miners did not entertain such reflections. They vanished each morning into the cavernous mountain-face, drew their wages, drank, gambled, fought, and came to various sticky ends. He basked in the warmth of their approbation, but one day young 'Chester' looked seriously at a drunken comrade and knew he did not want to end like that.

It was time to move on. He would try 'fossicking'. This meant living in the bush and looking for gold in crevices, shovelling hopeful-looking dust into long boxes and washing it out in rivers. With a partner called Dibbs Jones, Francis set off. They carried food and gear for eight hours through the wilderness to a hut long abandoned by previous diggers. Here they settled in. By day they dug, and searched, and washed out handfuls of glinting dust. At night they lay in exhausted slumber. Occasionally Dibbs went to town to buy food, but when he reached the shops he was inclined to go on a binge. Francis could never know when he would return or in what state. Once he was left alone in the bush for ten days and he hated it. Despite the beauty of these forests Francis was too young to relish solitude. The exquisite silvery notes dropped one by one by the bell birds increased his loneliness. His thinking slowed 'until it seemed to be done word by word with long periods between'. During the day he worked feverishly, half-expecting to strike it rich. At night, after cooking his supper he curled up miserably, longing for company. Once when he grew hungry he killed and ate a lovely kaka, the New Zealand parrot-bird, after attracting it by false squawks made by scratching a stone on a tin. Later he regretted this, just as he was sorry he had tormented the young schoolmaster in whom he had spotted weakness. Hunger is its own excuse, but Francis had a curious retentive mind. He never ceased to regret certain acts.

After Dibbs's return, much the worse for alcoholic wear, Francis insisted that in future he would make the eight-hour ration trek himself. Once he returned to find Dibbs had discovered a small tin of gold cached underneath the hut and long forgotten. This stimulated fresh hopes, but after another six months passed they had still found almost nothing. Eventually Francis returned to civilization carrying his biggest nugget; it weighed three-eighths of an ounce and later he made a ring out of it for a girl. A thin little ring for a thin little romance.

4. Fortune-hunting

Francis had left England with ten gold sovereigns – nothing but these and his dreams. At least there had been no tears, no emotional hold. Now three years spent earning his own living, with the roughest and strongest of men, had transformed the uneasy schoolboy into a husky fellow of twenty-one. 'Chich' as he would henceforth be called in New Zealand, revelled in the open-air life and above all in the excitement of searching for gold. He now possessed an extremely strong physique, but he longed to do something *clever*, to attain literary fame or to startle the world with some invention. To a certain extent he had emerged from that crisp English chrysalis, but he re-mained a late developer and pathetically naïve. Although still tongue-tied in the presence of pretty girls, he never learned to keep his face free of a beaming expression which caused parents to frown and whisk away their daughters.

Where lay fortune? And what *was* fortune? He set a target for himself of £20 000. With that capital he could regard himself as a rich man. New ideas excited him. 'Why don't you become a book agent?' asked a man in a pub. 'What's that?' A book agent appar-ently was a man who wandered about selling books, door to door. It could be done in Australia, *where people read*. Francis turned his face toward the ocean. But he only reached Christchurch. There a newspaper editor to whom he was trying to sell gold-dredging photographs, suggested that instead of sailing to Australia he should travel round canvassing for subscriptions for the *Weekly Press*. Francis gave it a try. When he started ringing doorbells in Wellington his sales talk proved so successful that the paper soon regretted having promised a big commission and called the whole thing off. Confident in his own power of persuasion, Francis then tried selling a system of book-keeping to farmers. It was onerous but he determined to stick it for one year. He bought a motor bicycle and set off to cover the whole of North Island. The motor cycle skidded on the clay roads after every shower of rain, so he paid out the frighteningly large sum of £120 for an old hooded Ford, put a bicycle and tent in it, and drove away to cover the territory systematically. He could pitch camp within half an hour. Then each morning he would pedal away on the bicycle to make personal contact. He devised a definite method of salesmanship. Each day he must visit five farms and obtain at least two sales. Then he would pack up. This self-imposed discipline prevented him either slacking or over-extending himself.

After a year he knew New Zealand extremely well and out of £700 earned he had saved £400. Once again he considered Australia, but on reaching Wellington he loitered there enjoyably with a friend, Harold Goodwin. Harold often took him sailing in a canvas canoe of his own design, but Francis did not seem particularly interested in sailing. He was restless, ambitious and determined to find something 'different'. Then Harold's brother Geoffrey asked him to become a partner in the land agency which he had recently started.

What was a land agent?

A book agent travelled round selling books. A land agent stayed put selling land.

Francis placed his entire year's savings into Geoffrey Goodwin's venture and this proved a financial success. 'Goodwin and Chichester' opened their office in a dilapidated old shop, and the commission they obtained through selling fire insurance paid the wages of an office girl. Francis had never taken any interest in houses, now he set about learning how they were built, which were likely to stand up and who wanted to buy them. Geoffrey Goodwin thought it amusing that his new business partner did not even know what a mortgage was! (Geoffrey knew little more himself.)

After three years devoted to purchasing land and real estate, Goodwin and Chichester Limited moved to grander premises. They bought an old wooden shop, had it jacked up, transported, and re-settled on concrete piles in the main street. The weatherboard sides of the dwelling were hidden by stucco on expanded wire netting. Francis proved an inflammable 'ideas man'. When Geoffrey suggested an eye-catching sign above the office veranda, Francis insisted that a large plywood top hat would arrest attention, and when they were promoting a series of land sales in sections he devised the idea (now often used in advertising) of writing every second FOR SALE upside down. Geoffrey was less willing to attract custom by the ridiculous, but he finally agreed to *one* notice being upside down. This was a mistake, because it looked like a mistake.

Goodwin and Chichester Limited rapidly became a 'smart firm'. Soon Geoffrey and Francis were able to purchase a beautiful fifty acres of wooded land lying beside a stream. They divided it into fifty allotments for weekend cottages. Francis regretted destroying the wonders of unspoilt nature, but he enjoyed working on this place during the planning period. He found this particular effort fulfilling and creative although he had to destroy in the process. Often he would picnic alone beside the stream, surrounded by tiny-leaved birch trees with cicadas buzzing in the heat, and wonder what kind of different careers might evolve from this present work. Occasionally when the chance came his way he enjoyed boxing. Less occasionally he had a fight. Francis seldom took a dislike to anyone, but he liked using his fists.

Then he and Geoffrey sold out their agency business to develop a big property of over a thousand acres. Francis grew pine trees from seed in his own back garden, and it was fun watching the little pine-needle seedlings emerge with the seeds on their backs. He planted out these experimental seedlings in rows six feet apart, with nine feet between seedlings. They grew well, so he started a tree nursery over a hill, and soon employed several men in planting. In the wonderful New Zealand climate pines could shoot up six feet in a year. Eventually they owned a million trees. It was a big project. Miles of roadway were laid down and three teams of surveyors kept at work. Small patches of embellished land had to be constantly sold off in order to pay for the whole scheme. In time they used a sales force of thirty, and Geoffrey proved himself the best of the lot. Francis discovered that he had no sales talk. He became embarrassed when lauding things which belonged to himself. By his twenty-sixth birthday his turnover equalled £10 000 a year. Geoffrey Goodwin says that his 'pranks and tempers' kept them all amused. But he amused men, not women. In close relationships he became shy and inhibited just as he did about selling his own property. Although Geoffrey was sometimes surprised at 'audacious remarks', young Francis could not be considered a success with the ladies. Women are not really attracted by muscle and vision. They like security. The initial attack was always too violent and he did not flatter them by a habit of suddenly losing interest and going off at a tangent concerning some plan which happened to catch *his* attention.

In business his vitality proved its own reward, in love he called himself a 'disastrous failure'. The trouble may have stemmed from a basic desire for Great Romance with capital letters. When Francis had finished work each evening he returned to his bed-sitter in a house possessing a marvellous view over the harbour. A strip of city lay below him with the wharves where liners and cargo ships were constantly docking, unloading, loading up, sailing off. At night the twinkling lights of the moving ships moved him to emotional despair and no one guessed his loneliness. A view is seldom enough. To a virile young man, highly ambitious, highly strung, it is worse than not enough. Beauty made Francis even more unhappy, by stirring up longings. It wasn't merely sex that Francis craved, but a woman he could talk to. A mature woman who would perceive the quixotic wit and the lion heart behind those thick lenses. As Tolstoy's aunt pointed out, *'Rien ne forme un jeune homme comme une liaison avec une femme comme il faut'*, but this type of woman hardly existed in Wellington. No one entertained the intelligentsia which he now imagined would develop him. In fact, few of his cronies entertained at all. At eighteen Francis had scorned dressing for dinner and only wanted miners for chums. Now he craved a salon of cosmopolitan houris.

Geoffrey Goodwin was contentedly married. Sometimes they went off on a male mountain climbing expedition, but Francis needed more! He embarked on what he describes as 'a wretched series of love affairs'. But such mawkish infatuations could hardly be termed 'love affairs'. In an almost hysterical sprint to ease emotional cravings, Francis fell in love with a woman whom he *thought* he hated. When she showed her utter boredom Francis thought he'd go mad. One night he motored forty miles just to stare in the dark at the window-pane of her bedroom. Then he motored back ill with unrequited love. Next morning he went to work looking haggard.

When the tall bored blonde sailed for Australia, Francis bought a ticket to Sydney, 1400 miles away, and hid in his cabin until the ship had sailed. The lady in question expressed extreme displeasure when he emerged to make his presence known. 'What was so maddening about this affair was that I knew all the time that we were not suited to each other', Francis would one day write, but he could not at the time organize his thoughts or abandon the chase.

On reaching Australia – that continent which had always lured him – Francis suffered from a loneliness even more piercing than that he had known in his bed-sit. He took himself to the theatre knowing she would be there, just for the agony, it seems, of watching her sit beside another man and hearing her laugh. 'It was a distinctive laugh, a ringing melody; it may have been too loud, but it slashed my heart in two that night. What a brutal thing modern love can be; how I wished I had been loving in the Stone Age so that I could have grabbed her by the hair, or dragged her off, or been killed in the process by a rival.' Sympathy must be extended to the blonde. Francis must, at this period, have been extremely tiresome.

Amidst other relationships, all far too platonic for a young man's taste, there occurred one hour of 'interesting adventure'. 'Chich' had motored a lady friend out to certain sand-dunes, a usual resort for sweethearts, and induced her to sit down beside him. Suddenly she whispered, 'Look! Over there.' It was a dark, overcast night and he could only see silhouetted on the crest of a sand-dune, the form of a man creeping on all fours. When he disappeared, Francis knew that he must be coming towards them. It was, for him, a thrilling moment. He was just in the mood for a fight. Not a sound could be heard above the subdued roar of the Pacific breakers and the rustle of dune grass in the breeze. Wondering if the stalker carried a gun or a knife, Francis took off his spectacles and passed them to his companion to hold. She squeezed his arm and whispered, 'There!' He stared into the dark until a black form appeared creeping nearer. When he reckoned the distance to be about six feet, Francis sprang. The man bolted away towards the beach and fell at full speed. Francis jumped on him, pinned down the spread-eagled arms with his knees, and seized his throat with both hands. Great fun. When the captive ceased struggling Francis lightened his hold. 'Now explain.' The fellow gasped some story about looking for his girl and staggered off. Francis really enjoyed the evening; it had not been dull. The actual sensation of hurling himself into physical combat enchanted him. This was what he really desired – to pummel some other male to pulp while a pretty girl looked on – holding his spectacles! How disappointing when she wanted to go home.

By now Francis had the makings of what careful parents could regard as a husband of substance. At the age of twenty-three he crowned a long series of frustrating liaisons by marrying a very young girl. He had met her when ringing doorbells for the newspaper. Muriel was one of eight children living with a widowed mother in financial straits. Her exquisite blue eyes framed by black lashes and magnolia skin enthralled every man who set eyes on her. Francis desired her passionately and as there were other suitors hanging around he asked her to marry him. Even before the marriage took place he sensed the mistake, but, unable to think clearly in the tangle of feelings and determined to have his way with her, he let the ceremony go through. It was most unfair of him. At this stage Francis was not fit to be anyone's husband, much less that of a naïve young girl who needed kindness and consideration. Like most men in their early twenties, he was exceedingly selfish. When Muriel bore a still-born son he appeared to be sorrier for himself than for her. Then later, when she bore another boy, he showed only moderate interest. In her gentle way Muriel tried to hold him, but his energy exhausted her and he hated a woman fussing around the house. He did not really want a home; it made him feel caged. Muriel needed a domesticated husband, not this tempestuous, highly sexed egoist. She was neither clever nor hard. Francis, unable to contain the seething cauldron of his own ideas, was incapable of being 'thought-ful' to a wife. Within three years the marriage was over. Muriel returned to her mother's house, taking baby George with her. Francis was glad that he was now earning enough to be able to provide an adequate allowance. The marriage had been a complete failure, so Francis crossly threw it out of his mind. Sometime, somewhere, he would find a woman he could talk to.

The first woman who really understood him, was Alice, Baroness von Zedlitz. She was perhaps twenty years older than Francis and her German husband, a most erudite and cultivated man, had settled in New Zealand before the war. The two von Zedlitz children were in their late teens – younger than Francis. When Louise, the daughter of the house, first saw him she reported: 'I met an extra-ordinary man today – very rough – carrying on like a working man – and yet somehow a gentleman. I can't think *what* he is.' Perhaps that would always be a description of Francis Chichester – no matter what he wore or how he behaved, somehow a gentleman.

Francis met the von Zedlitzes and was charmed by the baron's conversation and grateful at being allowed the run of his library. Then the baroness encouraged him to pour out his aspirations. It was extraordinary for Francis to find an older woman who listened to him and understood him. Baroness von Zedlitz soon discovered a very different young man to the tough, truculent one shown on the surface – different, but always difficult. There seemed to be many layers of Francis Chichester.

The von Zedlitzes had liked pretty little Muriel and they tried to befriend both sides during the hopeless struggle to 'make a go of it', but it was really Francis's conversation which made him so welcome in their house. These were the first people who recognized the originality of his mind.

5. Finding Wings

Geoffrey Goodwin was an enterprising fellow. Twice his ideas changed Francis's life. Geoffrey had become intrigued by the possibilities of flying, and he argued hopefully that a fortune might be made out of civil aviation. Francis had never been interested in aeroplanes and he did not immediately show enthusiasm. It was Geoffrey who held forth and Francis who queried. They were wonderfully different. 'You know,' said Francis, 'we are like Gilbert and Sullivan. We couldn't get on apart.' Then, together, they formed the Goodwin-Chichester Aviation Company Limited and bought two Avro Avians intended for lucrative joy-rides over the country. Geoffrey had an idea that later on an efficiently run service might be used for business purposes as well as for pleasure. It was a courageous venture, needing a lot of capital. To his surprise Francis discovered that his first flight made him 'wildly excited'.

The aim of this aviation company was simply to popularize pleasure flights. Having found a suitable landing-field, Geoffrey and Francis employed four top-class pilots. Six thousand people paid for joy-rides in their planes, but so much repair work was needed that the Company suffered financial loss. The pilots, experienced in handling heavier military planes, found the light Avians too fragile to land on grass and were continually smashing undercarriages. Exasperated, Francis and Geoffrey themselves went to the New Zealand Air Force station for flying lessons. They were taught in an Avro SO4K, a plane in which propeller and engine went round together, making it impossible to throttle back when landing; instead the ignition had to be cut and if a bad landing occurred the pilot would try to cut in again and hope for the best.

Francis showed no aptitude for flying. He took nearly three times

the time needed by the average pupil. Perhaps it was a curious perfectionist streak built deep in his nature that held him back. Unable
to take short cuts in learning, he had to master each step completely
and practise it over and over, carefully judging height and improving
his landings. After twenty-four hours of dual instruction he still could
not fly alone. It was really very peculiar. Many years later, in a
letter to the author, Geoffrey Goodwin would try to analyse this
unusual basic slowness.

Francis's chief credit lies in his determined will to master things he found
naturally most difficult. Generally I would say he could only concentrate
on one thing at a time, once he started to fly that was all he could think of.
He did not learn easily as we did. But in the end he went on and left us
'sitting' as it were.

Certainly Geoffrey had never guessed that this idea of plunging into
civil aviation would take 'Chich' right away from him. Once Francis
had the feel of flying, selling property would never interest him again.
'Making a fortune' now only meant a fortune to pay for his own
plane!

Meanwhile Messrs Goodwin and Chichester over-stretched their
resources by trying to run five different private companies. Trying
to kill so many birds with so many stones can result in a very small
bag, and Francis became over ready to hand all the boring financial
side to his partner while seeking fresh excitements himself.

Eventually 'Chich' announced that having earned his basic target
of £20 000, he ought to return to England to see his family. He tended
to ignore the fact that this capital was tied up in land purchased by
use of bank overdrafts, but he could not know that a world depression
was looming. Secretly Francis had resolved that by hook or by crook
he would finish his flying training, then buy a plane to fly back to
Australia himself. This would be a terrific adventure and if he could
break a record the flight might pay for itself. 'Only you would think
of breaking records before you're out of flying school,' teased
Geoffrey, but Francis was off. With about a thousand pounds
squeezed out of the various companies, he decided to travel slowly
across America looking at aircraft. No sooner did he reach Los
Angeles than he fell ill. In the long letters he wrote to Geoffrey from
hospital he poured out his heart, but he never said what was wrong
with him. After recovering, he travelled all over the continent trying
out the small planes which were on the American market. None of
those shown him in demonstration flights seemed quite suitable and
three machines crashed between the time of making an appointment

to view and his reaching the airfield. These were the very early days of flying, and plane firms were trying to prove how safe aviation was, while their models kept tumbling out of the air.

On 22 July 1929 he reached Southampton in the *Berengeria* to be met by his sister Barbara. They went to stay with Aunt Mary, their mother's sister, at 87 Cadogan Place, in London. Francis could talk of nothing but the joys of flying, and such was his enthusiasm that Aunt Mary announced she also wanted to take lessons. Every morning Francis travelled down to Brooklands where he found the flying lessons to be first-rate though painfully expensive. He had top-class instructors, and although still extraordinarily slow and over-conscientious, by 28 August, after a total of nearly forty hours' dual, he secured his 'A' licence which permitted him to fly solo.

On 8 September Francis bought the best plane that his rapidly deteriorating finances permitted. This was a Gipsy I Moth which weighed 880 lb unloaded. 'It was not the plane I wanted. I had left New Zealand with the idea in my mind of buying a bigger and better machine. It was by now perfectly apparent that financial reasons made its acquisition impossible.' The great slump was dramatically affecting real estate in New Zealand as elsewhere. Francis's earned capital of £20 000 was so completely tied up in housing that he could not extract sufficient cash to cover the outlay of his plane. 'Every available scrap of paper not filled already with notes on how to fly and how not to fly, I filled with countless budgets on cost, maintenance and (not least) expected repairs.' He determined to train himself to be a first-class navigator in four months. On the first occasion that he flew alone everything seemed to be a jumble. Then he picked out a railway line, the Thames, the Staines Reservoir. Flying at snail's pace he recognized other landmarks shown on the map. It was intoxicating. If he could do that on the first day, why should he not learn to guide himself over the world?

No one knew that in October he intended a flight around Europe, and by December he reckoned he would be ready to fly to Australia – a trip which had been made once only when Hinkler, a crack pilot, did it in fifteen and a half days. In 1929 a London to Sydney flight represented a fantastic feat and Francis had only a few days of solo experience. When he murmured about this project, one of his instructors retorted grimly: 'Look here, young man. First you've got to learn to get this plane off the ground in one lump and then you've got to get it back in one lump.' The small planes of 1929 might be compared with today's models as bicycles with racing cars.

Although fairly inexpensive, the little Moth with its Gipsy engine and Handley Page slots turned out to be a superb machine. Three days after buying it Francis flew it to Liverpool where he hoped to impress a certain actress. She proved totally uninterested so he turned round and flew to North Devon to visit his parents. The new plane had not yet been fitted with a compass. He was 'flying by Bradshaw', following the railway lines across country while wondering if he could fly by the sun without compass or instruments. He reckoned that if he got into trouble he could force the plane into a spin, that it was bound to spin round the vertical axis and that therefore he should be sure to emerge vertically from the cloud. That was how Francis's mind worked. After flying along for half an hour in sunshine, he climbed down through a deep layer of cloud. Then, wanting to find out how accurately he had carried out this manoeuvre, he fixed his position by the easiest method available – he flew round a railway station low down, and read the name off the platform. By some good luck he was right on course, and probably cried out for the first time in his life – 'Spot on!'

On that September day, Bill Wilkey, recently married, happened to be in Shirwell with his young wife and he heard the local postman alerting villagers. 'A telegram has come for Rector. Master Francis is arriving at Youlston in an aeroplane this afternoon.' So crowds of people who had known Francis since boyhood gathered on the wide hill inside the park of Youlston to await this momentous happening. The excitement when a faint buzz sounded and a real plane appeared in the sky and landed carefully on the greensward was intense. Bill Wilkey hurried forward to greet his old friend and Mrs Wilkey who had never seen Francis before remembers clearly the first words exchanged between Francis and the Rector, after a ten-year absence. Having brought the Gipsy Moth to a halt, Francis stepped out and something caught on a wing. 'Oh damn!' he exclaimed and then turned to his father to apologize for swearing, 'So sorry, sir.' New Zealand did not seem to have improved him at all. The welcome home was cool.

Next day, in front of a crowd of gaping villagers, Francis took his sisters up and showed off his wonderful new toy. Alas, when landing on a concealed cart track he split open the fuselage and came to rest like a winged partridge. He feared there would be many cries of 'I told 'ee so!' but friends rushed to his aid. George Moore, boyhood sparring partner and breaker of his nose, was now the local carpenter. He repaired the fractured ribs so well that eighteen hours later the Moth was in the air with splendid old Wilkey as a bewildered passenger.

When we landed again Wilkey said, 'Do you realize what this date is, Master Francis?' 'No,' says I. 'Well,' he replies, 'this is your birthday. Twenty-eight years ago this day 'twas that I was sent to fetch the doctor to help you make your first landing in this world. And I never did think that day that twenty-eight years later you'd be taking me up in an aeroplane.'

Shirwell village was charmed by all this but the Rectory atmosphere grew glacial. 'I had been away ten years and I arrived back thinking (privately) that I had a tremendous achievement behind me in building up a business and turning my £10 into £20 000. My family not only never mentioned this, but showed me plainly that I was an outsider as far as they were concerned.'

It was no good. Francis could not get on with his parents. Communication seemed impossible and faults lay on both sides. The cocky prodigal son talked too much and too loudly, purposely using a New Zealand twang which he could see annoyed. If the older Chichesters could be irritating, so could Francis.

After a few days of home life Francis was glad to fly his precious plane back to Brooklands. The take-off in a 35 m.p.h. wind proved both hair-raising and spectacular. He had to leave Youlston Park with Wilkey and his two sisters hanging onto the wings while he taxied into position. Suddenly the Moth seemed to rise vertically into the air. Then he was up and away over those valleys which had hidden him as a child, over the little church tower and that house of grim memories, away from all that for ever – into a new dream.

Arriving over Brooklands airfield he thought it would be great sport trying to land in a strong wind, but each time he nearly touched down a gust blew him up ten or fifteen feet into the air. Only after several tries did he bump successfully to a halt, and began taxi-ing proudly to the hangars. He did not realize what a crosswind could do until the port wingtip started to dip slowly and gracefully to the ground, where it dug in and crumpled up. The other wing rose equally slowly till the whole machine balanced on the tip of the port wingtip. Thence the Moth took a leap into the air, and landed fair and square on its nose, with the tail pointing to heaven. Francis found himself dangling in the safety-belt and looking down at the ground ten feet below.

Francis spent fifty hours working on the repairs, to the astonishment of the riggers who were less accustomed to pilots mending their own craft than blacksmiths are to gentlemen shoeing their own horses. After this exceedingly expensive lesson Francis settled down to serious training. For hours he practised landings, into the wind, across the wind, down wind, and then in a confined space. He would place his handkerchief ten yards inside a fence and try to touch down on it. Then he would move it 150 yards from the fence, and try to end his run exactly on it. For half an hour each day he practised forced landings, by climbing to 1000 feet, cutting the engine and landing on the best field he could see. At first he always overshot the field of his choice; gradually his skill improved so that he could just skim trees and fences and drop into the selected place. One day he was concentrating so hard on exactitude that he rolled to a halt beneath the walls of Windsor Castle. The guardians were not amused.

When attempting aerobatics Francis practised his loops over a straight stretch of railway line to check for accuracy as he flattened out. All England now seemed his playground. Throughout October, after installing a compass, he started to check on his navigational abilities and to study the plane's petrol consumption at different speeds. Then he tried night-flying and found that the feeling of complete isolation gave him enjoyment.

On 25 October, just two months after he had secured his 'A' licence, Francis left England for a trial spin around Europe. The great world slump was now hitting very hard and it was difficult for a novice pilot to insure an incompletely paid-for aeroplane, which he intended to fly over a variety of countries during the foggiest months. But youthful enthusiasm prevailed on one underwriter, whose only condition was that Francis should at any rate start off with an experienced commercial pilot, one Joe King.

The trip proved to be what Francis called 'great sport'. Apparently there was little discussion as to who should bring the plane into the air. When the two pilots were fastened in their seats Joe King said, 'Let her go' and pushed the throttle full open. In the company of an experienced pilot, Francis assumed that Joe would be flying the plane, so he dropped the controls. He did not want to appear presumptuous. The plane seemed to take rather a long time leaving the ground and then only just cleared the trees on St George's Hill by a foot. Francis thought that must be the way the professionals did it. Then Joe's voice roared through the intercom, 'What on earth are you doing?'

'I'm doing nothing,' replied Francis. 'Why, I'm not even touching any controls.'

'Nor am I,' exclaimed Joe.

This story of the dual-control take-off with each pilot presuming the other must be in command, and the plane just managing to do it alone, would become a legend in the R.A.F. during wartime training, when it was dinned into young pilots that the situation *had* occurred once and both pilots lived to tell the tale, but that such luck could never be repeated. (*If* the trim tabs on the elevators had not been absolutely correctly set, Francis's plane would have stalled or gone right on and smashed itself up.)

Hot under the collar, Francis now took over the controls with a vengeance. Never having flown over the sea before, he climbed to over 6000 feet over the Channel 'to feel safe'. As a result, the two pilots froze in the open cockpit. Joe did not seem to feel all that confident in his co-pilot. He kept asking Francis whether he knew his bearings. Finally they landed at Abbeville to warm up with cognac, and then hopped hilariously on to Paris. Here, Joe King, who had probably had enough of beginners, said that he must look up an old business friend. The lady in question demanded a great deal of time so Francis flew on solo. In twenty-five days he flew over eight countries. Of twenty-eight landings, eight were in fields and of these eight landings, three were 'for fun', two caused by fog, and three caused by fog and darkness combined.

At Nice, Francis came down on a deserted strip of beach, thumbed a lift into town and returned by taxi with tins of petrol. On he went via Milan and Venice into Yugoslavia. At Ljubljana, caught by mist and darkness, he had to land in ploughland and the Moth went onto her nose. For the second time in two months Francis found himself dangling above the ground in his safety-belt. It took ten days to get a new propeller. Then, after giving the village mayor a joy-ride, Francis flew on to Belgrade and then towards Lasi in the Prut Valley where he encountered a sea of white fog which sent an ice-cold wave of fear through him. But he was learning fast. He turned in a vertical bank and flew back to a treeless pasture he remembered. Dark had fallen but he managed to touch down safely. No one had seen the plane so Francis had to walk until a car came along carrying three fierce-looking, sheepskin-clad peasants. They conveyed him to a French-speaking official who explained to Francis they had thought he might be a Russian spy. A joke changed the atmosphere and Francis was hurried to the village, set before a mountain of goulash and bedded down in a tiny room beneath a huge *duvet*.

At another Roumanian town an officer invited him to stay and with an unusual hospitality arranged for him to spend two hours making conversation in German with a Russian belle while he worked in his cold office next door.

On 14 November 1929 the *Bukaresti Dimineata* carried a news item, the translation of which was handed to Francis:

Jassy 12 November: An English aeroplane landed here yesterday for a short visit, piloted by Mr Chichesters of New Zealand, director of the Godwin Chichesters Aviation Co. of London.

Mr Chichesters left New Zealand last week, touched at London, then at Paris, where he picked up another aviator. He continued over Milan to Jugo-Slavia. Then on approaching Zagreb his propeller broke at a height of some hundreds of feet and the aviators were in grave danger. The pilot succeeded in landing near Zagreb airport, and after repairs continued towards Roumania.

The aeroplane, of unusual shape and colour, attracted crowds to the aerodrome of Tecuci. At Vaslui the pilot met fog and was obliged to make a forced landing . . . At Jassy the aviator was met by the whole corps of officers headed by Major Argesecnu, Aviation Group Commander, and a reception was given in his honour.

After inspecting the hangars Mr Chichesters left for Warsaw and London.

What, wondered Francis, would Devon newspapers make of this?

On he flew to the boundaries of the Ukraine and then over hundreds of miles of dense forests to Warsaw and thence towards Leipzig. Occasionally, forced off route by fog, he would land frightened and hungry in unknown territory. Near Munster he very nearly came to grief when sudden fog closed in on all sides. Eventually he chose a likely field, landed, and was delightfully entertained by a small farmer who insisted that he spend the night under the same roof as his father, mother, grandmother and his children, *Gipsy Moth* and five cows. *Gipsy Moth* and the cows shared the hall!

On 20 November, after nearly a month of ceaseless flying, Francis re-crossed the English Channel at fifty feet above the water. He wished Joe King could have seen the improvement. Now he was ready for a greater project. One which he hardly *dared* mention.

6. London to Tripoli, Alone

He had, he thought, during this self-imposed crash course, shaped himself into a good navigator. He had the plane and the nerve and the inspiration. But what he now didn't have, was the money. Owing to the world slump, that £20 000 remained locked up in New Zealand land, producing no income. Geoffrey Goodwin telegraphed, envisaging possible crashes on jungly islands: 'Advise selling plane. Expensive salvage Malay aerodromes. No more money possible. All reserves used up. Expected £2000 loan unavailable.'

But Francis was absolutely determined. He slogged on applying for landing permits in Egypt, Iraq, Persia, India, Dutch East Indies, etc. and obtaining the necessary maps. The Shell Company agreed to lay down petrol supplies at a cheap basic rate when he could inform them which islands were usable, and de Havilland's made two extra tanks to give a total of fifty-nine gallons which would allow a range of 826 miles. His diary on 21 November recorded: 'Total load with boat will then be about 1800 lb. The plane weighs 915 lb. Have cast the die now although I won't have enough cash.' On top of financial worries, time pressed.

By mid-December he felt nearly ready to go but exceedingly tired. And if he wanted to beat the flying time of Hinkler, the only man who had flown solo from England to Australia, he would have to average more than 750 miles a day. This meant he must fly for at least twelve and a half hours each day. He decided to start every morning in the dark at about two o'clock and halt after six hours for a meal. Then he would fly on and ensure making the evening landing by daylight. As it was impossible to fit navigation lights on such a small plane, permission to fly unlit before dawn over various countries had to be obtained.

Gipsy Moth was indeed a miracle of engineering design, so delicately made and yet so strong. Her slender frame was built of inch-square spruce. This was covered with a skin of three-ply – almost like a kite – a kite with a superb engine as its heart.

For ten days before leaving he rose at 2 a.m. to work on maps and train himself to think clearly during the unusual hours when mental concentration would be so necessary. For London to Rangoon he obtained maps of 15·83 miles to the inch; for Rangoon to Darwin he could get only ones with 64 miles to the inch, and for Darwin on across the Australian desert it would be 45 miles to the inch. On forty-one maps he marked in every possible landing-ground. Then came meticulous perusal of the route and decisions on how to fly past mountains and over seas. He joined the maps together, cut them into a strip nine inches wide and divided the strip into five portions which could fit on the rollers of his map case. The total length of this map strip was seventy-one feet. He went over the whole route marking the magnetic variations for every hundred miles and every change of direction. Then he tried to learn the whole route by heart as there might not be time to study each day's map as he went along. During this process he marked off every fortieth mile so that he ought to know his correct position every half-hour after take-off.

Mid-December found him worn out by physical preparations and mental strain. The Air Ministry remained helpful but no one encouraged him to go. This flight was all his own idea, all his own responsibility.

Fearing trouble from the finance company who had loaned the last £275 and were now tiresomely demanding a guarantor in case of a 'complete write-off', Francis worked frantically to escape before they could find him. He felt he had 'about as much chance of finding a guarantor as of flying to the moon in a perambulator'.

On 18 December he flew the plane to Brooklands so that drift lines could be painted on the wings and a streamlined cover fitted over the front cockpit which he could quickly snap open to get out his rubber boat (into which went a ration of pumpernickel in case of a sea voyage in said boat!). A hole had to be cut in the back of the front cockpit so that he could keep food there and reach in to draw it out as he flew. Francis began to show extreme anxiety symptoms. He rushed about nervously, pulling out his watch every few minutes and forgetting the time immediately he returned it to his pocket. Infected by his sense of urgency, the mechanics worked like maniacs and eventually he literally tore the plane from their hands and flew it to Croydon where he was to spend his final hours before take-off.

He refuelled, collected journey log-book, *carnet de passage*, licence, and his passport endorsed for seventeen countries. Having cleared Customs he was walking across the aerodrome when he met a flying acquaintance of the early summer.

'I shall never forget your turning up at Liverpool in a new machine without a compass and that ridiculous map of yours,' the man laughed. 'Have you made any flights since?'

'Yes,' replied Francis modestly, 'I've flown around Europe.'

'Great heavens! But you've only just got your licence. Perhaps you're planning to fly back to New Zealand!' he joked.

'Well, as a matter of fact I am.'

'Not possible! When?'

'In about six hours.'

His acquaintance remained silent. It was not to be the last time that someone would wonder if Francis Chichester ought to have his head examined.

But now Francis needed what sleep his taut nerves would permit. He had not yet learned to deal with his own system; he could force it cruelly, but he would in time *have* to learn to rest.

Unable to relax or digest or cease fussing, he sat down to gobble his dinner. When summoned to the telephone panic smote him. Fearing the finance company were on his trail he told the message boy he could not take the call. Then he rushed out, alternately hot and cold with fear, wildly devising excuses, to snatch up the receiver. A cool, businesslike voice announced, 'This is the Meteorological Office . . .' They were merely ringing to give him a list of flooded islands in the Dutch East Indies. Faint with relief, Francis retired to bed and half-slept for a few hours. Bailiffs haunted his dreams.

At 1.30 a.m. he was up and exhaustedly trying to swallow bacon and eggs. Impressed by such pluck, his flying friend had risen in the early hours and come out to lend a hand. By the time Francis had got the weather reports and pushed the plane out of the hangar, it was 2.30. A man and a girl joined the party. The man helped by walking to the end of the aerodrome so that *Gipsy Moth* did not run into a hangar in the dark, for no floodlights were working at this hour. 'Good-bye,' said the girl. She was a stranger but her voice was gentle. Francis kept its memory. 'Cheerio,' was all he could call back.

The ground was frozen hard and bumpy. He did not realize that his prolonged take-off was due to the frozen ground having ripped a tyre. It was the first time he had flown the plane with a full load and the first time he had steered a course at night.

Moonlight glinted on the fields below, covered with hoar frost, then cloud descended and the horizon vanished. All he could see was a stretch of water. Francis had expected to cross the Channel in about fifteen minutes, but he had over-estimated the drift. Suddenly he realized the difficulties of flying in the dark, unable to use ruler or protractor. He would have to improve his night navigation if he was going to survive.

After being cramped four hours in the cockpit, Francis grew stiff with cold and most terribly sleepy, but he summoned his willpower and controlled the longing to doze. After seven and a half hours he landed at Lyons. Here the aerodrome staff mended his flat tyre while he enjoyed a delicious French meal. How, after so much stress, an omelette and a bottle of red wine, Francis could prevent himself falling into a bilious sleep is difficult to understand, but he was young and determined, and after two hours he was off again, wondering if the fully loaded plane would be able to climb to the 10 000 feet needed to cross the Alps. It seemed to take an age climbing each thousand feet, he could not take his eyes off the altimeter dial – or stop willing it to move. The Alps presented an impenetrable snow-capped wall. Francis drew in great lungfuls of crisp air. The 15 782-foot-high Mont Blanc looked as if at his wingtip, yet the mountain actually lay forty miles away. He almost felt as if he was skiing. He reached 10 000 feet but kept worrying lest bumpy air should lower the heavily loaded little plane. All remained smooth, however, until reaching rough air over Genoa. Then he flew with terrifying bumps to Pisa where he thought he saw the airfield all splendidly lit up for him. Unfortunately, this proved, on nearer inspection, to be a long illuminated hoarding, while the airfield remained just a black space. Sweating with trepidation, he touched down in the dark and felt the Moth's wheels getting bogged in mud. Then a swarm of soldiers sprang out of the shadows to push her out, but they broke a few of the Moth's ribs in their zeal. They were immensely kind, but talkative. Having explained in Italianized French that they had expected him to circle for half an hour while they found the landing-lights operator, they gabbled for over four hours. At 10 p.m., when he had refuelled, checked the motor and satisfied various over-enthusiastic authorities, Francis was led to a camp-bed and lay down to sleep. How little he knew himself! After twenty strenuous hours, after flying 780 miles in a cold cramped cockpit and being several times frightened out of his wits, Francis now found to his surprise that he was too tired to sleep. Soon after midnight he rose, tense and alert, to take off at 1.45 a.m. from a darkened airfield.

Passing Vesuvius, he flew on over the jet-black Bay of Salerno. Dawn found him battling in a rain cloud over barren mountains and once again sleepiness became an agony. He shifted about in the cockpit trying to wave his arms and stamp his feet. Some strange inner psychic force which has been noticed by other airmen including Lindbergh, during extreme fatigue, now rattled his subconscious. Each time he started to drop off he dreamt he heard explosions and awoke with a start. Such phenomena have been described to the author by an aviator as 'something like a guardian angel letting off squibs'. He tried watching the cliffs of Italy, but could not focus his eyes properly. When dawn broke, after six hours' flying, he feared he was losing the battle against sleep, but then after leaving the toe of Italy all drowsiness left him. His nervous system had changed gear.

At Catania in Sicily he landed. 'No petrol in the field, no Customs, no nothing.' However the pilots there welcomed him and produced an excellent meal. One officer lent his room for a ten-minute sleep. Even this could refresh him. Then when ready to leave Francis discovered that his log-book had been taken into the town, and it took an hour to trace it. After this maddening delay he could not possibly reach Africa before dark, but night-landing facilities at Homs were assured him. Off flew the Moth over a shadowy Mediterranean. As the sun set, Francis could see Africa beneath him but Homs looked terribly small and he could spot no airfield. Without any kind of radio communication he could not guess that a big red bonfire flickering in the desert had been lit to indicate a safe landing place. Knowing the Italian Air Force had a base at Tripoli, he turned westward along the coast, flying uncomfortably through cloud with no blind-flying instruments and broken altimeter. Eventually he thought he perceived a fine airfield with a rotating searchlight, but as he grew nearer this metamorphosed into Tripoli harbour and its lighthouse. Ten miles to the west another light flashed. He flew over to discover it was just a motor-car's headlight switching on and off. Then another searchlight appeared, and as he approached it, it lowered to illuminate the hangars 200 yards away. Francis feared this meant there was not room to land without hitting the hangars. He tried to think quickly and chose what appeared to be a large flat land surface nearby. He glided in steadily and then 'wonk!' – he felt *Gipsy Moth* tip over on her nose. Once again Francis found himself in the undignified position of dangling in his safety-belt ten feet above the ground.

Dead silence had succeeded to the roar of the engine. I was aware of the silence in spite of the rhythmic engine beat which seemed to continue not only in my brain, but in every part of my body. Nerves affected, I suppose. I fumbled with the safety-belt catch and pulled it. I was standing on the rudder bar and keeping my shoulders off the instrument board with one hand. I scrambled out, put a foot on one of the centre section struts, thence jumped to the ground.

To his amazement he landed with a splash. Floundering forward he reached a small bank and climbed onto it, squelching in his big sheepskin boots. Shakily Francis drew out his pipe and tried to light it. He wished to present the correct picture of a nonchalant Englishman. Meanwhile a searchlight flickered around and eventually it settled on the plane – alas, she showed tears in a wing and a broken strut. His heart turned to lead. This time she must be a write-off. Then what appeared to be a war-dance in silhouette was reflected on the wings as thirty excited Italian soldiers rushed from the airfield to help. Francis smiled jauntily, borrowed a match for his pipe, and was half carried to the Commandant who took him to an empty mess and there produced wine. This really did act as a soporific. Francis kept falling asleep as he drank. An orderly led him off to lie down in the room of an absent pilot. He woke to find himself groping along the wall suffering from his recurrent nightmare – of flying when suddenly visibility shut down and there was nothing to do but wait for the crash.

The fact that flying solo for twenty-six hours out of forty, and sleeping two and three-quarter hours out of that forty might disarrange his nervous system did not occur to him. All that Francis bothered about was his plane, and to his joy, when morning came and the Moth could be wheeled in by a crowd of soldiers, she had only damaged a front inter-wing strut and broken her propeller. Francis had landed in a dead-flat salt-pan covered by four inches of water. The wheel marks could be seen for thirty-five yards before she had nosed over.

Now he *had* to reassess his project. It would take ten days to get a new propeller out from England, and even if this accident had not occurred he realized that in such a small plane he could never surpass Hinkler's time. To do that he would have had to carry more petrol and fly 1000 miles each day, which meant twelve and a half hours non-stop. Despite his disregard for his own powers of endurance, he knew he could not have done this without a midday descent for a hot meal. At least he now knew his own limitation. After all he had only learned to fly in the last six months. For a makee-learn pilot he had not done badly.

Luckily the financiers back in England were spared the sight of *Gipsy Moth* turning on her nose in a salt-pan, and Francis could hope they read the *Daily Mail* of 21 December 1929 which, with inimitable Press exactitude, produced headlines:

RICH YOUNG MAN'S AMAZING FLIGHT

12 000 MILES DASH ALONE

'I'M GOING TO AUSTRALIA.'

3 a.m. START

ACROSS FRANCE IN A DAY

One of the most audacious flights ever attempted is now in progress. At three o'clock yesterday morning, as exclusively announced in later editions of the *Daily Mail*, Mr Francis Chichester, a rich young New Zealander, set out from Croydon aerodrome to fly alone to Australia . . .

For Francis the key word in all this was *rich*. Insurance brokers care less about audacity.

7. Tripoli to Sydney, Alone

He had reached Africa in two days covering nearly two thousand miles, but now a ten-day halt was forced upon him. Francis began to reflect on the effects of stress and fatigue. He was learning his lessons the hard way, by trial and error. Luck had allowed him to survive the errors, but his confidence was slightly shaken. He had actually broken three propellers in four months. Could he continue escaping each time *Gipsy Moth* turned on her nose?

The Italian pilots were men of understanding and their engineering department mended his plane free of charge. On 2 January 1930 Francis sat down in the Grand Hotel, Tripoli, and wrote a long letter to the agent who had most sportingly helped him to obtain insurance cover.

My dear Champness,

Thanks awfully for your two cables . . . I expect my cable mystified you. I hope they are sending the interplane strut I asked for, not the radius rods you speak of . . . I pictured de Havillands in consultation asking each other how the hell a feller could bust an interplane strut and nothing else. I'm not quite sure myself. I had a wonderfully interesting night down here but not so much pleasure in it. I shall be quite glad to proceed slowly.

He went on to describe the flight in detail and of his observations perhaps the most interesting are those which show his sense of being an absolute beginner.

It was my first point to point night flying and also my first full-load flight so it took me a few minutes to get the feel to keep the pace steady . . . I mucked my drift reading as the drift lines had only been painted on recently and I was not accustomed to them. There is no doubt I over corrected.

He described making a tentative line for Paris – but 'Paris wasn't there'. So he got a likely fix from a railroad, a canal and a town lying together and then shot straight for Lyons:

I might have some fun locating it but I could always land and ask a policeman . . . When dawn came I felt quite bucked up. Presently I was flying over some woods. 'Damned if I don't know these woods' says I to meself. 'If I'm right I shall find a river almost a mile ahead', and sure enough there it was. It was the exact spot I had flown over in the storm when I went on that tour round Europe. There are two rivers which flow Lyons way. This was the Westerly one – aviation was now like money from home . . .

On he goes relating episodes in detail until the splash down.

The facts of the case are as follows:
    Adjoining the aerodrome is a salt lake where they evaporate sea water to get the salt. It is almost 8 inches deep . . . Anyway it turned out that I had only broken my prop and a front interplane strut. So I was devilish lucky considering I had always had the presentiment I should be prevented by an accident from giving Hinkler a run for his money. I was not built to get anywhere quicker than the other fellow, only perhaps built just to get there, i.e. I have never yet succeeded in doing anything that other folk couldn't do better, quicker and easier than I. So I guess Minerva decided I was getting fresh with new ideas and stepped in. After sacrificing to her ladyship I shall hope finally to reach Sydney.

These were the early days of aviation when every flight was a strange adventure and every arrival a miracle. Francis pays the greatest compliment to de Havilland's when he writes in this personal letter, 'When it comes to forced landings I guess the Moth is miles ahead.'
    During the ten days he spent in Tripoli, several air disasters occurred which were far more tragic than his own mishap. Jones-Williams and Jenkins were killed in a long flight to South Africa. Then the pioneer French aviator Lasalle crashed with his crew trying to fly from France to Indo-China. Lasalle and his crew were buried with tremendous honours in Tripoli. Francis, asked by the French Consul to represent Britain's aviators, attended the service feeling somewhat conspicuous in the only suit he carried – a golfing outfit with plus-fours. Amidst glittering Italian uniforms and gentlemen in top hats the British representative stood out as rather too sporting.
    The new propeller arrived and was fitted. When Francis tried it out in flight he discovered a change in himself. He was far more nervous. During the test aerobatics which he attempted in front of

the Italian Air Force, he *thought* he flew badly. After a couple of stall turns he tried a loop down wind which proved a mistake. The Moth stood on her tail for a long time before falling over backwards, while Francis wondered if the rudder would tear off. Then putting her into a spin he found he could hardly pull her out of it.* When he came down the whole aerodrome staff had turned out to watch and applaud. Aware of this audience, and therefore self-conscious, he twice overshot the landing. Actually everyone thought he was stunting. He didn't tell them that something had gone wrong with himself.

Peace of mind seeped back when on 9 January 1930, having broken a bottle of brandy on the new propeller boss, he set off alone on the next 12 000 miles. The blue Mediterranean lay to his left, the deserts of Africa to his right. Sandstorms could be disagreeable, but on the whole the air remained clear. It took eight hours to cover the 570 miles to Benghazi, and here he spent the night with the British Consul. Without a record-breaking motive it was no longer necessary to drive himself to cover 800 miles in a day. In the morning the Consul told him that a message had arrived to say that Muriel had died during an operation in New Zealand. They had been separated for two years, but she had looked so young and pretty when he last saw her. The pathos of that hopeless match swept over him. And he thought of the little boy – *his* father had given him no affection, the chain of behaviour must not be repeated. Sadness and guilt filled him. He resolved that if he got back he would cherish the child.

There was quite a big IF to it as he left Benghazi in the golden desert light to fly 917 miles to the R.A.F. station at Abu-Sueir in the Sinai desert where his cousin Patrick Chichester happened to be stationed.

It took nine and a quarter hours and the last two hours were achingly disagreeable. He had discovered that after six hours in an open plane the engine beat had drummed itself into every nerve of the body. He kept squirming about trying to find a fresh part of his anatomy to sit on. It took an hour and twenty minutes to pump the lower tanks of petrol up into the top tank, and while doing this he had to keep his feet steady on the rudder-bars which meant no squirming. Young and strong as he was the soreness and aching cramp became almost unendurable.

It was a gruelling flight, for, after leaving Gaza, Francis made a

* In a 'slow roll', one of the most difficult manoeuvres, the action on the stick is almost circular and it took considerable strength when inverted to retain height as the plane would be *trimmed* for flying the other way up.

navigational mistake and found himself eighteen miles too far south. After this he had great difficulty in spotting the signs marking emergency landing grounds which were spaced along the desert track. According to his mental dead-reckoning, he expected to reach some hills marked on the map with a water course running through them. Eventually these hills appeared and after six and three quarter hours he landed at Rutbeh Wells, having flown 526 miles. An Imperial Airways mechanic issued from the post and they pushed the Moth through barbed-wire entanglements right up to the workshop window so that an electric inspection lamp could be fastened to a blade of the propeller, while they coped with a defective cylinder. They worked late, until the compression seemed perfect.

When Francis lay down in an Iraqi officer's room he heard flutes and tinkling bells, a strange eastern music which lulled him to sleep. He awoke refreshed for five o'clock breakfast. While eating, he inquired about the music, but he met blank faces. There had been no music in the Fort that night. Flying can produce a strange variety of hallucinations – the metallic plane sounds, the wood and wind, were vibrating in harmonious echoes through his tired eardrums.

Early morning in the desert can be bitterly cold and the Gipsy engine refused to start. Francis and a mechanic took turns at swinging the propeller until the oil warmed up. Then he soared off towards Baghdad where for once he found it possible to refuel, complete all formalities and get back into the air within fifty minutes. He ate as he flew. That night the Moth reached Bushire in Persia after eight and three quarter hours' flying, covering 772 miles. Francis took a nap and then went to the sea for a bathe. The warm water felt velvety to his skin after the physical beating he had taken. In those days of open cockpits the roaring exhaust and fierce wind made long flights hard on the human system.

Someone lent a camp-bed and as he fell asleep the same curious music filled his head. Fatigue seemed to open up a private wireless set in the back of his brain. At 6.15 a.m. he was in the air and after nine hours, having covered 740 miles, he landed at Chahbar. Next day he covered 430 miles to Karachi in six hours. Then he crossed India in five days, covering 3500 miles in forty-five hours' flying. He now realized that the chatter and negotiating forced on him at every landing were even more tiring than the long tense hours in the air. At Calcutta he got the valves of number two cylinder re-ground, which helped to reduce the increasing engine vibrations. There were several frightening moments during the five days over India; the worst being at the southernmost point of Burma where the landing ground was shut in by hills and palm jungle. His narrow escapes on arriving here and on leaving ruined all satisfaction in the day's flying. His nerves were getting jagged, and he began to reflect on the inadvisability of tempting luck too often.

During the eighty-mile crossing from Singapore to Sumatra Francis climbed high above gathering cloud until he concluded it must be time to zig-zag down into clear steam-like air. A column of rain, pouring from the centre of each flat cloud, made him feel that he was flying through a vast water forest. Beneath lay unmarked jungle. As the rain beat down and as he tried to escape visibility ceased and Francis, flying blind, realized he could not regain sense of direction or altitude. He checked each acceleration as smoothly as possible. If the speed increased till the struts screamed he eased up the nose, if accelerations built up sideways he rolled to what he hoped was level trim. If that put him upside down he looped: 'I knew that I was coming down but I could not tell how.' Once, suddenly, he saw that he was diving straight into the sea but he managed to flatten out and flew on until the hills of Western Java appeared. After eight hours thirty-five minutes, having covered 660 miles, he landed at Batavia, and to his amazement found himself in a modern airport surrounded by smartly dressed Dutchmen speaking perfect English. He stayed in a luxurious hotel for two nights and found no rest. After official calls and much conversation he became aware of a degree of nervous exhaustion never previously experienced. Whatever an aviator endured in the air he did not have to chat.

Information about future landing grounds seemed contradictory; so were the maps. Rainstorms proved unbelievably terrifying. He reached Surabaya 720 miles onward after six and a half hours of battling through monsoon conditions. Then on he flew with two night stops until he reached Timor Island. Here he stayed for a five-hour engine overhaul and the checking of his rubber boat for leaks before the long sea crossing of 320 miles to Australia.

Again he suffered from that horrible recurring dream of flying along until suddenly his vision gave out and there would be nothing to do but wait for the crash. On leaving Timor he flew 500 miles in six hours and ten minutes to Darwin. He had planned exactly how to act if the Moth came down in that sea which had claimed so many pilots, but in perfect weather this proved the easiest flight of the whole voyage.

Once he reached Australia Francis felt himself on home territory and he thought he might manage the Darwin–Sydney run in three days. But now he flew across the most difficult country for navigation he had ever met. There seemed to be no landmarks, just flat brown desert, and the river beds marked on maps were so dried out that they were impossible to spot from the air. He left Darwin at 6.45 a.m. and flew through a heat haze keeping so low that when passing an occasional drover the two men saluted each other as if they were both on horseback. It became so hot that he worried lest the top wing catch fire on the spot where the exhaust touched it. He flew for nearly nine hours following tracks by uncomfortable guesswork until he reached a borehole shown on the map as Anthony Lagoon – to his relief it actually had a lagoon. After landing on a hard patch Francis drank all his remaining water and crawled out of the plane to lie down under the shade of one wing.

After about twenty minutes a man appeared walking slowly towards *Gipsy Moth*. He appeared to have an enormous black beard, but on closer inspection this proved to be a fly-proof net round his face. Francis was excited. He asked about forty questions, but they all elicited the same answer, 'I don't know.' It seemed curious that a man living out in this blazing desert should neither know nor care who his next-door neighbour was.

Having emptied a can of oil into the sump and a tin of pineapple juice into himself, Francis flew away searching out a small town named Camooweal. He passed a few creek beds, some of which showed water, but it was impossible to tell whether they ought to be on the map. After a few hours Francis had the wind up well and truly. The petrol gauge showed practically empty, and the air currents were rough and tossed the plane about. He dared not stop watching for any signs of a track and ceased to give a damn about reaching Camooweal. All he hoped for was a sign of human beings so that he could descend before his tanks were empty.

When he had enough petrol for only another thirty miles, night began to fall and the air cooled, but Francis was sweating with fear. He whipped off his scarf to let his spine cool off. He was flying across a plain covered with boulders, then suddenly in the dusk he perceived a long straight shiny piece of road, apparently unused. It ended at a water bore with a shed and hut. Francis had been flying for eleven hours and feared his powers of judgement might be waning. He selected a green patch to land on hoping it would not prove swampy. A good landing was imperative. If he crash-landed far from assistance it could mean disaster and death. Now his brain cleared, he circled once and made a perfect landing. Francis would always react correctly in danger. It was when he thought people were *watching* that he did badly. He struggled out of the cockpit and dragged himself wearily to the shed which in the twilight looked quite close. It stood over a pumping engine, and the wind sighed mournfully through it. The flies were terrible, Francis had never seen so many before. They crawled ceaselessly over his eyeballs, filled up his ears, and tried to get into his dry swollen mouth. A bleaker, more unpleasant, stretch of desert would be hard to imagine. The water in the borehole proved thick and mud-coloured. He made a small fire and boiled the water for safety; it slaked his thirst whereas the Chianti brought from Tripoli repelled him. He was much too tired to eat. As dark fell he walked to the road he had seen from the air; it ran from the borehole into the plains and then apparently ended. A ghost road for non-existent traffic. Eerie. The wind blew strongly and as he had seen cattle in the distance Francis knew he could not safely leave *Gipsy Moth* in the open. Lifting up her tail he tried to push her to the shed, but he had not the strength, so he fastened a bit of rope to the tail skid and proceeded to pull her along in a series of jerks. It took him half an hour to shift the machine a distance that would have taken in ordinary circumstances thirty seconds.

As Francis blacked out he dropped to the ground. He felt panic-stricken and then disgusted with himself. It was hard to face the fact that he had allowed himself to get lost in the emptiest and driest of deserts. He had practically no petrol and this might well be the end of his life. Taking himself in hand, as he had done long before in the New Zealand jungle, he determined not to think about his predicament until he had had a sleep.

Having collected more wood for the fire Francis pulled his rubber boat out of the plane and pumped it half-full of air. Instead of floating him on a sea it was to rock him to sleep in a desert. As dark fell the flies vanished. Francis tumbled into his rubber nest and slept heavily, waking at intervals to slake his thirst with the boiled water. When dawn came he lay indolently on his back watching the sky change from dark to light grey through the dust haze. Then he examined the evidence. Had he overshot Camooweal? Had he missed the track leading to it? Had he sufficient petrol to fly on for a look-see? He tried to comfort himself with the thought that he could not die of thirst here, only of starvation. As the first fly buzzed, he jumped up to fetch a map from the plane to work out an estimate of his position while the details of yesterday's flight remained fresh in his memory.

His calculations (with drift corrected) placed Camooweal ten miles to the east of this borehole (if it was the one he thought it to be). Now he must measure what petrol remained. The gauge showed empty but there was a faint splash when he shook the plane by one wing. Slipping a shirt over his head to keep the flies off his face, he cleaned an old benzine tin and marked it off into four to represent gallons. Then he climbed on the wing, unscrewed the petrol-cock and held the tin under the tank while it slowly drained. He sweated with fear that it might slip and spill the contents. On these gallons his life depended. His arm muscles felt at breaking point before two gallons had been drawn off. These he emptied into the back tanks with infinite caution, begrudging even the evaporation that must take place. Checking with a foot-rule showed exactly one gallon more. Total – three gallons!

This meant thirty-six minutes' flying – twenty miles out, twenty miles back. He had to decide whether to wait until the dusty atmosphere cleared sufficiently to allow an air view of maybe ten miles and risk the embarrassment of search parties and a broadcasting of his incompetence, or to take to the air at once in the haze, fly east for fifteen minutes looking for Camooweal and back to the waterhole if he did not find it.

He decided to leave at once. He searched for the best place from which to get off and to use for a landing on return. Then he packed everything up, taking especial care to wrap up the wine. He thought of leaving a note at the waterhole to say he had been there, but that seemed too cocksure, as if taking for granted that he would not have to come back. Francis did not wish to tempt Providence; he even left a tinful of boiled water ready for his return.

The three minutes spent warming up the engine seemed an age. Then he took off with a strong wind blowing from the south. The dust haze proved very thick. Five minutes went by – not a sign of anything. Nine minutes went by and he saw a fence. His heart pounded with hope but he had to realize that a fence might be a hundred miles from any settlement. Eleven minutes went by and he thought he saw a man walking. He strained his eyes; it turned out to be a small horse which promptly bolted. At fourteen minutes and a half he saw a creek. One minute to go. Then he must return and wait by the waterhole. No more use reasoning, arguing, debating. He decided to cross the creek and turn on the other side. As he went into the bank for turning he caught the dull glint of light on an iron roof. He felt himself give a jolt of excitement. An iron shed! another – five, six, seven of them!

He landed. It took three tries in that wind. Then not liking to taxi towards the buildings he sat in the plane and waited. A truck rolled out to him packed with shouting men. He had reached a homestead called Rocklands, 'quite small – only 3400 square miles', which lay four miles north of Camooweal. The waterhole where he had spent the night would not have been visited for six weeks so Francis would have had time to grow extremely hungry. The mysterious metalled road was the work of a fire-plough – drawn across the desert as a barrier – leading from nowhere to nowhere.

The cattle station manager took him in for a meal. Francis found it hard to stop talking. He had suffered a real scare. This day he had made his shortest run – nineteen miles. 'Short,' he said, 'and very very sweet.'

During the long terrifying day's flying out of Darwin Francis had made his first serious exercise in dead-reckoning. It was also an exercise in decision and resolution.

The remaining 1380 miles to Sydney Francis took in three un-hurried stages. A strange mental torpor was affecting him. The nearer he got to Sydney the more depressed he became.

I was a human 22-day clock beginning to run down. After being wound up at Tripoli I had been ticking away every day from before dawn till an hour or two after sunset. It had become a habit. And now the clock was just about to stop, to leave a desolation, an emptiness, a solitariness in place of its steady tick.

But when he saw the suburbs of Sydney excitement became the overriding sensation.

A monoplane came out to meet him over Sydney Harbour and lead him to the aerodrome. Then Francis saw a stream of planes leaving the ground to escort him in. As they began to fly around him he grew increasingly nervous. After escorting *Gipsy Moth* to her desired runway the planes landed one after another. Then it was Francis's turn. He knew that several thousand people were watching him and he became feverishly anxious to perform perfectly. Francis could keep a cool head in danger, but he always suffered from stage fright in front of an audience. Bump, bump, bump! To his embar-rassment *Gipsy Moth* hopped like a rabbit to her standstill. But he had got there. By the grace of God he had got there.

8. Across the Tasman Sea

On 20 December 1929, Francis Chichester had been an unknown beginner pilot, who could not quite pay for his plane, dismally break-fasting alone in England. A month later, on 19 January 1930, he found himself famous. The drama of nineteen days' solo flight in a tiny plane, buzzing like a mosquito around monsoon cloudbursts, and over trackless desert, caught the public imagination. So did the fact that he had earned (almost!) the money to finance his own flight. His smiling photographs appeared on the front pages of newspapers throughout the world – a young man with fine features, skin rather tightly drawn, large spectacles – a handsome dragonfly, essentially male. He could not help enjoying the novelty of acclaim and wonder-ing if certain belles now regretted their snubs. Francis would through-out this period complain of non-success with women, but did he realize that although the ladies might be flattered by his willingness to fly to their vicinity, they noticed the less flattering eagerness with which he was ready to fly off again?

Shipping his plane back to New Zealand, he collected George from Muriel's home. The child, who hardly knew his father, was reluctant to leave and the von Zedlitzes disapproved of plucking him away. But Francis could be obstinate. He was determined to have little George around while he sat in the von Zedlitzes' garden writing a book in which he tried to explain the appeal of tasting danger. He wrote and re-wrote and read aloud. Everyone grew exhausted by Francis and his precious saga. Curiously, reviewers of *Solo to Sydney*, when it appeared, ignored the description of the recurrent nightmare which had woken him up for weeks on end – the horrible repetition of loss of vision while flying and the helpless wait for the crash. The dream was so vivid that he would wake up clawing at the wall. It is impossible to explain the strange string of presentiment tied into his brain. When eventually he did crash it would be due to outside circumstances which he could not possibly have foreseen; there could have been no half-knowledge of an error in flight instructions.

With the diligence usual in new authors Francis collected enthusiastic reviews of *Solo to Sydney* and pasted them into his own copy which survives. The praise was particularly gratifying for one who had craved to be a novelist. 'Aviation classic – a jolly light-hearted narrative that is immensely taking – engrossing . . . will rank with *War Birds* as one of the extraordinarily few classics of aviation literature.' Beside the *Bookman*'s pontifical judgement – 'The book is not quite as successful as the flight' Francis scrawled, 'Ha, ha!' – this expressed his attitude to uncomplimentary remarks at the time.

Francis was now using Louise, the von Zedlitzes' nineteen-year-old daughter, to slave for him. He made her ask her parents to allow him to rent the studio-cottage in their garden, and there, again not entirely to their approval, he brought the four-year-old George. He meant well by his son and he sincerely believed that a child ought to flourish amidst the boisterous good times he arranged. But George was a timid little fellow and he had been perfectly happy living with his grandmother and aunts. The sudden appearance of this energetic father frightened the wits out of him. It is curious that Francis, who was basically high-strung and sensitive and who had suffered from his own father's intolerance, should not have realized that this was an exceptionally nervous little boy. Although not afraid of the dark as most children are, George seemed frightened of almost everything else – of entering the water, of catching a ball, of new people, even of mechanical toys. Francis had known fear, but it had always been logical fear of punishment. He wanted a daredevil son, and the crash-course in daredevilry which he devised for George proved disastrous. Louise von Zedlitz watched appalled while this rumbustious father, who had appeared literally out of thin air, tried to teach George to resemble himself. Everything that Francis would have liked to do as a boy he tried to lure George into trying. *He* couldn't see a fast ball, but George's eyes were all right, so he must learn to catch. Francis had never been taken to swimming pools, so George must enjoy plunging in. When finally Francis decided his son would benefit from games with other children, he arranged to drive him away to stay with friends who owned a lovely country home with big nurseries. Louise hearing George bellowing at the front door, flared up: 'Can't you see he is terrified of going to a new place?'

'But there are other children and lots to do.'

But George did not want lots to do. He preferred clinging to the skirts of people he knew. Soon after this he started to have asthma. Louise never liked Francis in the way that her parents did; she noted with asperity that with that 'disarming smile' he could get away with anything. He drank very little but drove much too fast. One midnight, after he had borrowed her car to attend an all-male binge, she heard sounds as of jingling saucepans on the drive. There stood a crestfallen Francis with her broken car, which he had turned upside down, lifted back on to its wheels and bent into sufficient shape to drive home. Not too steady on his feet, he began to apologize. 'I would drive anywhere with you,' snapped Louise, 'or fly in your wretched plane as long as *you* were in it. You're a SURVIVOR.'

When not working with Geoffrey or climbing a mountain with him, Francis sketched out new plans. Now he knew what he hungered for – it was supreme achievement alone in the air. Von Zedlitz, listening to his outpourings, wondered if this difficult young man might become the great aviator of the age, and he pondered the qualities which can set one man above others in the same endeavours. Quick mathematical thinking? Ability to concentrate and reason and improvise as danger closed in? Sheer determination could not be enough. Some strange mainspring must be wound tight to enable a man to go through with such projects as Francis hungered for. The earth and its wild adventures he had always loved, romance he hankered after, hard work and practical achievement came easier to him than to most. The admiration aroused by his solo flight from England, done on the cheap, gave him fresh confidence. He felt an enhanced love of the air and the stars and the sea. Using his own hard-earned savings and his own willpower he could enter a new dimension.

Perhaps it was easier for Francis Chichester to face dangers and hardships because everything had always been difficult for him – it was difficult to be a sensitive child in an unappreciative family, difficult to play football with short sight, difficult to earn a fortune from scratch and extremely difficult to finance hare-brained flights when personal capital had been frozen. Von Zedlitz sensed that Francis possessed an extraordinary talent, above that of other men, for assessing wind, sun and stars and for keeping his sense of direction – like a bird, like a fish. What makes a pianist great? Not just playing fast and accurately. There is more to it and that extra-sensory brilliance was what Francis had in dead-reckoning.

Now he knew the elation of making two dramatic plans in which he could reasonably expect to succeed. He wanted to fly right around the world alone in *Gipsy Moth*, and he wanted to be the first to fly across the Tasman Sea from New Zealand to Australia. At that time only one great ocean had been flown solo – the Atlantic crossed by Lindbergh whose plane *Spirit of St Louis* (paid for by door-to-door subscriptions) was a far stronger machine than *Gipsy Moth*. Francis thought day and night about the stretch of ocean he wished to cover, *alone* and *first*. The Tasman was three-quarters as wide as the Atlantic and *Gipsy Moth* could only carry sixty gallons of petrol, and that meant taking off with a load equal to her own weight. To cross the Tasman Sea demanded one hundred gallons.

One day, while shaving, Francis felt his eyes wander from the mirror to a big globe standing nearby and suddenly he was struck by two specks on the blue Tasman Sea – Norfolk Island, 481 miles from New Zealand's tip, and Lord Howe Island 575 miles farther on. Then came a stretch of only 480 miles to Australia. These divisions compared favourably with the daily hops he had made on his flight from England. If he could make pin-point landfalls, it *would* be possible for little *Gipsy Moth* to make the crossing in three separate flights. No plane had ever landed on either island, and he could not discover if any suitable landing places existed unless he spent a couple of months examining them by steamer. Then came a brainwave. Why shouldn't *Gipsy Moth* be converted into a seaplane and land in the lagoons which these islands must surely possess?

But as his entire capital remained tied up in real estate he must first find £500 to buy floats. As the slump continued to prevent any property sales, he attempted to earn that sum by taking passengers joy-riding, but after the bashing his Moth had received during her long flight from England, clients were not eager.

Then one day Francis noticed a pair of old floats lying in a warehouse, which a naval seaplane had accidentally dropped twenty feet onto the deck of a cruiser. He tried to purchase them cheap, but the officials would not play. However useless they might be, discarded floats remained government property.

Petulantly, Francis made off into the mountains where he lived alone in a tent while sublimating his exasperation in a fortnight's hard bush-felling. As he sweated away in the scorching heat of summer he felt the 'poison of worry' drain out of his system. He revelled in this life, in the hard physical work and the plunges into icy mountain streams, in the peace of each evening meal by a camp fire. Now, bursting with vitality, he tried to assess how much he

Francis, aged three

The Rev. Charles Chichester, Emily, and their children Barbara (left) and Francis outside Shirwell Rectory

Above Francis standing on the float of his Gipsy Moth plane

Above right Francis, aggressive (left) and Geoffrey Goodwin, pensive (right) with some of the employees in their timber business in New Zealand.

Right Twenty minutes after the Gipsy Moth's crash in Japan

Above Family group: Sheila, Francis and baby Giles

Right Francis with his bees

Above left The wedding of Francis and Sheila, 1937

Left Giles Chichester's christening, 1946

Left Outside the front door of 9 St James's Place

Right At sea

Below Discussing the transatlantic race with the French mariner Bernard Moitessier

Four competitors in the first solo transatlantic race. Left to right: Francis, 'Blondie' Hasler, David Lewis and Val Howells.

really wanted to return to flying – 'to the terrible fatigue at dawn, to nerves wearing thin through sixteen hours of strain each day, to wondering how much longer one's luck could hold?' Here, in New Zealand, he had found a life that he loved – why eat his heart out over no money; no floats; no encouragement! But it was no good – the longing to turn his toy into a seaplane never left him. 'I felt that I *had* to make the flight and could not escape it.'

Finally, a practical idea struck him. As he belonged to the Territorial Air Force and had a great friend in its Director of Aviation, he would ask permission to do practice training in seaplanes. Down from the mountains came Mr Chichester. His request was granted. Francis found the flying of seaplanes to be even more thrilling for it demanded increased flying skill.

During this period, when Francis was fussing about his floats, Kingsford-Smith flew the Tasman from west to east in a big record-breaking plane. Francis felt this to be a blow but he retained his determination to be the first across in the opposite direction and worked on assiduously at his charts.

Professionally he received only discouragement. As it was impossible to carry enough petrol in so small a plane to make it in one hop, what did he imagine he was going to do if he missed each tiny island? There were no radio aids at that time and after leaving the tip of New Zealand, the slightest inaccuracy must mean death in the ocean. Francis settled down to intensive study of astronavigation. No one had ever before tried to pinpoint such targets in the last hour of their petrol supply.

To fly a small plane single-handed across a vast windy ocean and make a landfall on a minute island required not only expertise and cold courage and unusual luck but a new line of navigational thought. The pilot would have simultaneously to fly a bouncing machine and work out the complicated problems of course, speed, wind-drift and position. He would in fact be a one-man band in cramped discomfort and in constant peril. Francis reckoned he could make adaptations of age-old sea lore. A ship when seeking a small island can find its landfall by the method known as 'Aim-Off'. The theory is simple and logical. If a skipper aims directly at a small target and arrives where it should be and cannot see it, he then has to decide whether he shall search to the right or the left. If he guesses wrong he will be sailing ever farther away. If, however, the ship is aimed not directly at the target, but at a position say 100 miles to the left of that target, when the ship reaches what it thinks *is* 100 miles to the left, it can after taking a sunsight, turn and sweep along the position line until the island is *seen*. In other words, it gives the ship a definite direction in which to *search*.

Francis adapted this method in a unique way for his own venture. But a ship which missed an island would not sink, whereas an aircraft which missed an island would run out of petrol and drop into the sea. Bold and inventive as he was, Francis had to face the fact that no compass could be considered absolutely reliable in a small plane. It would be an extremely hazardous enterprise depending on absolute accuracy in calculations made beforehand. His only chance of finding the islands would be by taking shots at the sun and then working out his own position. He would try to do this every hour in order to be certain of where he was when the vital moment to turn off arrived. The experts said that it was impossible for a lone man flying in an open cockpit to use a sextant and work out sights. A plane simply could not be navigated like a boat. Francis queried this. He said that a plane perfectly trimmed could hold course for thirty seconds or more in calm weather during which he could take a sextant shot. He began to practise fast mathematics.

The object in using a sextant is to obtain a position. It is a small instrument consisting of a telescope and reflecting mirrors to measure the angle between sun or moon or stars and the horizon. The navigator has to catch the sun as you would catch a sunbeam on the wall from a well-polished knife. As Francis reckoned a marine sextant might prove impossible to use from his cockpit, he bought one of the newly developed 'bubble sextants' which had an artificial horizon in the form of a built-in bubble level. He carried this around with him while motoring and running. With practice his skill increased. Louise grew weary of bouncing her car over rough roads while Francis stood in the back trying to see if he could obtain a sunsight. Even less amusing was his command that she accompany him on his rubber-dinghy trial. Two people were needed to right the dinghy if it overturned, and no men friends seemed anxious to spare the time. Louise went out with him on a cold March day and as soon as he put up the sail, over went the dinghy. Francis's expression of disgust as he toppled backwards into the sea caused Louise to give a hoot of laughter even as she herself submerged. They climbed back onto the upturned dinghy, disentangled themselves from ropes and then had to plunge back into the icy water to right it. 'How useful you are, Louise. One person could not have done it,' Francis approvingly remarked. Frozen and sopping they rowed back and tried to run home but cramp gripped their leg muscles. Both of them hoped this little episode might pass unobserved, but next day friends who had been out to watch the 'dinghy test' with binoculars greeted them with shouts of laughter – their agonies of cramp on the roadside had appeared especially comic.

Francis could take chaff but he was hard hit when his first flying trial with the new bubble-sextant resulted in an error of 770 miles. Now his good friend the Director of Aviation wrote a stern letter in which he advised abandoning the whole project. Two famous aviators, Hood and Moncrieff, had recently disappeared in the Tasman Sea and it was feared that 'aviation would receive a setback if any more publicity occurred concerning lost airmen'.

Francis replied to this official damper with an assurance that he could work an ordinary sextant by flying very low and using the sea horizon just as a ship did. All that he begged for now was the loan of those old floats. He would secure them with wires under *Gipsy Moth*. Softened by such determination, the Director replied that he would 'praise Chichester's useful experimental work in navigation' and recommend that the floats be lent.*

---

* For the completely uninformed general reader here is an appreciation of Francis Chichester's early feats of navigation contributed by Lieutenant Commander Oliver Stoney of County Mayo. The author has deliberately retained Commander Stoney's first and last sentences:

At the risk of being a bore I shall start at the beginning: A position on the earth's surface is fixed by the intersection of Latitude and Longitude lines. Latitudes are the lines girdling the earth parallel to the Equator, which is Lat. 0°. Longitudes are the north-south lines, running from pole to pole like the sections of a peeled orange. 0° Longitude runs through the Royal Observatory at Greenwich. It may be the most lasting monument to the British Empire; when its civilisation is forgotten the 'pyramid' at Greenwich will remain. You can't rocket to the moon without G.M.T. to the umpteenth fraction of one second.

Fixing your position at sea or in the air is done when out of sight of land by Observation of Heavenly Bodies. This is the authentic term used by the most pedantic navigation instructors or the fullest textbook. An observation is a combination of sextant altitude of the sun or a star and simultaneous measurement of time. The sextant measures the angle of the heavenly body above the horizon. If at the same time you record the time, you can, after some involved sums with 5-figure logarithmic tables, calculate your latitude and longitude.

Working a sextant from a pier looking out to sea is straightforward if you are on a stable platform and the horizon is steady, so that 'bringing the sun down to the horizon' in order to measure its angular altitude by an arrangement of reflection mirrors and a telescope is relatively easy. On the bridge of an ocean liner it is more difficult. In a yacht it has always struck me as being so difficult as to verge on the impossible. Because of the violent motion of a small boat, a bubble sextant is usual – this introduces an artificial horizon into the sextant by means of a spirit level.

Anyone who has used a builder's spirit level, or measured a house, knows how difficult it is to get the bubble central and still. If at the same time you are trying to get the reflected image of the sun to coincide with it from the cockpit of a yacht the problem is increased. When Francis Chichester tried his bubble sextant in the air he found that by introducing

Francis then collapsed with a mysterious undiagnosable illness. Maybe it was caused by frustration or by the fears secretly creeping up on him about those thoughtless small mistakes in spherical calculation which could so easily lead to disaster. Whatever the cause he suddenly revived when he learned that the Government had graciously decided to lend their old floats. He was then seized by a strong presentiment that 28 March would be right for the first lap of this amazing flight. He sat down and worked out the position of the sun for his navigational chart on that date. Strangely enough, a wireless message then arrived from the Meteorological Office auguring a favourable wind for 28 March. This gave him two days in which to get ready.

Francis went straight to Squadron-Leader Isitt, the Commandant of the Air Base and asked if he could turn the Moth into a seaplane in the time. This very experienced veteran flying-boat pilot replied bluntly: 'I don't like this flight of yours. I doubt if you can find your way alone by sextant. Even if you can, suppose there is no sun? If you reach Norfolk Island there is nowhere to put down a seaplane. If you succeed in getting down, you won't be able to take off again, because of the swell. If there should chance to be no swell, it would be impossible to take off a Moth loaded up like yours unless a stiff wind was blowing. That might not happen.'

After this cascade of warnings, the Commandant set about working on the plane himself along with his aircraftmen. They were at it till midnight. Next afternoon the Moth had been tied to her floats and a wading party wheeled her down the slipway. Francis saw that his swallow had turned into a seagull! But could she rise when loaded with food, water, navigation instruments, boat, anchor, ropes and fifty gallons of petrol? According to previous tests with other planes the answer was No. But this *Gipsy Moth* knew nothing of other planes.

---

an artificial horizon he also introduced large errors and he fell back on swift visual recordings with an ordinary sextant.

Then after the sun has been caught accurately in the sextant come the 5-figure logarithmic tables and complicated calculations which must be done at speed. In an aircraft your desk for this wizardry can only be a small writing pad strapped to your right thigh. It is easiest to appreciate the magnitude of the necessary skill by considering the effect of any minute mistake in observation. An error of 1/60th of one degree in measuring the sextant altitude will place your position one nautical mile wrong. Simultaneously an error of one second of time will give you an error on the earth's surface of a quarter of a mile at the Equator and much more at other latitudes.

So absolute accuracy is essential not only in catching the sun but in quick mathematical calculation. To manage this in a little plane bobbing about in the wind was an extraordinary feat of skill and of mental endurance.

On no account submit my explanations to an expert navigator!

She rose at the first attempt. 'Don't forget that you have ideal conditions now,' warned Commandant Isett. 'It could be different without that strong breeze to head into and the right tide behind and the choppy sea to break suction.'

Of course it would be wise to make tests to make certain the old floats did not leak and to make several long flights testing Francis's navigation system. But then the perfect weather conditions might change. 'I'll do a test tomorrow,' murmured Francis, and Isett, by the look in his eyes, suspected that might mean not seeing him again.

Again they all worked till midnight, and on the morning of Saturday, 28 March 1931, Francis arose at 4 a.m., ate bacon and eggs by candlelight and walked out to where *Gipsy Moth* sat bobbing in the water. 'I'll just try her out properly,' he said innocently. He faced her into the wind and she rose with ease. Flying over Auckland he noted the time was 6.45 a.m. It would be sunset at Norfolk Island exactly twelve hours later. This was the magic date. He would go. On reaching the northern tip of New Zealand he had to descend to fill up with petrol. The sensible thing was to rest there overnight and leave fresh in the morning, but he did not want to recalculate his sextant sun-shots.

This fuelling stop proved unexpectedly complicated and long drawn out. He landed safely but his anchor dragged and the Maoris who rowed out to help him secure the plane were not prepared for his arrival. In leisurely fashion they fetched the fuel cases and then announced they possessed no funnel or hammer. Francis, standing on the bobbing seaplane had the greatest difficulty in pouring heavy tins of petrol into the tanks while a curious conversation took place.

'You going far?'

'To Australia.'

'Ho, Australia, hey! You give me that benzine tin when it empty, hey?'

'How many miles this Australia?'

'Fifteen hundred the way I am going.'

'Py corry! That th' phlurry long way to swim, I tink.'

The Moth now had fifty gallons in her tanks. She could not rise from the water with more. It was getting on for noon. Reason said Stay. Instinct said Fly. A launch chugged up with a telegram. 'Weather expected fine; fresh to strong south-easterly breeze; seas moderate becoming rough.' That was it. He opened the throttle but to his surprise the plane did not respond gladly as she had in the morning. It was only at the third attempt that she dragged herself

out of the water. It never entered his head that the carefully tested
floats might already be leaking.

Once in the air elation filled him. 'The flap I got into before starting had now disappeared, and my brain was ticking over cool and
steady. I knew that everything depended solely on accurate work.'
Conditions were perfect, the sun shone in a cloudless light-blue sky.
The exhausts gave off a steady rolling roar. The needle of the revolution indicator might have been the hand of a clock, it kept so steady.
The time for the fast sextant work on which everything depended
was rapidly approaching. The smallest error meant death and if the
sun hid herself at the vital turning point it meant death. But despite
fear (which Francis always knew, and considered importantly astrin-
gent) he remained basically confident and serene, feeling his master-
ship of this half-psychic art. He would attempt the nearly impossible,
the sun would come to his aid, the plane *would* hold a level course for
thirty seconds for his shots and he *would* get there. Flying over the
cloud-wrapped face of the rotating earth Francis Chichester believed
that by a mingling of skill and instinct he would find his way.

He was heading for an imaginary point ninety miles to the left of
Norfolk Island which he had calculated as the correct turn-off point.
He descended close to the sea to reset his altimeter and felt the Moth
rising and falling to the huge swell below. A perfect tail-wind
continued. After three o'clock, having taken several shots at the sun,
and recorded the sextant, watch and altimeter readings, he felt his
brain begin to flag. It was wearying trying to plot two sets of drift
readings, and although he could not receive any messages he continued trying to transmit a radio message every hour. Then a
muffled knocking sounded in number three cylinder. He forced himself to relax while reviewing fuel gauge, oil pressure, engine revs,
height, compass and chart.

The wind was hurrying him along so well that maybe he felt he
ought to make a fresh set of calculations for the turn-off point and
take it at four o'clock instead of at five o'clock. Quickly he worked
out the sun's position for the earlier hour and at four o'clock he
obtained four shots from 100 to 150 feet up, turning his plane in a
steep bank so as to catch the sun abeam. After each shot he turned
on course again to write down the sextant and watch readings.
When he plotted the result it showed his dead-reckoning to be nineteen miles out. It was no good worrying about the cause.* Now he
must rely entirely upon the sextant. This showed him to be forty-five

* Later he discovered his outboard air-speed indicator was over-reading by five
m.p.h. which had built up during four hours' flying.

miles from that vital turning-off point. He slowed the plane to give him half an hour to compute the work for another sextant sight at the exact moment for turn-off. The whole success or failure, his own life or death, depended on that moment. If he turned and missed the island he was done for. The plane would run out of petrol, land on the sea and there he could float or sink or starve in his rubber dinghy hundreds of miles from land. He remembered 'More missing airmen publicity would be bad for aviation.'

Now his mind worked coldly and clearly. The calculations he had made would give the true bearing of the island at the turn-off point because it would then be at right-angles to the direction of the sun. And that turn-off point was growing nearer and nearer. A few minutes before he was to reach it, when everything depended on a sight, clouds obscured the sun. He swung the plane to the left towards a white cloud, and then glimpsed sunlight on the sea five miles away. Opening the throttle he raced for this precious sparkling patch, and used his feet on the rudder while he worked the sextant with both hands. He got four shots in the sunlight, flying round in a tight circle, and each time he flew out into cloud to read the instruments. The shots compared exactly with the figure already computed. He was on the line. With a gasp of joy and relief he swung the Moth around on the new course. And now a strange madness filled him, he *knew* he was right and yet his very being cried out with despair at having to change from the straight line he had been flying all the way from New Zealand. Just before five o'clock he again glimpsed the sun and obtained one more sextant shot. It tallied exactly with the calculations he had made at the start of the flight. He must be dead on to that tiny island. And ninety minutes of light remained. He felt wildly excited. The island *must* be there.

Every minute seemed a lifetime, as I scanned the horizon ahead. The wind was dropping with approaching nightfall, and the drift was now only ten degrees. The sea looked grey-blue, cold and hostile. If I missed the island, what should I do? My brain was numb, and I could think of nothing . . . At 5.12 I knew the island ought to have been in sight fifteen minutes earlier. Surely that was land to the left – two hill cones, above a barren land of grey cloud with a dark purple coast below? But it was only another cloud.

As there was no use in worrying Francis deliberately relaxed. He needed his faculties in perfect control. Then the cloud lifted and he was looking down on an island – the only island for over five hundred miles. His navigational system had proved right.

As the Moth circled Norfolk Island, seeking some bay sheltered from the south-south-east swell, the wind, which had been behind him all the way from New Zealand, dropped completely. Francis glided down through bumpy air without mishap into Cascade Bay where he saw a jetty and a moving boat. He landed at 5.40 p.m., an hour before sunset. The memory of eleven hours before, when he had risen over sleeping Auckland in the grey morning light seemed too strange to believe.

9. Island to Island

A boat resembling a big whaler swept out to meet him, the crew bending to their long oars while a helmsman stood in the stern. Reassured by the sight of expert boatmen, Francis asked if he could immediately refuel so as to be ready for an early start next morning. They fetched him petrol within minutes. Then, with appalling difficulty, Francis sat astride the plane which was rolling in the swell and poured the four-gallon tins of petrol into a perpetually collapsing funnel. Soaked with petrol and seawater, he slithered about the fuselage until long after dark. After this the islanders escorted him to 'Government House' for the night. The old stone edifice had been built for the Prison Governor when the island was used as a penal settlement. Francis slept heavily within the thick walls.

At 4 a.m. he had to be woken from a deep sleep to drag on his sticky salt-encrusted clothes, swallow a confection of bacon and eggs and whisky, and drive to the jetty where the stalwart boatmen rowed him out and helped him onto the plane. Now that Francis felt absolutely confident of his navigation system, he did not suffer the extreme tension of the previous day. He expected to cover the next lap of 575 miles in eight hours. However, new worries beset him. Two of the cylinders had no compression. They improved when warmed up but he knew the engine was not absolutely perfect. After checking the oil and the petrol filter and finishing off refuelling, he taxied out to sea where just the right off-shore breeze was blowing, but when turned into the wind *Gipsy Moth* ploughed unevenly through the rough waves, struggled to rise, and could not. Then as the float settled horrifyingly deep in the water the propeller began to hit the wave crests which made the frail fuselage shudder. Poor little Moth – she felt strangely heavy, as if waterlogged. While Francis frantically drove her out to sea, improvising by use of difficult and usually forbidden emergency techniques to raise her from the water in a cross-wind take-off, she swayed and jumped and fell back into the water. In despair he decided to stop and see if any water could have got into the floats. He did this by inserting a rubber tube into each compartment and sucking. Sure enough one float had mysteriously filled with seawater. For half an hour he sucked and spat until his mouth ached and his jaw muscles got cramp. There was nothing for it but to taxi away to calmer waters. Dodging rocks he made a couple more attempts to raise *Gipsy Moth* into the air, but although once she leaped from the crest of the swell, she had not enough speed to stay airborne and fell back pitifully into the sea. On the final attempt she broke an inter-float bracing-wire and the floats began to spread apart beneath her. With difficulty Francis drove his battered seahorse back into Cascade Bay.

During the next two days, 29 and 30 March, the inhabitants of Norfolk Island slaved to help Francis Chichester repair his plane. A crack mechanic among them discovered that the metal seating of the exhaust valve had begun to unscrew and was indeed likely to jam the valve post and break up the engine. New wires were procured to hold the floats and everybody tried to discover how water could possibly have entered these supposedly waterproof objects. This was certainly a puzzle. In New Zealand, meticulous tests had proved these second-hand floats absolutely watertight – and yet here they were taking in gallons! When re-tested by filling with water, no leak showed. Their water absorption seemed inexplicable. Larger screws were fitted into the inspection plates on each float in case worn screw threads had allowed the plates to lift on being submerged. How could water get into the floats and yet not run out? The leaking remained a mystery, and the best that Francis's friends could do was to present him with a bilge pump made by reversing the valve in a bicycle pump so that at least he would not have to use his own mouth for suction.

With a hundred and forty letters to post for the islanders, Francis intended to set off on the morning of 31 March, but as no breeze blew he could not induce the plane to rise out of the water. In desperation he jettisoned the heavy rubber dinghy and an hour's petrol, but to no avail. Then again a bracing wire snapped, so he deferred departure until the morrow, which, being April Fools' Day, he thought might prove auspicious. He removed all heavy gear and flew the Moth to a coral bay on the other side of the island. There everything was re-stowed, and he tried to memorize the under-water coral reefs because he would not be able to see them when motoring out in his plane. Before dawn on 1 April Francis walked from his lodging and looked up at the dark, star-studded sky. He felt a fine breeze blowing from the south-east, perfect for take-off. His team of enthusiastic helpers towed the Moth to a neck in the lagoon and Francis climbed onto a float, swung the propeller and jumped back into the cockpit. Then to his horror a friendly swimmer half-climbed onto the plane unable to see the rotating propeller and for several minutes Francis expected to see a smiling face decapitated. But the man swam merrily away without ever knowing the danger he had been in. Francis opened the throttle and signalled for the rope to be dropped. *Gipsy Moth* gathered speed and rose wearily from the lagoon. He regretted having to leave that rubber dinghy, but the old elation filled him. After three days of mind-cracking struggles he was again in the air. Now 575 miles of ocean stretched between the two islands. His navigation system would remain the same. After a few hours he noticed a puff of smoke on the ocean which could only be a steamer and he tapped out a message on his wireless key. It gave him comical delight when the ship belched out a big smoke notifying reception.

Now there began a new and most terrifying experience. Although the engine was running perfectly, the plane's entire fuselage began to vibrate. He guessed it must be the result of weakening the propeller by thrashing through the waves in attempts to rise from the sea. Whatever the cause, these vibrations managed to rattle out the holding screws of the compass and break both airspeed indicator and altimeter whose needles started to jerk in crazy circles. His anxiety, added to the roaring engine noise and the wind on his head, caused Francis to make a mistake when plotting the drift lines. This puzzled him for some time. Then he perceived the foolish error and began worrying about his own waning sense of judgement.

He had expected to reach the vital turn-off point when six hours out. At 5.10 he took three shots of the sun and found that he was twenty-six miles short of his dead-reckoning position. He sweated with fear at this inaccuracy until he remembered that now the strut air-speed indicator was over-reading five miles an hour. As the all-important turn-off moment approached, black clouds blotted out the sun and raindrops hard as hailstones stung his forehead. It seemed too cruel that the sun god would hide when a brief glimpse of him meant life or death. He spotted a fragment of sunlight upwind and raced towards it at full speed hoping this would not cause the propeller to disintegrate. But the sun patch was moving fast in front of the wind and he could not reach it. Each time he caught a glimpse of golden light he banked steeply and tried to obtain a shot with the sextant but clouds always closed in.

Like a mad creature the plane turned and raced for each shaft of light which could mean life. At last from a vertical bank, diving near the sea, Francis obtained a single sunsight; he got it four and a half minutes late, but at least he got it. Making due allowance for the time difference he compared it with his calculations for 5 p.m. It showed him to be twenty-one miles short of the turn-off point and he had to rely on that one shot taken in a second of faint sunlight. There was nothing for it but to change course seventy degrees on the single calculation.

Clouds thickened. Then suddenly a burst of sunrays poured down as in a holy picture. He raced to the golden shaft, took three shots and computed the observations. The result placed Lord Howe Island exactly ahead. Wild excitement seized him as he put away his sextant. Once again Francis knew that his system had worked.

The last hour passed slowly. Then suddenly he saw a big rock and the island was there beneath him. Wild with joy he circled the lagoon till a sudden air bump threw the plane downwards, and he landed on the clear water and realized the plane was drifting fast astern. Scrambling out of the cockpit he heaved the anchor overboard.

This day's flight of 575 miles had taken him seven hours and forty minutes. Two launches drew out and men shouted instructions. One man picked up the anchor line and towed the plane to a mooring of two great anchors. Then the launch took Francis ashore. Dark was falling. He had only just made it.

A kindly Mr Dignam, in charge of his refuelling, invited the triumphant pilot to spend the night at his house. Hardly able to register, Francis fell into bed and slept fitfully. There were squalls all night. He heard them even in his dreams.

Early next morning he went out with Dignam to examine the plane.

'She looks queer,' said Francis.

'She looks queer to me too,' said Dignam.

Gipsy Moth had sunk. Only her tail remained above the water, as if she had been just too tired and battered to hold her head up any longer.

10. Tasman Accomplished

Each of the three days in which Francis Chichester flew across the Tasman Sea represented a small lifetime of incredible experience. Each minute of 28 March, 1 April and 10 June 1931 resembled no other minute of his or any other man's existence. He would for ever remember the rain storms so likely to bring death, the uncertainty, the elusive shafts of sunlight that alone gave his sextant guidance, the wild triumph of his navigation and the horrible fears caused by technical aircraft difficulties.

Now, when two fantastic laps had been completed came an unexpected interlude of happiness and calm imposed by cruel circumstance. The hundred-odd islanders were aching to help this strange adventurer who had landed in their midst. As Francis reeled at the sight which met his eyes, kindly voices were trying to soften the blow, voices which encouraged him to salvage the plane and rebuild her with their help.

After returning silently to Mr Dignam's house and finding that, strangely enough, he was able to consume the large second breakfast set before him, Francis went out to re-examine his plane now lying upside down on the sea bottom. It was unbelievable! How could a plane sitting on waterproof floats have *sunk*!

Strong hands dragged her inshore and half the island's population splashed around eager to salvage every possible piece. The islanders showed much practical genius. They unscrewed, unbolted and lifted with intelligence. Two parties worked in relays, carrying objects ashore. The motor was placed in a cargo shed to be carefully dismantled. Heartened by so much industry and kindness and yet dazed with disappointment, Francis stared at the body of his Moth lying in the grass stripped of her wings and her beating heart. Was there a chance of salvage? In her construction the thin plywood skin of the fuselage was tacked and glued to the framework, the strength of the whole depending on its rigidity. The glue did not appear to have been destroyed by salt water. So, if the motor could be overhauled, and new wings and ailerons sent out by steamer, he might perhaps paste his broken toy together and fly on the remaining 600 miles to Australia. New struts, spars and bracing wires would not cost a great deal but new wings certainly would. He pondered wistfully. Maddening not to have been born a millionaire.

Seeing his downcast face the islandmen encouraged him further; they swore they were sufficiently knowledgeable to rebuild the wings themselves.

'There must be four thousand different pieces of wood in those wings, a lot of them only half as thick as a pencil . . . there's the fabric covering to be sewn on, not to mention half a dozen coats of dope,' said Francis. Each wing would have to be painted with three coats of red dope followed by five coats of aluminium dope, but it was worth trying. He made out a fourteen-page list of materials and replacements and telegraphed it to Sydney. Then he relaxed. Francis was very partial to laughing people, and Fate had dropped him from the skies amidst cheerful boatmen and fisherfolk. The girls looked handsome, and two splendid seamstresses volunteered to undertake the stiff job of sewing all the fabric which would cover the wings.

Francis's spirits flickered up. This rest on a small island waiting for materials to arrive by steamer from Sydney would give him the chance to revive. He had been very near snapping point. The joy of intricate craftsmanship soothed him. It was what a later generation might call occupational therapy. Valves had to be ground and cylinders polished. Then blueprints for wing-construction arrived from de Havilland's to be studied and discussed. There is real drama in putting together a plane that means to break records with do-it-yourself kit! After the long days' work with his jolly companions Francis would go for a two-mile barefoot run along the beach. He had a particularly devoted gang of young admirers. One of them, Maurice Wilson, who was a schoolboy at the time, writes: 'Often on a moonlight night he would get me out of bed to walk along the beach and would tell me all about his travels and adventures.' The youth of Lord Howe island would never forget his visit. Francis slept well and ceased to feel tense. These nine weeks were among the happiest he would ever know. However, the season was getting on, winds were becoming cooler at night and the great fat clouds of the Westerlies started to roll across the stars; he kept an anxious eye on the skies.

Winter storms would soon be breaking and the constant reminder of deteriorating weather drove him.

At last the time came when four wings and two ailerons had been reconstructed and painted with oil and then with dope-resisting paint. To finish the job, seven coats of dope had to be applied to all surfaces. Then came the fitting of automatic slots, fixtures, struts, rigging wires and aileron controls. After a meticulous overhaul the motor was put back in place, the fuselage enamelled inside and out, the floats carefully painted and ninety-six new screw threads inserted through the manhole rims. As soon as the wings could be attached to the fuselage the Moth would be launched on the lagoon. Then as quickly as possible she must fly away.

Everything seemed to be in order, but the first trial produced a nasty shock when the engine suddenly stopped. Luckily Francis was still over the lagoon and could glide down onto the water. Inspection of the carburettor revealed that it had been wiped clean with a rag soaked in linseed oil, and this oil had then dried into a skin, bits of which had blocked the jets. Francis wiped the carburettor carefully hoping that no tiny invisible fragments remained. If the jets got blocked far out over the ocean the Moth would fall into the water and he would die.

Towards the end of his stay he indulged in two days of merry joy-rides for the islanders, but something in his plane's performance made Francis uneasy. The Moth pulled more to the right and seemed to take longer to leave the water each time he took off. It was as if some part of her was again getting waterlogged. Francis pumped out the bilges with his new specially converted bicycle pump and found very little water, yet several islanders insisted they could see water trickling off one float when he flew low. 'But it is impossible for these floats to leak,' said Francis. 'It feels as if one of them was filling with water but when I use the bilge pump I only draw air.' And yet, and yet . . . the Moth seemed to grow heavier and more lop-sided every hour she sat on water.

On the night of 9 June Francis went for his last jogtrot along the beach. How sad he felt to be leaving this happy island – and for what a wildcat leap! Before this he had at least known that his plane had been put together by experts, certainly it had never spent a night bumping on the bottom of a lagoon. But the lure of finishing this adventure and of being the first man to fly the whole Tasman Sea from east to west solo, wiped out misgivings. Just before take-off, a storm of curious contradictions flooded his mind. One moment Francis felt that Fate would decide on whether or not he reached

Australia. Then came the opposite idea – this venture was nothing to do with Fate and depended entirely on himself. If he had made mistakes in rebuilding the plane, if he became slack in his calculations, if he let any part of his mind forget an essential – then he was for it and Fate had no part in the outcome. He had not long to indulge in such reflections. He walked with his friends to the jetty, rowed out in the dinghy, broke a bottle of brandy on the propeller-boss and cast off.

The engine started obediently and he began to taxi down wind to the reef. But something was wrong. The Moth would not turn properly and as she gathered speed Francis felt her slewing round to starboard. In fact she nearly overturned. After meticulous examination, knowing that he had pumped all the float compartments dry, Francis could not accept the possibility that one of them was filling up with water. It just couldn't happen. He must go on. He must force her up. He tried again and again, almost capsizing each time, but *Gipsy Moth* refused to rise. Heartbroken, he let her drift back towards the reef. When dangerously near he slipped out of his seat to swing the propeller and the Moth thrashed with wild effort across the lagoon. He noticed then the two mountains had shed their usual cloud caps as if to salute him. In desperation he decided to jettison fuel and food until his plane grew light enough to get out of the water. He syphoned out petrol until he had enough for only eight hours' flying, but he kept two homing pigeons, they weighed so little in their light box, and they might convey his last message to the living world. Anxious friends rowed out in a dinghy to suggest that he dump his kit of spare parts for these were really heavy. Reluctantly he did so.

The nightmare of trying to get off ended when he tried a new tactic – that of keeping the plane down until she had long outrun the distance usually needed. Straining every nerve he eventually got her to rise from the surface, though rather slowly. She nearly crashed into the palm-covered mountainside but a strong gust of wind lifted her just in time. Francis puzzled at the plane's uncontrollability. He kept looking at the revolution indicator to see if the engine was turning properly. It showed a steady 18·00. There seemed no explanation. There simply could not be a rush of water in the float as she changed tilt, and yet that was what it felt like.

It was 9.30 a.m. when the Moth finally cleared the twin peaks of the island and turned resolutely towards Australia. When 160 miles out she backfired and Francis hoped this was just a defective magneto and not the engine packing up. Then came a battle with rain clouds, and for a time he had to fly blind while fighting the panic which rose up within him. He would remember saying to himself out loud, 'Keep cool! Keep cool!' When he emerged from the first storm he found that the wind had changed by forty-five degrees, so that he was fifty-five degrees off course. After correcting this error he saw storm clouds ahead and quivered with trepidation.

We flew through the curtain of rain into an immense cavern of space between the illimitable vault of dull sky above, and the immeasurable floor of dull water below. It was solitary in that great space. Some slanting pillars of rain leaned against the wind, trailing across the dull floor of water like spirits of the dead drifting from the infernal regions. Water spouts rose like great columns and then suddenly ahead several bright flashes as if a heliograph was signalling, and a pearly-grey-white airship.

At that time the Flying-Saucer cult had not been heard of and as this is Francis Chichester's personal Flying Saucer story it *must* be recorded in his own words:

I looked around, sometimes catching a flash or a glint, and turning again to look at the airship I found that it had disappeared. I screwed up my eyes unable to believe them, and twisted the seaplane this way and that, thinking that the airship must be hidden by a blind spot. Dazzling flashes continued in four or five different places, but I still could not pick out any planes. Then, out of some clouds to my right front I saw another, or the same airship advancing. I watched it intently, determined not to look away for a fraction of a second: I'd see what happened to this one, if I had to chase it. It drew steadily closer, until perhaps a mile away when suddenly it vanished. Then it reappeared, close to where it had vanished. I watched with angry intentness. It drew closer, and I could see the dull gleam of light on its nose and back. It came on, but instead of increasing in size, it diminished as it approached. When quite near, it suddenly became its own ghost – one second I could see through it, and the next it had vanished. I decided that it would only be a diminutive cloud, perfectly shaped like an airship and then dissolving, but it was uncanny that it should exactly resume the same shape after it had once vanished.

This experience remained unique in his life. He kept wondering what it was. Fatigue? Hallucination? Electrical cloud phenomena? Or some super-sensory perception of an activity beyond man's usual ken?

After six lonely hours, the wound-up pilot gave a gasp. A long, dark line marked the horizon. It was Australia! Having the luxury of a whole coast for landing instead of one tiny island, he had not made a definite choice but it had been his intention to reach Sydney. However, looking down, he noticed a big bay to the south and in it spied five warships lying at anchor. This was fantastic luck. The Navy understood people of his kind and would surely welcome him. What guardian angel had led him here? He dropped the Moth down beside a cruiser on whose bow he read H.M.A.S. *Australia*. *Gipsy Moth* drifted past the vast grey sides while Francis stood on the cockpit edge frantically signalling with his handkerchief, 'How far is Sydney?' An Aldis lamp flashed back from the bridge and within seconds a motor launch swept around the bows. Sydney was eighty miles to the north. He was in Jervis Bay. As the sailors towed the Moth to the shelter of the breakwater where Francis could swing the propeller and fly off, an absolute longing to remain filled his heart. When he swung the propeller the engine responded but the Moth shivered and seemed unable to rise from the pounding swell. He did not care. The first solo flight from New Zealand to Australia had been accomplished. He had flown the Tasman Sea and achieved his aim. The tremendous experience could never be taken away from him. Not only was he the first man to accomplish this flight but he had done it in a way which no other human being would ever dream of attempting to emulate. The fantastic drive of his own will had got him into the air, onto the islands, over the disintegration of his frail plane and on to his destination. With hardly any money, with borrowed defective floats, with cheerful amateurs to help him stick his plane together, he had achieved a world record. What peace of mind. Or so one would think.

Seeing that he was in difficulties, the launch reappeared and an officer offered to tow him to the aircraft-carrier H.M.A.S. *Albatross*. He knew it would be bliss to be the guest of these efficient naval men, men who would understand and care!

After making fast to a rope dangling from a long boom, Francis freed the two pigeons who must have undergone many an anxious moment during the flight, while their little personal compasses gave them no comfort at all. Up they flew and one can only hope that chums in their home-loft believed the story they had to tell.

Now a sailor let down a rope ladder and Francis climbed up it to greet Captain Feakes, the commanding officer of H.M.A.S. *Albatross*. 'Doctor Livingstone I assume,' he said, looking hard at the dishevelled pilot on his quarterdeck. 'At any rate, you have managed to discover the only aircraft-carrier in the Southern Hemisphere. Come along to my cabin.' There he turned casually. 'Did I say, when you came aboard, "Doctor Livingstone I *assume*"? Of course, I meant Doctor Livingstone I *pre*sume.' He produced a whisky and soda and made Francis feel like a long-expected guest.

A squadron-leader of the Air Force breezed in to discuss lifting the plane onto the deck of *Albatross*. Francis wished to do the hooking on himself and climbed down in the dark to his bobbing Moth, where he stood on her engine reaching out for the iron hook lowered from the carrier. It was difficult to catch the heavy hook but after a few tries he managed to grab it and slide it under the two taut sling wires. At this second the swell caused a sudden roll and the hook snatched right on his fingers. The scream that Francis gave alerted the winchman to immediately lower the hook. Sick with pain Francis leant against the petrol tank holding the iron hook in his right hand and resting the wires in the crook of his left thumb. The sea held still a moment. 'Lift!' he called, and the plane went up, hung over the deck and settled gently on the padded mats just meant for such as she. Francis heard his voice saying from far off: 'Help me down, will you? I'm going to faint.'

When he came to he was in the ship's hospital. The surgeon had removed the top of one crushed finger and neatly sewed up the rest. No one could choose such a way of entering naval society but this accident proved a blessing in disguise. Francis became a guest of the wardroom and he revelled in the comradeship shown him. These were men who could evaluate what he had achieved; men who liked him and rejoiced with him; men he could talk to. That open friendship which Francis so desperately needed became his. 'It was like staying in the best club with the mysterious fascination of naval life added,' he said, but within the wardroom it was Francis who seemed mysterious and fascinating. The naval officers were not only impressed by his use of the 'Aim-Off' system in the open cockpit of a tiny vibrating plane, but filled with secret trepidation at the thought of his future. He had done what the experts said was absolutely impossible, but that was not enough. Francis was all set to go on around the world in little *Gipsy Moth*. They liked him and could not help fearing for his fearlessness.

11. From Australia to Japan

What sort of tattered hero eventually arrived in Sydney? What had it *done* to him, this gruelling battle across that sea which had claimed so many pilots' lives? What elation and what triumph of spirit mingled with the fatigue he suffered? In mind he remained balanced; he could take strain. It was on his physical system that the engine vibrations, the over-endurance and worry had adverse effects. Francis Chichester understood the trembling feel of his *Gipsy Moth* while he forced her components to hold together, but of those effects in himself, which might compare to metal-fatigue in a plane, he was unaware. Observers could see a tense, girl-shy, muscular young man burning with ambitious ideas, but his secret iron reserves and self-control were never immediately evident.

In a fairly clear, introspective assessment, he would later write of the moodiness which tempered his pleasure in adulation.

Yet I felt isolated, and drained of personality, horribly cut off from other people by some queer gulf of loneliness. I had achieved my great ambition, to fly across the Tasman Sea alone, I had found the islands by my own system of navigation which depended on accurate sun-sights worked out while flying alone, something which no one ever would do in similar circumstances. I had not then learned that I would feel an intense depression every time I achieved a great ambition. I had not then discovered that the joy of living comes from action, from making the attempt, from the effort, not from success.

But this was not entirely true. The joy of living does to a certain extent depend on success, in that it does not flourish in repeated failure. What Francis suffered from was simply nervous reaction. He had undergone an ordeal which might be compared to playing a Beethoven sonata with one hand while doing a complicated crossword puzzle with the other – and this while being flung around on a switchback railway. It was natural to be keyed up.

Captain Feakes brought his aircraft-carrier to Sydney with *Gipsy Moth* resting in her interior, and Francis enjoying himself in the wardroom. A flight-sergeant attending the Moth found one of the bilge compartments full of water, but the naval experts could not discover any actual leaks in the float. They puzzled; how *did* the water get there? De Havilland's also examined the float while overhauling the engine, but could not find any reason why it should not be waterproof. It remained a maddening mystery.

Meanwhile Francis grappled with plans for his next lap around the world. First he had to work out refuelling stops between Sydney and Japan. It would be very different from flying the Moth as a land plane. With her reduced range he must discover some sheltered bay or inlet every 500 miles or so where petrol could be waiting. This meant coping not only with the elements, but with many foreign peoples and in their own languages.

The first 2000 miles of his intended flight would follow the coastline of Australia northwards to its farthest point. Then leaving Thursday Island he would skirt New Guinea and hop along the Dutch East Indies to the Philippines and on to China and Japan.

There were gloomy prognostications and Admiralty Sailing Directions noted the New Guinea coast as 'everywhere covered with dense jungle and so marshy as to be almost inaccessible . . . natives hostile . . . boats and bivouacs repeatedly shot at . . .' An experienced skipper marked out the worst places for cannibals and the best places to refuel.

The Dutch government proved most reluctant to grant permission for a little plane to fly over New Guinea, and asked the destitute Francis if he could guarantee payment for searches which might have to be made for him! Blithely he signed a form absolving all authorities of all responsibility. When issuing the permit, they did not tell him that two stalwart friends, Eric C. Riddiford and Grant-Dalton, had secretly guaranteed to pay for any searches. He spent a month doing repair work and fretting over finances. There was even some small hold-up over the small amount of money due to be sent out from New Zealand and eventually Francis had to borrow £44 off Major Hereward de Havilland with which to buy petrol and food on his way to Japan.

By 3 July everything that could be done had been done. One chilly early morning the great hatches were rolled back, and *Gipsy Moth* hauled up from the giant hold of *Albatross*. When Francis tried to thank his host, Captain Feakes, he drew him aside and said quietly 'If you find it's impossible, you *will* give it up, won't you?' These were the sort of men Francis wished he could live with, men who understood the fantastic dangers and difficulties of what he tried to do, who advised and warned but did not seek to hold him back against his will. Only men who knew about navigation could appreciate the near-impossibility of completing his venture. He had tempted Fate in crossing the Tasman Sea – must he go on tempting right round the world? With a loan of £44 in his pocket the answer was Yes!

Gipsy Moth swung out on the crane hook and landed in the glassy water beside the aircraft carrier. Francis feared he might not be able to rise from the suction without a wind – and he dreaded this when Captain Feakes and all his naval friends were watching. However, when he turned her towards Sydney Harbour bridge, he spotted the wake-waves of a ferry steamer and he chased them. The slight bumping enabled the plane to soar off the water. He dipped his wings to *Albatross* and headed north. In his log he wrote: 'This is the supreme ecstasy of life!'

Near Brisbane he alighted in the big river. Next morning, with again no wind, he had great difficulty in taking off, in fact to force her up he had to use a right-angle bend which was forbidden in seaplane flying instructions. That night he spent in a strange little sea-coast town called Rockhampton. The people sat him on a beer-barrel to answer their questions, just as if he was a stranded Hottentot. On he flew, inside the Great Barrier Reef, to land near Gloucester Island and eat a peaceful meal alone. He was learning how important it was to be alone occasionally – just to recharge his own batteries.

Next day everything appeared to be perfect for take-off, with the right sort of choppy waves, but to his surprise the Moth remained heavier than ever in the water, and when she reached the open seas he felt her swing reasonlessly to starboard. By jamming on the opposite rudder Francis pulled her round and managed to climb into the air. He wrote in his log: 'Horrible! Cannot understand it; I must have been flying atrociously, yet did not think so.' Again there had been some inexplicable weight change in her – the mystery was beginning to drive him mad.

That day he covered 623 miles in eight hours and landed with nearly empty tanks at a town called Cairns where it proved very difficult to find any petrol whatever and impossible to procure a bed. The few hotels were overflowing with tourists. The weary Francis was extremely grateful when eventually a sympathetic lady took him in, produced supper and rose before dawn to cook him a breakfast next morning.

Leaving the northernmost point of Australia, Francis flew on to Thursday Island where a pearl merchant invited him to dine sumptuously in Dutch style. Then with only £18 left for fuel he flew to Merauke, a Dutch settlement on the New Guinea coast. Here he spent the night in a stone guesthouse and watched with amusement the jovial countenances of cannibal prisoners going out to work. They were hillmen unable to resist the occasional capture of a plump town boy for the pot. The Dutch considered it unfair to execute natives for indulging in the natural habits of their tribe. Cannibals, when caught, were merely sentenced to a few years' road-making, an exercise which they rather enjoyed, particularly as abundant meals were provided without the trouble of a stalk.

On and on flew Francis, from one island to another, from one strange world to a stranger. Sometimes he slept in weird discomfort, sometimes he would be magnificently entertained by the magnates of pearling stations.

The longest sea stretch he covered was 139 miles from Ternate in the Moluccas to the Talauer Islands. On the way he grew rather sleepy and looking down on the blue ocean he decided to satisfy a growing curiosity as to whether he could alight on the open Pacific and rise again. He found the waves bigger than he had expected and as the Moth rolled he logged: 'Funny how she always rides beam to the wind.' The plane bumped hard when taking off, but he felt sure of getting her up when he had such firm waves to turn into. Then he noticed the unbelievable happening again, and logged: 'Can see water running from the tail of the starboard float all the time.'

This was proof that an unidentifiable crack existed and that his island friends had not been imagining water running out of the floats. But how could it happen? If neither de Havilland's nor the naval experts in Australia had been able to discover a leak in the floats and if the pump only produced air, what demon lurked in those compartments?

During his night in Mati the President gave him dinner, and the Postmaster, a very important personage, insisted on throwing a dance. Although dropping with fatigue after the long hours of flight in moist heat, Francis brightened at the prospect of dancing with pretty native girls. To his chagrin, they had learned Spanish ways. All were dressed in stiff brocade and watched by strict chaperones.

At Ormoc Bay in Leyte he spent a terrible five hours trying to take off from the glassy surface. He had just pumped the bilges but the suction of the water seemed to hold the heels of the floats. After struggling fifteen miles across the bay, heavy rain started and broke the surface just enough to reduce suction and he flew on three hours to Mashate. Next morning the get-off proved even worse; after nearly four hours of trying to rise, the starboard float drove under the water and went on submerging until the wing dipped under the surface and one propeller tip was chipped by a piece of floating wood. He had to ask a motor boat to tow the Moth back to the wharf. Here he decided that he must open that starboard float and see what in heaven's name was weighing it down. The bilge was dry but he continued to open up until he reached the large middle compartment. 'When I saw what was inside I just stayed on one knee staring . . . This middle compartment, about six feet long, was half full of water; there must have been fifty gallons in it, equal to nearly half the weight of the whole plane.' At last he understood the cause of the plane nearly capsizing and not being able to rise. He could see that the metal bilge pipe had once been cracked, probably when the float had originally been dropped in its old naval days. This explained how he had been misled when his pump sucked up air instead of water. But he still could not imagine how the crack which let water in when the plane was sitting, could then close up and not let it out, thus defying detection.

It seemed most cruel that having discovered the reason for the Moth's reluctance to rise from the water, he had now chipped the propeller. He spent a hellish night going over the possibility of mending it himself while mosquitoes bit his feet sticking out from a too-short net.

Next morning, in the blazing heat, he pumped the float dry – so simple now he had realized what the trouble was – and then he removed the propeller. He cut a piece out of a petrol tin and worked it into a sheath and the local native Governor produced some shoe tacks with which to hammer it onto the blade. To balance the other blade which then caused an uneven violent vibration, he sheathed its tip also with tin, and drove in tacks until it seemed to balance perfectly when threaded on his walking stick between two chairs. When he replaced this tinkered-up propeller, the plane flew perfectly. He gave the jubilant Governor a joy-ride around the harbour, nearly sank the plane on a coral reef, and next day took off for Manila.

As *Gipsy Moth* approached Manila, she was welcomed by an escort of American fighter planes. Francis felt immensely excited as they flew above him in formation – such a reward for his little plane, who tried so hard!

Manila society descended on the new arrival. Francis was rushed from luncheons to dinners, to clubs, to boxing matches, to swimming pools and cocktail parties. When surrounded by 'attractive girls in bathing suits' he grew introspective. He had thought this was what he wanted but when lionizing happened, he hated it. He did not want parties. He did not want to be a lion. No, he wanted a wonderful wild lover – and if he could not have one, he'd rather be alone. Whatever amorous adventures Francis had pursued in New Zealand and England, they had left him unsophisticated, susceptible as a schoolboy to the opposite sex and unable to deal with his own feelings – so of course he got gloomy. It was better to concentrate on floats and typhoons.

Reports of an approaching typhoon were at this moment discussed at every party. Manila longed for it to arrive and dispel the sultry heat. Francis thought it might be wise to fly off soon, and he overhauled the Moth as fast as possible. *Gipsy Moth* was wheeled into a seaplane hangar and suspended from the roof so that those odious, unpredictable floats could be removed from her tummy. Generously, the U.S. Air Corps offered to test each float and an army lorry arrived to take them away. The Air Corps experts requested several days to spend patching, screwing new plates and driving rivets. Francis felt dazed by their efficiency. The home-made tin tips of his damaged propeller were replaced by copper sheaths which ought to stand up to lashing waves at take-off, and although heavier, these blades were so perfectly balanced on their spindle that when he breathed on one tip it started to revolve. While these exquisite adjustments were being made, Francis could keep his mind off the cocktail-party girls he so disliked, by grinding valves with first-class mechanics.

Father Selga, Director of the Weather Bureau, brought daily reports of the slowly approaching typhoon (which, soon after Francis had gone, was to wreck the city). On the day after the propeller and floats were returned to him, Francis departed. He reached the Aparri River on the northernmost tip of the main island in five hours.

When he came to take off on the following morning it was to find that the starboard float, which had just been overhauled by American Air Corps experts, was leaking worse than ever. It actually submerged when he stepped on it. He pumped for ten minutes but could see the water was gaining. There was nothing for it but to tow the plane to shallow water and, standing deep in slime, to remove the manhole and then bale with a tobacco tin – the only thing of a size which could go through the hole at the top. But water continued to enter at some invisible point beneath a girder. He sat back, trying to think of some way to pinpoint and stop this crack which he could neither see nor feel. Eager helpers flocked out and together they pulled the plane up a slippery bank and onto a bed of coconut husks, but when Francis washed the mud away he could not perceive any hole in either float. Then once again he filled the floats with water – it did not run out. After emptying both tanks completely, he took one of the helpers for a short flight up the river and when the plane resettled on the water her floats appeared absolutely buoyant and water-proof.

As dusk was now approaching Francis had to spend the night on shore. At dawn next morning he returned to the plane, stepped on the float and down it went waterlogged! It was beyond reason. He had at last discovered that the starboard float filled with water, but he couldn't discover how or where. If water could come in why didn't it go *out* through the same hole? Sweating in the damp heat, he sought to stuff rags under the girder whence it appeared to be welling, climbed, mud-covered and filthy as he was, into the cockpit and flew off with the lightest possible petrol load for Tamsui in Formosa.

Here, having landed in shallow water, the hot, dirty, exasperated pilot found himself facing ceremonious welcome from launch after launch of Japanese officials in spotless white uniforms. With im-perturbable good manners they bowed and made speeches while ignoring his piteous cries of 'My plane is sinking!'

Then the British Consul arrived on the scene and stared in painful embarrassment at the oily, mud-covered pilot. An Englishman dressed like this would lower prestige.

Trying to be polite Francis finally persuaded his hosts to tow *Gipsy Moth* to a mooring, and continue interrogations in the Customs House. After politely drinking a toast in sweet port wine, they started a barrage of questions which seemed anything but friendly. Had he been spying on their fortifications? 'No,' retorted Francis – he hated port, especially in that heat, and could think of nothing but his diabolical floats.

As weather reports remained good and he felt exhausted by so much questioning, Francis decided to remain resting for a day. But rest was not a word that the Japanese understood. Commands to appear before the Governor-General and sip warm champagne were impossible to refuse. Francis conducted himself with suitable deco-rum, and after a hot night he rose to be again toasted in port wine while a gang of coolies lifted his plane on bamboo poles back into the water. On reaching open sea the Moth, with her floats all light and dry after a night on land, rose easily into the air and headed for China. His advent was, of course, expected, and as he flew over his first Chinese island, Tung Yung, a red and black Chinese flag broke out on the lighthouse in his honour. With a proud heartbeat he dipped his wings to return the salute. Then, growing drowsy, he picked out a bay devoid of shipping and slid down for a brief rest. He lit a pipe and stood peacefully on a float listening to the lapping waves until a junk came up and dropped off a sampan of eager and curious Chinese. Then he swung the propeller and taxied off seaward to rise from the wave bumps.

On reaching Shanghai, Francis flew ten miles to the south of the Wusung River and landed. A sampan sculled by one old Chinese woman approached the plane, and its only passenger, whom Francis took to be an important harbour official, shouted instructions and ordered Francis to move from the harbour shipping lane. He kept drawing up on the windward side and banging into *Gipsy Moth*. After a wingtip had been buckled and several ribs in the leading edge smashed, Francis started to yell, 'You bastard, if you barge into me again I'll wring your neck.' The important personage seemed nonplussed. 'What do you want then?' he asked. 'Come up from astern, you bloody fool,' Francis bellowed. The old woman, her wrinkled face cracked into smiles, skilfully sculled to the other side. 'Who *are* you?' Francis asked. 'I represent the *North China Daily News*. I am a globe-trotter like yourself and a keen airman like yourself.' There was no time for Francis to vent his feelings in words – nor indeed did words exist to suitably describe such feelings!

After discussion with the Shanghai Volunteer Corps and a Shell Oil man, it was decided that he would fly the plane up river to the Shell jetty. Now that the floats were dry and light he could take off within 150 yards. What bliss that knowledge was. Although water still inexplicably poured in when the Moth sat overnight in water, he now knew which compartment to pump out, and whenever possible she would be lifted out onto dry land for her sleep – all the way across the world!*

* The *real* trouble, which had eluded all the technicians who handled and examined these floats was worked out many months later. After the floats had been dropped on the deck of the cruiser, the keels had been replaced with stainless steel, and electrolytic action (which no one thought about in those days) had corroded away the rivets and some of the thin duralumin skin of the float. When the floats were in the water, the thin sides were pressed away from the keel, and the water flowed in. As soon as they came out of the water, the water inside pushed the sides of the float against the keel thus almost entirely stopping the leak. Ordinary tests could not reveal this.

With the Moth tied up securely on a grass bank beside the Shell jetty, Francis spent the next day studying weather reports at the Jesuit Monastery Observatory at Siccawei outside the International Settlement. Here, in the cool silent stone-built room, surrounded by a deserted garden, Father Gherzi, priest and scientist, gave him advice. There was a typhoon east of Formosa travelling fast for Shanghai. The plane could not fly 538 miles to Japan against a head-wind of 35 m.p.h. and must be fastened down yet more securely. At 4.30 p.m. on 10 August, the day that the worst typhoon of the century sank ships and devastated Manila, the typhoon gun was fired at Shanghai and Francis kept watch over his plane all night. If he could face her into the wind and weigh her down with a ton the Moth could endure a 100 m.p.h. gale safely. After a night in a shed listening to the ceaseless roar he thought it would be wise to take off soon and turn for Korea if a head-wind prevented him reaching Japan. But Father Gherzi still reported a 60 to 70 m.p.h. wind against him, and fretfully, he had to remain. He spent the enforced waiting time examining his plane on dry land. The fabric appeared to be peeling off the underside of the fuselage and the exposed plywood looked sodden, which made him fear that, if the glue had been weakened by seawater, the tail might break off in a sudden gust. The Moth had not been constructed to be a seaplane. He felt uncomfortable about these obvious ravages, and after ripping off the rotted fabric he brushed the plywood with bituminous paint. Then he began discussing the swerves of the typhoon with Father Gherzi. Instinctively Francis liked this man, liked his fire and his intellect and his goodness. Each time he parted from the Jesuit he felt curiously different and inspired. Francis was sensitive to the magnetic qualities of other human beings. Perhaps that was why he suffered such nervous irritation at the trite comments and the flippant talk of the girls who physically attracted him. He could not always tune in to the ordinary, and women especially resented his obvious lack of ease in their company.

On 13 August, still unaware of the havoc that the typhoon was creating in those ports through which the Moth had just passed, Father Gherzi announced that it might be possible to fly off although it meant facing a strong head-wind for half the journey. Once again Francis knew the joy of feeling his plane rise bird-like with dry floats.

Leaving Shanghai, he headed for Japan, carefully checking the drift which was very strong. He flew at 5000 feet for just over three hours. At this point he felt certain the head-wind was not sufficient to force him to deviate to Korea. He could dare to continue straight to Japan. Descending to 800 feet, he brought out his sextant and took a sunsight. He had not practised this for some time, but as soon as he caught the sun on the horizon in the sextant the drill came back to him, and he quickly worked out results on the slide-rule. He still had 270 miles to fly but could reach Japan if no head-wind sprang up. Father Gherzi had forecast more favourable conditions from now on and he felt complete confidence in the scientific Jesuit's judgement, so he decided on the direct course between Shanghai and Kagoshima in Japan. When he identified the first tiny island he was only one and a half degrees out. He lit a cigar and drank a small brandy. He reached Kagoshima harbour in the dusk and its beauty took his breath away. He knew that it was always much harder to touch down correctly after a long flight, and so he swooped around carefully before settling in a small creek where he could hope for half an hour's peace before the officials reached him.

After mooring for the night he faced the usual questioning, apparently intended to discover if he was an officer of the British armed forces. The Territorial Air Force to which he did indeed belong seemed impossible to explain, so he answered, 'No, I am not an officer in the Army.'

'You are a government fly.'

'No, I am a private fly.'

After sipping the usual sweet champagne, Francis was driven by his interpreter Hayashi and a policeman to a hotel where a line of exquisite geisha girls knelt bowing their ornate black heads to the floor. Francis watched the men doing return bows and copied them. Then, having had his shoes daintily removed, he was led away for the longed-for bath. A Japanese bath is sunk in the floor and it was the policeman who led him to it, wrapped a kimono around him, summoned the scrubber and personally dried him in a rough towel. Then wrapping Francis up in a flowing kimono he led him back to the enchanting waitresses who served him a Japanese dinner in different bowls. A geisha girl squatted on a cushion beside him filling his delicate porcelain *sake* bowl and instructing him how to neatly handle chopsticks. It was so polite and so peaceful, entirely different from the brassy hurry of European hotels. Led to his bedroom, where a flower-like maiden pointed out the huge brass bedstead reserved for foreigners, Francis realized that his policeman intended to remain there, on guard, fanning himself all night. Touching the walls he found them to be thin sliding panels. Out of curiosity, Francis slid one back to find himself staring at a Japanese couple asleep in the middle of the floor of their room. Hastily he closed it. Curiosity was so impolite in Japan!

Despite the five hours of interrogation obviously designed to discover what type of spying this private fly intended, this was a tranquil interlude for Francis – a step into a quiet world of different standards.

Next day he flew on in bright sunshine. The earth looked incredibly lovely and the fact that he could now rise lightly from the water made Francis himself feel light-hearted. This day demanded a flight of only 300 miles and Francis wrung joy out of it. For sheer delight he brought the Moth down to skim the surface and the ocean's strength seemed to fill his being. On this morning, of all mornings he felt himself master of the art of flying.

The little fishing port of Katsuura had been selected for his landing by the Japanese authorities. He had orders just where to alight. The town lay on the edge of a crater-like bay and as the welcoming launch came out, he saw one man wave a flag and another an umbrella. In fluent English, the umbrella-man, Mr Suzuki, invited Francis to stay the night. Francis thought it would be fascinating to be a guest in a private home and gladly accepted. The two men sat down peacefully while the lady of the house cooked their dinner on a small brazier. Then, clad in kimono and wooden sandals, Francis was taken out to see the town. Suzuki was so charming that Francis hated to refuse his request to be given a lift to Tokyo on the morrow. Hoping not to seem churlish Francis explained that if a crash occurred it was usually the person in the front cockpit who got killed. The responsibility of carrying Suzuki as passenger was too great.

Next morning, after complimentary farewells to Madame, Francis returned to his plane. Suzuki and his friends helped in every way they could. They were touching and attractively eager.

'Will you make circles round the town? The peoples would like to see your aeroplane,' Suzuki shouted as the propeller whirred. In the most perfect form on this miraculous sunlit morning, the Moth, light and dry after a night ashore, rose from the water. Francis flew straight out across the harbour. He believed speed to be more important than height before manoeuvring. He pulled back the control stick and the plane started to climb. After obtaining the necessary height he would return and circle the town to please the 'peoples'. It was the least he could do in return for Suzuki's kindness. Then it would be straight on to Tokyo. How good it felt to have the Moth light-footed and copper-tipped and her old glue seams bitumen-painted.

Glancing round in final check-up he noted that he had everything he needed for survival – sextant, slide-rule, nautical almanac, log-tables, watch, barometer, log-book, charts, dividers. All was well on this glittering morning. Ahead lay Tokyo and then the world.

Far beneath him in Katsuura hundreds of beaming faces were turned upwards. They watched the Moth fly round into the valley between the harbour rock peak and the inland hills. Suddenly they saw the plane stop in mid-air as if catapulted backwards, and then forwards. Like a dead bird it dropped from the sky and landed in a crumbled heap on the concrete harbour edge.

12. The Crash

For Francis there had been a repetition of the old dream sequence. One moment he was thinking how pretty the little town looked beside the green water and then suddenly his sight went black. It was the moment he had known before – usually at four in the morning. There was nothing to do but wait for the crash. Vaguely reaching at lifeless controls he became aware not of fear, but of an intense loneliness and sense of loss of friends.

He regained consciousness briefly in fiery brightness which he thought must be the brightness of heaven. But hands clutched him. There was terrible pain. Now he was being stitched up and sometimes he counted the stitches. This *couldn't* be heaven! Then a new fear seized him. This kind of pain must mean that he had become a eunuch. All right in heaven but not at all right on earth.

Night fell. He lived through it. Suzuki never left his side. In the morning, Francis resolved to speak.

'Suzuki, my eye . . .'

'The doctor say he think you save that.'

The stitching of his testicles had been done without anaesthetic. He had felt the needle. He asked the vital question.

'He says he think you save everything.'

So it was worth while trying to live. Deep in himself, Francis switched on those healing taps available to a being who *wants* to get well.

Now for weeks he must endure the kindness of incessant Japanese visitors who arrived in hundreds almost as if doing a pilgrimage. All day long they would pass through his room, pausing at the end of his bed to express sympathy or just to stand silently watching. Francis would drift out of a doze to see the endless procession of well-wishers dressed in their robes of ceremony – the men wearing black kimonos, with a skirt suspended outside by two black bands from the shoulders. There would be a faint hiss of indrawn breath as they stood there in black silk stockings with separate big toes. All of them men and women, carried fans. All behaved with perfect decorum.

If he appeared to be awake, Suzuki would chant introductions. 'This is director of the ice factory at Katsuura; they pray to God for you, and send you ice every day.'

'This is lady who has hotel outside what you fall.'

'Here is a priest of Buddha; they pray to God for you that you get well soon.'

The people laid their little tributes near him; fans, fruit, dolls, photographs, *sake*. They were so thoughtful, so kind, but the patient's nerves were raw and he longed to be alone, not always watched by those black eyes shining with mingled tenderness and curiosity. Francis had to get used to having his intimate wounds dressed while women and young girls stood at the foot of his bed. Gradually he grew accustomed to being watched as he grew used to Japanese food. The European reaction to nakedness did not exist – these people were innocent.

In his mangled state – he had thirteen broken bones including his right arm, and countless cuts and gashes – Francis remained sensitive to spiritual radiance. There was an old lady, a practising Shintoist, who was able to put him into a peaceful sleep by gliding her hands over his body and softly droning prayers. An extraordinary feeling of lightness, of melting dis-ease would sweep over him.

Among the hundreds of touching tributes and letters came a note from the interpreter who had looked after him at Kagoshima two nights before the crash. Hayashi poured out his feelings:

Sir, receiving the report of the mishap I have profound regret which never could be forgotten. I expected you will success as I said you, I hope you will success, when bid farewell on the beach. I hope you will buy fresh eggs with money that I present to you (I enclose a money order, ten yen, which you must ask for post office) and take them to make you healthy.

> Yours truly,
> M. Hayashi.

As Francis strengthened he found his mind growing interested in reconstructing the accident. It had actually occurred because when ordering him to land at Katsuura, the Japanese officials had not thought it necessary to inform him that a half-mile span of steel telephone wires hung from the high harbour rim to the top of the hill behind the town. He had flown straight into them. Suzuki gave a graphic account: 'You have wonderful good luck. Nobody understands. They rush to pull you out before the fire catches. You must be dead. Great is their wonder to find you still alive. It was a terrible sight. I am nearly sick. Everybodies is so sorry for you. Everybodies prays to God for you. The doctor thinks you do not live for ten, twenty minutes . . . All young men carry you to train, very careful. They carry you all way one hour train journey.'

His crash must have been a riveting sight from the ground. Francis lay back visualizing it. As it had to happen, he only wished that he had been able to watch it himself.

Amy Johnson had just flown out from England with her engineer, Humphrys. They had reached Tokyo in ten days and Amy was very famous indeed. When she heard of Chichester's crash, she and Humphrys travelled across Japan to sit by his bedside. Not a rich girl, Amy had struggled as hard as Francis to become a pilot. She tried to comfort him and explained how much she had learnt from studying his exploits. She said: 'You know I've watched your career and learned by your mistakes. Last year you left London without a spare propeller and had to wait ten days in Africa, so when I started my London to Darwin flight I had one tied to the fuselage.'

'Learn not to fly into telephone wires too,' said Francis. He admired this dedicated girl who had worked hard and saved money in order to learn to fly. Courage and artistry always fascinated him and so did Amy's wistful feminine charm. She remained completely unspoiled by the adulation to which she was subjected.

After Amy departed, Francis lay back to assess the realities of his own life. If it was records he was after he had gained two. He had made the first solo flight from Australia to Japan, and he had also achieved the first solo long-distance flight made in a seaplane. The fact that *Gipsy Moth* was really not even a seaplane but a land plane dressed up in borrowed floats added a sort of mini-record that no future person could ever desire to emulate. The magnitude of his feats would be remembered in flying circles for ever.

He had done all this but his precious plane was finished. He had bought her with his own hard-earned money, alone he had hopped her all the way from England to Australia, and alone he had flown her across the Tasman Sea, and alone he had got her here. Now there was nothing for it but to give her crumpled remains to the local grammar school. He was hard hit in spirit and battered in body.

The Crash

In left-handed script, his right arm having been broken, Francis Chichester wrote: 'Every flight is moulded into a perfect short story; for you begin, and you are bound to lead up to a climax.'

This short story had reached its end in bitter disappointment. He had terribly wanted to get *Gipsy Moth* around the world.

13. Interlude

Francis had left New Zealand in *Gipsy Moth* on 28 March and he crashed in Japan on 14 August. The flight with long halts for repair work had taken nearly five months. These months were encrusted with memories both terrifying and precious.

When he could walk he bade farewell to his doctor and his friends and forlornly boarded a P. & O. steamer for England. It was the autumn of 1931 and Francis had not seen his land since that dark morning of 29 December 1929 when he had flown off before dawn, unable to digest his bacon and eggs, and nervous of bailiffs seizing a not-quite-paid-for plane.

Now he was thirty years old and his strong body had been smashed to pieces. He needed absolute rest, his bones would knit and his flesh heal because he was healthy, but beneath flesh and bone lay a shattered nervous system. Willpower alone could not mend him – other forces, spiritual forces perhaps, the forces of the beautiful earth would have to heal the deep invisible wounding.

Amidst a variety of aches and pains his most serious injury, which was to his back, had not yet been diagnosed. It would, in fact, take him ten years to get over it. Strangely, he still suffered from the identical nightmare of suddenly losing his vision and having to wait for the crash. He had suffered this dream perhaps fifty times in the past. Then in the accident it came true, and now maddeningly it continued. It was as if he had been deliberately brought to the moment of death, shown death and allowed not to die. As if his inner being had always known this moment would arrive and that a lesson must be learnt from it. So that he should recognize the moment of peril and release from peril, he had to have it dinned into him in advance and now repeated. But what was the lesson?

Not to fear death? He was always far too brave for his friends' comfort. To understand the force of destiny? Maybe, but to what ends?

He reached England in a golden October and crept back to his country home. Once again he stayed in his parents' house at Shirwell and this time the visit proved an absolute fiasco. Francis had always been regarded as tiresomely unconventional, but he could speak of materialistic success in New Zealand. Now he returned to North Devon a nervous wreck yet not at all humble. Francis sat at the dining table holding forth on the exhilaration of attempting the near-impossible, describing strange lands, strange people and strange faiths – Jesuits and Shintoists! It was really too much. To cap it all, he cast a critical eye over his family! Although he still always addressed his father as 'Sir', he now assumed airs which made it obvious that he thought most members of the ancient Chichester family were narrow-minded bores. His face showed what he thought. Mealtime conversation in the Rectory appalled him. How was it possible to be interested in who had come to church and who had stayed away? The family did not listen to his stories (entrancing stories, thought Francis, likely to broaden the horizons of stay-at-homes), and he pulled a wry face when neighbours dropped in for local tittle-tattle. Francis wondered how he could have sprung from such stock, and they wondered how this eccentric had emerged from their line. They would never understand his questing spirit.

Family discord reached a climax over his choice of a funeral wreath. He happened to have been particularly fond of a great-aunt who had died aged ninety while he was in New Zealand. Before visiting her grave he bought the biggest, brightest, most gorgeous wreath of flowers he could find in London. The Rector pulled a face. How brash! How vulgar! What would the village think? Francis didn't care what the village thought. The tribute might seem flamboyant, but it expressed his feelings.

A major row occurred because, although his mother still fussed over spots on the tablecloth, she insisted on using an ugly scullery lamp in the dining-room. The Chichester fortunes had deteriorated steadily after 1918. Francis considered the way in which his mother ran the house with reduced staff to be unimaginative. There was no need to place unlovely objects in view just because bank balances went down. Peasants made beautiful things, quite poor people put flowers on the table. It was no longer the coldness of his parents which afflicted him, but what he called their mental dampness, a sort of mildew. Francis could not talk to his father about how frightening it was to be nearly castrated. And his back hurt! It was all too depressing.

Anxious to show his family the stuff he was made of, Francis openly rejoiced when the Guild of Air Pilots, presenting for the first time the Johnston Memorial Trophy* for the best feat of air navigation in the British Empire, chose him to be the recipient. The Prince of Wales personally presented the trophy and photographs of a beaming Francis receiving it appeared in the newspapers. The brilliance of his feat in flying over the Tasman Sea, the feat which would cause later navigation manuals to refer to him as 'the greatest lone navigator the world has ever seen', had not been understood in the Rectory, but a presentation by the heir to the throne did make an impression.

Francis fled from Shirwell to stay with his favourite and very glamorous cousin Angela, now Lady Slade and living at Instow, her own North Devon home. Here he was able to settle down to write a book called *Seaplane Solo* in which he endeavoured to describe his efforts in crossing the Tasman Sea. He hoped this book would make money, but the gift of writing was not his. The artistic streak in him registered this fact and fluttered with annoyance at his own inability to express a fantastic adventure in moving prose.

Months passed. Imperceptibly he was recovering, but in secret he still suffered from horrible illogical fears. On train journeys he would sweat with terror lest another train crashed into his, and tunnels had become a torture impossible to describe. The humiliation of his inability to control inner panic was particularly galling for Francis Chichester who had brought self-control to a fine art.

During the 1930s aviators were regarded as a strange glamorous race of beings. Flying was not merely an exceedingly dangerous activity, it was novel. People seldom met a flyer. When they did they held their breath in awe, and the Press tried to build up all airmen dramatically. Francis did not easily fit into the category of popular heroes. He was quiet, unassuming, unflamboyant (except at home). Journalists did not quite know how to serve him up, and he made no effort to help them. When in London he frequently visited the Royal Aero Club and there he made a very different impression to that he left in the Rectory. Among men aware of the magnitude of his achievement, Francis appeared to be extremely humble. He would slip in and out of the club, eyed with reverence by other flyers. Although ready to discuss flying, yet he seemed rather distant. At least that is how he struck Nigel Tangye, the famous test pilot whose

* Johnston had been navigator of the airship R101 destroyed over France.

friendship with him started at this date. Francis was always eager to
thrash out an idea or indulge in technical argument. He appreciated
Nigel's story of Amy Johnson's humility – that of the truly great
artist – when, on returning from her triumphant flight to Australia,
she asked Tangye to give her flying lessons, because, she said, 'I'm not
quite satisfied with the *way I handle my plane*'!

Within a year, having finished his book (which sold very few copies
because no ordinary readers could grasp the drama of his achievement from its pages), and soothed himself with some dinghy sailing,
Francis returned to New Zealand. It was strange to arrive back
planeless in that country from which he had set off with such high
hopes in brave little *Gispy Moth*.

The slump still held real estate in fetters. There was not much to
do except plant trees and scheme to sell an occasional property.
Geoffrey and Harold Goodwin remained his stalwart friends. Geoffrey
would say to him: 'You deserve the greatest credit for your determination to master the things you find most difficult.' During Francis's
absence, Geoffrey had had to cope with many financial difficulties
and would eventually be forced to wind up their pioneer Aviation
Company. Although it had carried 9000 passengers without an
accident, the Government refused to issue a licence. Geoffrey, defend-
ing the case himself, found he had to compete with the best known
barrister in New Zealand who represented a large company wishing
to take over. Geoffrey maintained that this company was ignorant of
aviation, but their K.C. knew how to argue. Geoffrey lost the case,
and with bitterness had to watch others reap enormous benefits later
on.

Francis lived between the von Zedlitzes, and his mountain hut, and
friends at Masterton. He knew he had changed. A certain wildness
had gone out of him. Once he had thought he could not live without
action. Now he enjoyed reading and trout fishing. Could he lay by his
talent? His most extraordinary talent? Had ambition been broken in
him? Was he happier now that he seemed able just to enjoy the feel
of the sun and the sea, to go in for ordinary living as ordinary people
do? Without lusting for adventure? It seemed so. There seemed no
reason why, after the horrific experience in those telephone wires,
he should ever again feel the urge to fly. This seemed a pity. Despite
continuous improvement in instruments, fliers maintained that
navigation in small planes remained an almost psychic art. The man
who knew where he was at a given time by some inner ear, while he
worked out lightning calculations, was the *great navigator* – he had the
extra-sensing not quite possible to put into words. Perhaps fitness and

concentration could increase this sense, but it was no more explainable than the perfect hitting of a musical note.

Four years passed – years of quiet, moderately remunerative business, of fishing and camping in the wilds. His aches and pains diminished except for those in his back. It would be a long time before X-rays would reveal that he had cracked it. Young George spent holidays with him. He had learned to regard his father as an extraordinary personage, one who had accomplished a feat which other little boys – who heard *their* fathers talking – greatly admired. But the bond between them was tenuous. George's asthma made Francis unhappy. He could not help him. And perhaps the boy resented those early days of fear when his father urged him to be daring.

During all the early part of his life Francis was full of complaints about his lack of success with women; a closer investigation leads one to believe, however, that he merely suffered from that affliction of ninety per cent of the male world – that is, insufficient success with large numbers of ladies. But whether he was a successful wolf or an unsuccessful wolf or just a wolf in lamb's clothing, by 1936 he had again become restive.

One day, a plan developed swiftly. While visiting a friend, a big sheep farmer named Frank Herrick, Francis held forth on how delightful it would be to fly back to England across Siberia. He could argue most enticingly. Frank Herrick listened, lulled his wife Flora into a sense of security, and purchased a plane which Francis could pilot. Remonstrations from Mrs Herrick were brushed aside. Francis should certainly know how to get there, but in those days all planes were prone to mysterious accidents. Test pilots so often got killed while trying to discover defects that weaknesses remained undiagnosed.

Mr Herrick's purchase was a second-hand Puss Moth, a high-winged monoplane with a Gipsy Major engine. Francis had not flown for five years, so he spent many hours on simple landing practice. This plane was bigger and more expensive than his old *Gipsy Moth*, with an enclosed cockpit for two. He would not have to stuff his ears against the roar of exhausts and wind, that roar which he feared because he knew it deadened the brain during flight.

They shipped the Puss Moth across the Tasman Sea to Sydney and then the two of them, jubilant as schoolboys, set off across Australia to Darwin and on through the East Indies, enjoying themselves every mile of the way. They intended it to be a light-hearted trip – no records to break, no hardship, no glue-pot repairs. The

most enthralling of many stops proved to be Peking, which Francis
deemed the most romantic city in the world. Feeling exuberant in
the electric-dry air, he accepted the invitation of a Chinese girl to
visit her in the old walled city. Such visits, by rickshaw at night,
were dangerous for foreigners which, of course, added spice to what
was a curious, but never to be forgotten, romance. 'This enchanting
young lady was so small that my two hands could meet round her
waist.' His feeling for the city of Peking would remain a feeling apart
for ever.

While a host of difficulties arose regarding permits to fly across
Siberia, Frank and Francis dawdled around sightseeing. Eventually,
determined to avoid red tape and to keep the whole venture 'a lark',
they flew back across China and took the more ordinary route to
England. Off the coast of Indo-China they encountered a typhoon
which caused Francis some uneasy moments. He was always aware
of the possibility of de-winging, but they climbed high and turned
safely into still air.

All went well until, on reaching Bushire in Persia, suspicious authorities detained them for five days in a terrible heat-wave. Without
being very superstitious, Francis had noticed how often omens
seemed to warn him at certain times and if he ignored them things
went wrong. It was almost as if some outside watcher occasionally
pulled him by the sleeve to say 'Don't'.

When, on the fifth day in this furnace-like place, permission to
proceed actually arrived, Francis inadvertently dropped his watch
between his belt and his shorts instead of into his pocket. It fell and
broke. As they faced a 500-mile flight and it was already 1.30 p.m. –
late in the day for starting – he suggested deferring the flight till
next morning. But Frank Herrick, suffering intensely from the heat,
expostulated: 'Let's get out of this hell-hole at any cost.' They flew
against a head-wind all the way to Baghdad and were getting short
of petrol when they landed on the unlit aerodrome. It was not quite
dark. 'Take a torch, Frank, and walk ahead of the plane towards the
hangar so that I don't taxi into anything.' Herrick opened the cabin
door and as he stepped out he did not turn sharply out of range of
the revolving propeller. Francis heard a sickening noise and saw his
friend stagger. Thinking he must have been killed, instantaneous
misery filled him. He jumped out and found Frank huddled on the
ground holding his left forearm which appeared to be torn off. Two
ends of bone were showing. A car drove out and quickly took him to
hospital. Frank Herrick was not a young man, and it seemed quite
likely that he would die of shock if not of the actual wound, in this

sultry summer heat. Francis spent the most agonizing night of his life, but next morning when he reached the hospital room Herrick cheerfully greeted him with 'Where's that propeller? I want it as a souvenir.' He had the stuffing which makes people survive.

Both blades of the propeller had been broken on impact but Francis reckoned that the first blade, in striking a silver cigarette box in a pocket, had halted Herrick just in time, or the second blade would have cut through his shoulder instead of falling lengthwise on his forearm.

The R.A.F. provided a new propeller and from now on they thought only of escaping the heat. On reaching Cairo Herrick rested in a hospital, but the arm did not heal, so they decided to hasten to England. It took them twenty-nine and a half hours' flying time. They had left Sydney on 26 June and they reached England on 2 October. Frank Herrick recovered completely and returned to New Zealand with the broken propeller to put on his mantelpiece, and a good yarn. Francis ventured to pay one more visit to his father. Now the two men looked at each other in puzzlement rather than dislike. They simply had no line of communication. Francis moved on to stay with cousins. Probably he would never be able to afford another plane of his own, and enthralled as he had been by China and Malaya, he felt he was closing a chapter. He was, but a surprise chapter of happiness was about to open.

14. Marriage

It was the autumn of 1936. Francis Chichester was now thirty-five years old. Despite his impetuous nature, all through the hair-raising adventures of his adult years he had remained shy and lonely. In New Zealand he could be hail-fellow-well-met. There he was well liked, especially by men who were not fatigued by his ebullience. In serious flying circles he was quiet, diffident, regarded as a genius. Right through boyhood he had known the prick of loneliness and it did not cease now that his mind could put his teeming ideas in order. It may have been this loneliness which had stirred up a little sadistic streak when at home. Now he had outgrown the urge to annoy. He was fond of his sisters and could regard his parents through uncritical eyes; they were old people, rather sick and not particularly happy. His father, that disapproving father whose sepulchral voice during long Sunday services had turned Francis against church worship, now seemed rather pathetic. Francis no longer fretted, but accepted people as they were. His relationship with brother James remained a void. Later on, when Mrs Bill Wilkey happened to remark, 'I never knew your brother,' Francis would reply laughingly, 'Well, neither did I.'

Soon after Christmas, while staying with cousins and walking through the North Devon countryside, which evoked so many childhood memories, Francis found himself inadvertently listening to talk about a girl who was coming to stay. One might say that he had a preconceived notion of Sheila Craven, although all he gathered was that she was *unusual*. He did not know that she loved wild animals and hated all forms of killing. Francis enjoyed wildfowling, and during Christmas week he went out with his gun every day. One evening he returned carrying a wild goose he had shot and as he walked into the room carrying the dead bird he saw Sheila for the first time. She recoiled, but in spite of this he thought she liked him, or at least liked something about him.

On New Year's Eve, the house party attended a hunt ball. Francis, dancing attendance, discovered that Sheila had just journeyed alone though India and Abyssinia. He liked adventurous girls. And there were other things which attracted him. Her elegance, her original views. He found her feminine but outspoken, mysterious and yet jagged. The jaggedness in particular appealed to him, and her independence.

When, a few days later, she left for another dance some distance away, she put her car on the train with her so as to arrive fresh. Francis listened in, noted her mode of travel and managed to board the same train. He found her compartment, entered and announced, 'I've got £100 in the bank, an overdraft of £14 000 and some trees. Will you marry me?'

'But I spend £50 a year on my hair,' Sheila murmured.

'Do just that,' said Francis, 'I like it.' He reckoned he'd won.

Actually she was drawn to this odd fellow. Sheila always confided in her mother's old maid, Hester, who looked after her London flat. On return, she tried to describe Mr Chichester and asked Hester for her opinion of the latest marriage proposal. 'Well, I like the sound of it; quite different from all the others you've had. I always worried about you taking up with those married men,' replied that oracle who had disapproved of quite a number of gentlemen. Perhaps because she had known no father, Sheila had always turned to older men, several of whom wished to divorce for her sake. This suitor was only four years her senior and free.

Francis telephoned, re-proposed, and asked if he might dine at her flat. By chance she had been given a theatre box that night, and this came in useful because her swain arrived in one of his wound-up, super-practical, flight-planning moods and proceeded to de-propose. Happily, Sheila was sufficiently sought-after and mature to be amused. He sat down to explain that he didn't really think he was the right type for her after all, and unlikely to make a good husband. 'I am so used to being alone,' he said rather wistfully.

Anxious to see the play, Sheila hurried through coffee. 'I absolutely understand, don't feel tied. And now let's go to the theatre.' The evening passed off easily but she thanked heaven for those tickets.

Next morning Francis arrived back at her flat in reverse gear. He'd spent a sleepless night. He would be a dreadful husband but she'd got to marry him all the same. They were both old enough to understand themselves, he said, echoing her words. And she would love New Zealand.

'So you've changed your lordly mind,' commented Sheila. 'All my friends are warning me against you – only Hester approves.'

Then in some extraordinary way, she found that she had accepted him and the engagement was officially announced. Sheila knew that Francis had flown back from New Zealand, and had previously won renown as an aviator, but she had no idea that his flights had made history. It was the Press who rang up and told her about the Tasman Sea.

Her own story, which, psychologically, was intensely interesting, they could not publish. Miss Sheila Craven appeared before the public only as a young woman who had emerged as a débutante in London society, whose grandfather, Mr Craven of Kirklington Hall, Nottinghamshire, had been a millionaire. She now seemed to live a rather bohemian artistic life of her own choice. The queer tragedy of her personal family history remained secret.

From babyhood Sheila had known that some cloud hung over her and her older sister. 'Poor little Miss Kathleen – poor little Miss Sheila' the servants would whisper. When she grew older she had suspected that they might be illegitimate because an icy silence fell whenever their father happened to be mentioned. Not until she reached the age of eighteen did Sheila learn the truth – and that quite by chance – when a young man told her that three days after she was born her father, a younger son of this self-made millionaire, had committed suicide. Young Mrs Craven may have half-feared this might happen, for her sister-in-law Edith had come to stay during the confinement. The women had been a little worried over Gerald's occasional talk about debts and Mrs Craven did not want her handsome husband to feel lonely when the baby arrived. A few hours before his death Edith bade her brother good night without noticing anything strained in his expression. In fact she went up to bed thinking how charming he was looking. In the morning they found him. Sister and wife had to guess at the inner despair which had made him reach for the gun.

Ominous whispering had been bad enough for the children who dared not ask firm questions about their father. Worse was the punishment inflicted on the widow by her rich father-in-law. Outraged by the scandal of a suicide, old Craven decreed she should receive only a very small allowance. 'With Gerald's death all my responsibility to you and the children ceases,' he wrote. Mrs Gerald

Craven was left with little more than her own fifty pounds a year to bring up two daughters. Within circles of rich aunts and cousins they found themselves the poorest of poor relations. It was a heartless arrangement inflicting the maximum of social embarrassment.

That was how Sheila Craven grew up, in a welter of false standards and un-Christian charity. 'The family' saw that she was educated, of course, and sent to a smart finishing school – not to do *that* might have reflected on *them*. But she could not go to the Opera every week as the 'richer girls' did, and even when invited to be bridesmaid at her step-aunt's grand wedding at St Margaret's, Westminster, *she* had to make her own dress. It could not have been a more odious set-up, this having no money and yet being surrounded by rich conde-scending relatives. Sheila's nanny would relate years later how scornfully the other nannies and servants treated her when she took her charges to stay in grand family houses. By the time Sheila reached eighteen, old Mr Craven was living in a large London house – 12A Kensington Palace Gardens (now the Nepalese Embassy) – and occasionally he desired his daughter-in-law to bring the girls to see him. Dazed by her own tragedy and submitting to the social stand-ards surrounding her, Mrs Craven vainly hoped that her daughters' 'prettiness' would induce the old man to allow them an income approaching that of his other grandchildren.

Sheila showed great talent in drawing. She could also design and make clothes. Friends offered to finance her in a dress shop, but to see her daughter earning her own living would have been the last blow to Mrs Craven's pride, so, as she loved her mother, and did not want to cause her pain, Sheila did not insist on a career. She sup-pressed her irritation, and occasionally earned a few pounds making clothes for other people – or worked as a model – an activity less lucrative then than it is now. Her wages were £3 a week. Several photographs of her draped in the 'smart clothes' of the 1920s survive, in some she wears a cloche hat pulled down over her nose, the eyes peep forth wistfully – 'looking for Prince Charming' is her present comment.

When her mother died Sheila inherited a small sum and spent it on travel. While she was staying with the Viceroy in Delhi, Lady Willingdon had arranged for her to see the Taj Mahal and told her, 'Either you must go with your sweetheart or on your own.' Sheila understood exactly what the Vicereine meant. She accepted the ex-perience *completely alone*. So she knew what Francis sought to imply when he talked about loneliness, and how he had grown accustomed to self-sufficiency. Yet she had too many men on her tracks to take umbrage when he burst in saying that perhaps they ought not to marry after all. She let him blow himself hot and cold by turn, amused by the originality of this approach. What she did not understand was flying. When Francis announced a treat – he would take her up in Herrick's Puss Moth – she dressed herself smartly, wishing to look nice for his sake, and then nearly died of terror and cold. When Francis did a loop she thought she was going to fall out. In one morning Sheila learned that aeronautics were not for her. But the art of flying and the skills of navigation began to intrigue her.

When she gave an engagement party in her London flat, Amy Johnson came and sat on the sofa beside her: 'Do you realize you are marrying the greatest navigator in the world? I came to London specially to ask him to give me lessons. Now you are marrying him and leaving for New Zealand so I will have to learn in America. No one could teach me like him.'

Unable to visualize life in New Zealand, Sheila bought a somewhat exotic trousseau with money recently inherited from her aunt Edith (who had been in the house the night her father killed himself), and proudly she wore her aquamarine engagement ring. Naturally, Francis had to take his fiancée to meet his parents in Devon. The Rector's eyes fell on Sheila's fingers, red-tipped in the fashion of the day. 'I don't like the colour of your nails,' he said.

'Oh don't you? I do rather.' Francis kept his face straight whilst inwardly revelling at the dialogue. When Greek meets Greek, however, one of them has to give ground, and after a day of polite skirmishing the Rector intimated that it was his wish to travel to London and conduct the ceremony. Even so there were complications. Sheila was intensely sincere about her religion, so much so that she did not really like vows – which, such being the frailty of human nature, were so often broken – to be made in church. Unexpectedly, it was Francis who wanted a white wedding and flowers and music. His boyish enthusiasm proved so endearing that Sheila forbore to say, 'But you know perfectly well you are no churchman and *I* am seriously religious in my own special way.' Eventually, on 25 February 1937, just six weeks after she had first set eyes on Francis, they were married in Chelsea Old Church. It was the most floral and white of weddings. While the groom radiated content the bride kept wondering why the Rector's hands trembled when he made them man and wife – was it the sight of coral-tinted fingertips when she held out her hand for the ring, or was he just getting old?

The honeymoon was passed in snow-covered Cumberland and a fortnight later they sailed for New Zealand with all their possessions

– Sheila's antique furniture as well as her trousseau. She was longing for the new country – her own mother and father had travelled through New Zealand on *their* honeymoon, in that far-off time so impossible to visualize before her sister and herself were born. Had they been happy there, and seen what she and Francis would see? She had, of course, related the whole story to Francis and he knew that she had very little money, while all her relations were immensely rich. Her old grandfather, Mr Craven, had seemed to take deliberate pleasure in imparting the information that, after her mother's death, she would inherit nothing at all, but he had forgotten making a small settlement in one of his more amiable moods. So when he died, Sir Charles Craven, a kindly cousin, rang up: 'You're all right, you've been left a few hundred a year, you and your sister.' Francis did not care. He was sure he could support a wife in the style to which she at any rate, had been accustomed.

Sheila knew little about children but she immensely looked forward to meeting George. Of the day when they fetched him from prep school, she would write: 'It was very touching how pleased he was to see a younger woman and to come to live with us. I always remember that I did a room ready for him and he said, "Is this my very *own* room?" which went to my heart.' That was the beginning of a very close relationship. She understood the high-strung asthmatic boy as Francis did not. He had suffered from his own father's coldness, but even now he could not establish contact with his son. So uneasy was George with his father that Sheila had some difficulty in persuading him to call him 'Daddy'.

While the forestry business remained tied up, they lived in a small house in the suburbs of Wellington. Because Sheila had known such a difficult life, perhaps she would be able to manage a difficult husband. Francis's New Zealander friends waited agog to see how this sophisticated woman would respond to life in Wellington. What she really wanted was to explore the wilds, but Francis had to buckle down and attend to a turmoil of business difficulties with Geoffrey Goodwin.

The pain of watching George struggling for breath during asthma attacks affected Sheila deeply. Could this terrible affliction be due to losing his mother so early? Or to babyhood knowledge of tension between his parents? Did it stem from unhealthy feeding or was it purely psychological? As Sheila sat with George during his breathing crises she felt for the first time in her life that she was failing a human being. This was the beginning of her belief in herself as a person whose job in life was to help others by prayer.

The year in New Zealand was not a success. Sheila adjusted herself
to running the small house, but she did resent the false image
aroused when the Press incessantly wrote her up as the 'grand-
daughter of a millionaire' ('which, of course, I was, but they didn't
say I hadn't inherited any of the money!'). As a result of this unwanted publicity people expected her to entertain lavishly, and she
just could not do so. The von Zedlitzes became her closest friends,
and when George's health permitted she attempted camping and
fishing trips, but they couldn't live perpetually in the mountains.
Sheila would later assess this period with Francis:

I realized that he was a genius, but I thought he was wasting his talents out
there and felt my work was really to look after him and build him up for
what he was later able to do. After all, he'd lived half a lifetime of adventure before he ever met me – a most extraordinary career starting things
up and letting them run down, making successful flights and smashing up
his planes, this kind of pattern, and he'd never had any real support
behind him.

Francis detested domestic women. Ignoring the fact that he was
a full-time job for any woman, he liked them romantic, extravagant-
ly dressed, artistic in taste, full of ideas and adoring.

Within a year they had decided to sell up and return to England
with George. Sheila insisted on travelling first class and seeing the
Great Barrier Reef, Bali and Batavia. 'We may never have another
chance like this, let's blow the money.' Francis liked to be led into
extravagance – he had always had to be so careful. London seemed
the obvious place in which to settle. It was the world's capital. There
must be scope for a proven genius. But once there, material worries
seemed overwhelming. Francis, who had such experience and initiative in his specialized branch of knowledge, found it almost impossible to get a job. Never was there a man with more vision, but he
did not quite fit into any category. Certain that war lay ahead, he
tried to join the R.A.F. as a fighter pilot. Ruefully he has described
the result of this application: 'I thought that my flying experience,
combined with my capability at shooting, would be just what they
wanted. I was surprised and chagrined to be told that I was too old.
I was thirty-seven, and the idea of being too old for *anything* just had
not occurred to me.'

He wanted to earn money, but on his own terms. He felt that life
– that tenuous string onto which he had held so hard – was too
precious to be used merely for money-making. He longed for
creative work, in which he could use his skill, but where did such

work exist? Francis tried in vain to form his own company for making flying instruments. No one would produce capital. Eventually he found a post as a navigation specialist in Henry Hughes and Son, the famous makers of navigational instruments, at a salary which hardly exceeded the rent of their Chelsea flat, but at least he would be working in a right element, flying many hours a week, taking sun-sights and using his brain on the development of a new bubble sextant for Hughes and Son to produce. They were very lucky to have him. No other living man could tell them so much about sextant experiments. Sheila could enjoy London, but she noticed how sorely the weekends irked her husband. He had for years been accustomed to tough physical activity and to frequent escapes into the New Zealand mountains; he liked to be close to nature, to camp and swim and fish and shoot for the pot. There just didn't seem enough room for this restless spirit in southern England. And then George's ailment tore their heartstrings.

High over their own problems of finance and health hung the cloud of approaching war. Feeling that it must be absolutely inevitable, Francis, still smarting at being turned down as a fighter pilot, wrote a set of articles describing a system of navigation he had personally evolved for bombing targets by star-navigation. These were published in a magazine called *Flight*. He would get up at 5 a.m. and scribble until he had to leave for his office. During these months of insecurity, so humiliating to a man of his stature, he also produced four small volumes on aero-navigation, containing instructions on how to navigate by the sun and the stars, volumes which he thought could not fail to catch the attention of the Air Force.

The social London whirl continued right through the summer of 1939 – as indeed it had during the summer of 1914. Magnificent balls and parties were constantly given by Sheila's relations. She could only arrange small dinners in her flat, but her friends were interesting and Francis saw a new kind of life.

As weekends had to be spent in town, they attempted to impart a slight *douceur de vivre* into the London Sunday by taking George to Battersea Park. There they would hire a boat and row around the lake eating sandwiches out of a paper bag. This was their regular treat. It was a frustrating but not an unhappy period. Francis could be quite content rowing in Battersea Park if only his knife-like mind could find worthwhile employ. And Sheila thought that in looking after this man and this boy she had found fulfilment.

15. The War Years

When war finally broke, Francis could not believe it possible that the Air Force would not recant and immediately welcome his talents – his extraordinary talent for navigation and his talent for improvising in emergency and his indisputable talent for survival. He had proved all these in tests of ultimate human endurance. He was a legend in flying circles. He *must* be used.

Although he had trained himself to be a crack shot when wearing two pairs of glasses, Francis knew that in official tests his eyesight must receive very low marks, so he began by asking the Air Ministry to form a Special Squadron of experienced pilots who, on account of some physical disability, were considered unacceptable. 'The object of this Squadron would be to bomb valuable pinpoint targets in enemy country, flying in alone by precise navigation.' The idea was turned down.

Francis fumed at the Ministry's lack of imagination. To him it seemed obvious that such a Squadron could not fail to execute work of inestimable value, and being expendable they could attack with individual daring. He stamped back to the Hughes factory muttering: 'If they want me after this they can damn well come and get me.'

During the next few months he devoted himself more assiduously than ever to his bees, who always charmed him by their own tiny navigational lore, and who dutifully produced honey in a sugar-rationed England. He also wrote two short books which became bestsellers – *The Spotter's Handbook* and *Night and Fire Spotting*. Everyone wanted to know which planes were overhead – the subjects had become *topical*! These short books – 'boshy' as Francis called them – did indeed evoke the interest of the R.A.F. and at long last a summons came. Francis found himself commissioned as a Flying Officer and ordered to write navigation notes for instructors and students. Once in uniform he felt certain that he could wriggle into combat planes, but he gradually became aware of the bias against civilian navigators, especially those with independent views and a tendency to criticize superiors. For a time he worked happily enough with the Wing-Commander who was rewriting the *Manual of Air Navigation A.P. 1234* (an officer who would introduce a system of navigation drill for Coastal Command resembling that which Francis had used when pinpointing the Tasman Sea islands). Frantically, he snatched at every chance to take part in a sortie over the Atlantic, but he was not officially allowed to fly and therefore wore no pilot's wings on his tunic. This rankled. He just could not philosophically accept the fact that in the mess and at the bar operational pilots did not always know who he was, and would talk shop in front of him as if he was a *non-flying man*. Sometimes however he could not resist propping himself up against the bar to obtain amusement from egging on young pilots who had just got their wings and were shooting awful lines.

By mid-1943, he had written some 500 000 words on navigation and was sick to death of so doing. What he wanted, and what he was sure he could do better than any other man, was to pioneer the art of pinpoint bombing. He tried to become Navigating Officer at an operational post but again the eyesight test stymied him. Finally he was given the arduous and interesting post of Navigation Officer at the Empire Central Flying School. His job was to brief pilots from every branch of the Service and of every Allied nationality, and to devise navigation exercises for them. As the Air Force had in the end snatched him up in rather a hurry, he had been popped straight into uniform and set to work without the ordinary training course. It was a slight shock to arrive at the Flying School and learn that on the following evening he would be Duty Officer. He had not drilled a squad since he was a schoolboy, but by intense concentration while watching the preceding Duty Officer, he memorized the commands, and when the time came he marched onto the parade ground and shouted orders accurately in a proper sergeant-major voice.

Peter Bristow,* who was a kind of instructor of instructors, has donated his memories of that time at the Empire Flying School.

This was a fairly star-spangled unit where the key chaps from all over the Commonwealth Air Training schemes and European and U.S. flying training people came on a three-month, post-post-graduate course, partly to see a little at first hand of the operations over Europe that they were

* Sir Peter Bristow, Q.C.

training their boys for. Most of the instruction staff were squadron-leaders or higher. Many were decorated. All were pilots. A few were pre-war R.A.F. regulars.

Into the galaxy, Francis arrived, a middle-aged Flying Officer with one ring on his sleeves and no wings, for by reason of his eyesight the R.A.F. would not let him fly operationally. He brought with him in the back of his car two hives of bees. Within a fortnight the Staff, without exception, were eating out of his hand. Within a month they were thrilled with his low level navigation exercises. These were done on days when the cloud was too low for any other aerial activity. Blenheim Palace was one of the turning points, and one of our rougher Canadian ex-bush-pilots commented that you had to fly so low that you could see the Duchess in her bath, etc. etc. . . . .

At the end of the first three months, graduation proceedings were enlivened by a navigation race in light aircraft flown by officers who were not officially supposed to fly.

One of the tasks Francis immediately and obviously excelled in lay in devising methods to teach 'nought feet navigation' for pilots flying over enemy territory when they might be unable to take their eyes off the ground ahead, and had to keep jinking to avoid anti-aircraft fire. 'It amounted to map-reading without maps, in other words all the map-reading had to be done on the ground before taking off. It sounds an impossible requirement but, with the right methods, and plenty of drill, pilots could find a haystack fifty miles off while dodging about all the way to it.'

Happily for Flying Officer Chichester, the Commandant soon realized that it is not possible to instruct in 'the impossible' unless the teacher is himself allowed to fly and navigate. Henceforth Francis found himself continuously trying out navigation in different aircraft (there were thirty-seven types at that camp!), and he was given his own light plane for solo flying and experimental work. In this he could prepare the flight tracks and instructional films, work up a variety of exercises and occasionally fly back to Sheila at Chigwell, outside London.

Having succeeded in getting himself in the air again, Francis tried to teach himself to feel amused and not resentful when, having flown his light plane to operational stations to discuss navigational developments, the Duty Officer would look questioningly at his wingless tunic and say, 'Where's your pilot?' To the end of the war Francis continually tried to sneak into a raid over Germany as a navigator, but he never quite managed it.

The author's brother, who was a fighter pilot during the war, received his training in America, not at the Empire School, but he remembers the 'legend of Chichester' – he who had once taken off with a second pilot, each thinking the other was at the controls and lived to tell the tale, who had incredibly navigated his tiny *Gipsy Moth* across the Tasman Sea, and who would scoot off in a plane alone, when chaps were missing, trying to calculate their possible errors as he flew.

Chichester stories entered R.A.F. folklore and there were many young men like my brother who could write of the state of affairs in wartime:

When we came home from flying training in America we used to get hopelessly lost and used to 'Bradshaw' as we called flying along railway lines, incessantly. Rather annoying when following a railway to a town which the map clearly showed as having three lines leading in, to find it has four or five so it must be the wrong town and probably not even on your map and you hadn't a clue where you were. When lost it became our habit to call up on the radio and ask for 'practice homing fix' pretending we knew where we were all along but just wanted a little more experience at flying along a radio beam. One very senior officer landed at our station airfield, rushed to the Officers' Mess to read the station name on the Notice Board, then flew away hoping his trick had not been observed because he was too embarrassed to ask for a 'radio fix'. Good navigation is a sort of psychic art. I've known pilots who'd lose themselves on the sunniest day ten miles from the field but we had a C.O. who'd bring us back across the Channel from France at fifty feet in mist and hit spot on the expected landmark. It was horribly easy to fly out of a tiny misty country like England and cross the Channel without knowing. More than one pilot came down to refuel at an airstrip which, too late, he saw was manned by Germans rushing out, but not with petrol.

Amy Johnson stayed with the Chichesters shortly before she was killed. Sheila again noticed what beautiful hands and feet she had. Delicately made fragile hands, sensitive to the controls, show more clearly in a woman. And Francis – who had made his first flight to Australia only months before she made hers – always felt touched by Amy with her great blue eyes and long oval face that was so wistful in repose.

Meanwhile, George, for safety's sake, had been sent to live with old Mrs Chichester in Devonshire, and Sheila worked driving a mobile canteen in the incessantly bombed London docks. She seldom took shelter, detesting the atmosphere of a stuffy refuge. Her home in Chigwell Row, Essex, received bomb damage eight times and she had to sleep alone there with Dimbleby, her spaniel, after long hours of driving in even more dangerous areas.

Francis's war letters to Geoffrey Goodwin, who was in the R.A.F. in the Far East, describe his rare days off when after sleeping for a solid ten hours he would go out with his gun to shoot pheasants and partridge, 'incidentally a useful addition to the larder in these times . . . my little shoot is $11\frac{1}{2}$ miles from the Bank of England which never ceases to be a source of wonder to me'.

At the Empire School, pilots had to fly many different types of plane while undergoing an intensive lecture course. Francis considered the high casualty rate due to insufficient drill in handling so many types of aircraft during a period of hard study, and he said so. The airing of personal views on training losses irritated some of his superiors who maintained the war could not be won by playing safe at any stage. No one could accuse Francis Chichester of ever having played safe, but he played careful, which is a different matter. When pilot students were missing on practice flights Francis would zoom off in his plane alone trying to reconstruct the trouble they might have got into.

At least he spent these years working full out, and using his skill to increase the skill of younger men. But although he was doing a job of great value, the war, for Francis, must have been a period of long-drawn-out frustration. The role of a great combat hero is admired by most, desired by many and lies within the capacity of very few. Francis knew beyond doubt that his natural position lay among those few. A man cast by nature in the heroic mould could not easily accept a non-combatant role.

Francis was glad to shed his blue uniform in 1945. He never really got over not being allowed to go out on operations against the enemy, and not wearing the wings which would automatically have brought him into the vortex of flying talk in any R.A.F. mess. No wings for the jacket of Francis Chichester! No wings for him of all people!

16. After the War

During the first few months of peace, the Chichesters, like almost everyone else in England, were simply trying to find their feet in a new world. At least they possessed a new lovely home, for in 1944 they had with perspicacity bought a house off Piccadilly. Francis had gone on occasional house-hunting expeditions through the deserted city while the V.1s (known as doodle-bugs) were falling and exploding with devastating effect. Strolling the empty street around the Ritz Hotel he noticed several dilapidated houses with For Sale signs. There was one of particularly elegant William and Mary proportions. Discreet enquiries revealed it possessed a repair licence. Jubilantly he described 9 St James's Place to Sheila.

He said to me, 'There's a wonderful room will do for your drawing-room, with three long windows and a balcony', and I pictured all this as any woman would, and there indeed it was. In ten minutes I said, 'Let's buy it.' We went round to the Ritz and offered considerably less than was being asked, but in the whole of St James's Place there were houses to let and for sale, and the street was practically deserted except for the Stafford Hotel which was occupied by American soldiers.

A year later, in the spring of 1945, when the doodle-bugs with their odd moment of silence prior to explosion had been replaced by the V.2s – those great shells that whistled down from the skies without warning – Francis had obtained a few days' leave and they moved in, complete with spaniel and a buzzing beehive, which Francis placed on the roof.

George was growing up. He had, at sixteen, become an apprentice at de Havilland's aircraft factory, but he yearned to enter the Merchant Navy. Sheila thought it vital for a boy to be encouraged to tackle whatever career appealed to him, and she kept him as calm as possible so as to get through his naval interview day without developing nervous asthma. He returned to her exclaiming triumph- antly, 'I'm Grade A!' She said, 'Marvellous! You'll probably never have asthma again.' He never did when at sea.

For Francis there could be no question of returning to the naviga- tional instruments firm, Henry Hughes and Son. He was determined to invent a business in which he could be his own boss. The Francis Chichester Map and Guide publishing house started in 1945 – the day after Francis Chichester was demobbed from the Royal Air Force. He was map designer, publisher, salesman, secretary and office boy rolled into one. His first office had to be one room on the ground floor, and here Sheila hung her white satin curtains – old favourites although not exactly suitable for an office. Typing went on all day and dinner parties at night! Francis's first commercial undertaking in 1945 consisted of turning 15 000 obsolete wartime Air Ministry maps into jigsaw puzzles and selling them to the big London stores.

He then proceeded to design other maps for jigsaws – the Heart of London, Heart of Paris, Shakespeare's Country, and the London Zoo were all map jigsaws. Francis had held strong views on what should be put into and what left out of maps for fighter pilots. Experience taught him that the whole value of a map lay in simpli- city – the eye must be able to take in main points quickly. So now he devised a large-scale map of the Heart of London, with small draw- ings of prominent buildings. The eye would go straight to one of these, making it easy to find nearby streets. A map, maintained Francis, ought to resemble a poster rather than a telephone directory.

One day a man walked into the ground-floor office exclaiming: 'This picture map of London is the best I've seen; if you will take it off this lousy piece of cardboard I'll order 5000.' And so it was that Francis Chichester, in his own words, 'became a map publisher by accident'. The business was hard work but it expanded steadily.

In time Sheila would join in the enterprise, designing maps attrac- tive enough to hang on the walls as a decoration. But before this, in the autumn of 1945, something happened to her – something un- expected and immensely exciting. Only her own words could describe this event:

Driving back from one of our visits to the West Country, I suddenly noticed a heightened pleasure in everything. The trees looked more brilliant, the autumn tints and sky looked brighter, everything seemed marvellous. Later, I connected this intense feeling of joy in living to the fact that I had become pregnant.

Sheila's views were unorthodox on many subjects. Experience in her youth had driven her to beware of conventional medicine. She was determined to have her child born in her own home, but the gynaecologist she visited in Harley Street had no time for this self-arranged programme. She heard of the famous vegetarian Dr Pink – an early advocate of 'natural childbirth' – who believed that the home was the right place in which to welcome a baby. As the hour approached one of the upstairs tenants grew most apprehensive, but all went exactly as Dr Pink maintained things should. He only arrived ten minutes before Sheila's son was born and soon after him came Dimbleby her adored spaniel creeping into the room literally on tiptoe to lie down under the baby's cot as if he owned the new arrival.

The surprise of a child in their lives made for a change in domestic arrangements. They rented a water bailiff's cottage on the River Kennet beside Savernake Forest, so Sheila let most of the rooms in 9 St James's Place and moved with her baby. Francis travelled down for weekends to enjoy the fishing and rough shooting. Although the strictest of vegetarians and at one time a vegan, Sheila agreed to cook the game he shot. For seven years Sheila lived by the river, letting little Giles know a wild paradise. Because she remembered fearing the dark she always left his curtains open at night and explained as best she could to a child the celestial bodies which remain such honest guides to an adventuring man!

Francis found it hard enough to make money with his map business, but he laboured on, typing out the invoices himself. Never much of a typist, the hero of the Tasman could make very heavy weather of this sort of work, but he had resilience and faced his large overdraft lightly.

When Monica Cooper first came to him as a young secretary she was dumbfounded at the firm's apparent financial insecurity, but she responded to Francis's driving force and eventually she became a director of the world's most interesting map business. Many people thought Chichester difficult to get on with, but Monica understood him. He could not abide red tape, nor could she. He drove himself hard and drove others hard. He exasperated or exhilarated. Sometimes he would throw work aside and reminisce with a sort of passionate intensity – as if he wanted to wring some new truth out of remembering. Although he seldom returned to North Devon, he often talked about it – the soft air and the mists – the sweet damp smells – the greenness – all the enchantments of his boyhood would come surging back. 'In New Zealand,' he told her, 'I yearned for the soft rain and the skies that rolled in from the Atlantic – the sun was too harsh out there and the winds too hard – one never heard the gentle murmur of insects – it was beautiful but not my landscape.'

When Geoffrey Goodwin (who was still running the forestry business in New Zealand) came to London, he went around with the famous Chichester Map of London with its landmarks. Eventually he grew tired of standing on a windy corner holding a flapping map and suggested that it might be produced in pocket-book form. It took two years to get the sales going, but these would eventually reach a million. Today Francis Chichester Limited publish eight city pocket maps and guides which are sold throughout the world because they are so easy to read.

While forced to live in the city, Francis snatched at opportunities to try every kind of sport. On an Alpine holiday he taught himself to ski – or so he said – in sixty hard falls. What really appealed to him was overcoming ineptitude. If he found he *couldn't* do a thing he'd work at it until he could. As Geoffrey Goodwin enjoyed skating, he accompanied him to the rink and had a try. Circling seemed much more difficult than it looked. From that moment he *had* to master 'edges'. Geoffrey describes him at this time: 'He was always asking me to go to the rink with him and when I finally introduced him to the instructress who was teaching me, he could not get over my prowess and boldness. For a time Francis was blissfully absorbed. "I find it so difficult," he would say.' But as soon as he could waltz he lost interest. He could do that – what next?

Francis now had many friends, and was regarded as a most stimulating companion. He never accepted anything until he had shaken it to pieces with his own logic. The delights of converse with this penetrating, technically unbiassed mind were on the whole for males. Francis adored women but he was still not quite at ease with those he did not know very well indeed. And the feminine mind was inclined to lose the thread of his logical deductions.

In 1947 Mr Francis Chichester modestly presented a paper at a meeting of the Royal Geographical Society, entitled *Is Forecasting Necessary?* He maintained that while forecasting might remain necessary for light aircraft, things were evolving so fast that soon automatic landing methods must be invented and used. The argument appeared novel at the time. Most of his audience were members of the Institute of Navigation; they found themselves absolutely enthralled by Chichester's turn of thought. Michael Richey, the Executive Secretary, struck up a friendship which would last till Francis died. 'During all the years in which our lives were entwined in the navigation world I never ceased to enjoy his originality. Francis refreshed one by always finding a new way of looking at a subject. He could take nothing for granted.'

While Francis discovered that he could live happily even when enclosed by London streets, Sheila discovered that she could reconcile herself to conventional prayer. Little Giles liked going to church with her. Francis couldn't stand it. He'd had an overdose of 'services' in boyhood. He shared Sheila's nature-loving philosophy but he did not become a strict vegetarian, and he did not feel it incumbent on him to kneel by her side in prayer. He thought it was cruelty to animals rather than the fact of killing that mattered. It seemed one thing to bring a bird down unwounded out of doors and another to transport terrified animals to be butchered. His mind was too exact to be able to put aside the vision of animals he had seen slaughtered, and, indeed, had to slaughter himself. He felt ever more intensely with the years. 'I think that few mature people would eat beef or lamb if they had to kill the animals first,' he repeated.

News came from Australia. George had left the Merchant Navy to settle in the dry air and sunshine. Eventually he intended to run a fruit farm. He wished he could see his little half-brother, but now he had broken away to run a life of his own at the other side of the globe.

About this time Francis suffered several bad attacks of gall-stones. Despite his rugged appearance and capacity to accept physical hardship, Francis had never been constitutionally strong, and the injury to his back in the plane crash had not been properly diagnosed. Now the strain of past exploits, the inhuman driving of himself to the end of endurance, began to tell. And constant financial worry acted as a corrosive. Over the years, Francis had, when he did not feel well, taken to the usual male solace of pipe-smoking and whisky. He would write of gall-stones: 'I have been told this is the greatest pain known to man; I believe it.' The first doctor he consulted wanted to operate but advocates of nature cure deplore the cutting out of a mistreated organ. They believe the *cause* should be removed. So Francis found himself with no pipe and no Scotch, and no meat either. His sense of humour carried him through, and Sheila's earnestness when offering him a lettuce leaf and an apple, enabled him to accept her orders with a smile. Under this austere regime the gall-stones disappeared, and henceforth his adviser was a nature cure friend – Dr Gordon Latto.

When Giles reached the age of seven, it was considered necessary for him to attend a London school. Neither parent approved of sending small boys to boarding school, thus risking the cruelty and queerness which Francis himself had encountered, so Sheila made arrangements to move back into St James's Place. Siglinda who had been her au pair girl in the cottage did not always appreciate vegetarian fare and had left long ago.

Now that Francis was over fifty, his mind teemed with projects more concise in their nature than when he was young. He remained fascinated by the exactitude of navigation and wondered if he might perhaps edge into the yachting world as a navigator.

He advertised his services, but no one answered for a long time. Then Mike Richey suggested that he act as crew for a yacht owner who was a retired P. & O. Commodore. Sheila received comical accounts of Francis's first voyage with this elderly gentleman. A long letter written after sailing to Holland gives the picture.

The skipper has gone ashore to buy potatoes and, I suspect, yoghurt, which he likes, and I am therefore eating chocolate on the sly because I am not allowed to eat any when he is about. Everything has to last him three months so I had to buy some chocolate (also butter) on the quiet, although he has a large tin full of each commodity. I felt starved because I was not allowed to eat anything except white bread bought eight days ago and cold meat or bacon, cooked by him before we left, none of which I like. There was a frightful row because I bought a brown loaf before the white one was finished, because Dutch bread was 'no good'. Dutch tomatoes, strawberries, peas and beans (all of which I bought) are 'no good'. I was also ticked off for eating an apple and refusing an orange, so you won't be surprised to hear that finally I told him not to be such a damned skinflint and *I* was going to buy something to eat anyway. That wasn't the end of it, however, because I found, to my cost, that if I handed over my purchases they disappeared into the store chest and I still got nothing to eat. So now, like Siglinda, I have bits hidden away all over the cabin, and whenever he is not looking, I gobble an apple, biscuit or dried prune etc. How Siglinda would fare under these conditions, I cannot imagine. I really am a little schoolboy again with a very strict 'headmaster' who gives me hell at all hours. No shore leave for a drink, or a meal. No tipping of bridge keepers etc. As a result my initiative is paralysed. I dare not touch a rope without an order, so now we have a split bowsprit. Just before the crash I saw the old boy was tilting a barge; I shouted 'look out', it being his side, whereas normally I would have just grabbed the tiller and done a little good. Luckily he does not seem to worry about his bowsprit, at least nothing like so much as he does over throwing away the scraped-off mould on cheese. (You will be amused to hear that I have never been allowed to cook or do the final washing-up – I scrape potatoes and do the first wash-up in the sea. Anyway, he bust a bowsprit last trip so feels at home. In spite of all this I do like him and the trip is great fun. I feel pretty confident about the handling and the navigation is quite interesting, not at all difficult. I am trying to pick up as much as possible about the customs and habits of the seafaring world.

After this kind of cruising, Francis yearned for a boat of his own, and in September 1953 he purchased a day cruiser for £1150.

Sheila was packing up the cottage prior to moving back to St James's Place when he telephoned her rather nervously: 'I have bought a boat.' He was amazed when his wife exclaimed, 'How wonderful! I've always wanted one.'

A boat would compensate for the restrictions of London life. Now Francis could creep out of the city to revive his spirit amidst natural elements. He was feeling his way back to the sea – he who had known the ocean as a seagull soaring over the waves would find another sensation – that of the dolphin, rolling in star-mist spray.

Francis re-named his boat calling her *Gipsy Moth II*, for he could not forget that wonderful, fragile little plane whose fragments he had left in Japan. She would have to be converted for night sailing and ocean racing. Until she went into dock Francis kept her at a mooring at Brightlingsea on the east coast.

At the first possible opportunity Sheila parked Giles with friends and travelled to Brightlingsea; it was a darkening November evening when she reached the jetty where Francis had ordered her to wait – but there was no sign of *Gipsy Moth*. Fog descended, and she made enquiries of an old fisherman who murmured soothingly, 'Oh, you mean that there blue boat? She be lying on Buxey Sands, and it's lucky 'tis fine weather, otherwise she'd be sunk when t'sea rises. What's more, there be thick fog coming up, and if she do get off the sands, it'll be a long time before you see her in Brightlingsea.' Sheila drove away through ever denser fog to a cousin in Colchester, where she was revived with strong martinis and advice to consider divorce.

In the morning Francis telephoned that he had reached harbour. 'You give him hell!' advised the cousin. But Sheila didn't. She accepted his invitation to join him for an immediate sail, and that was the beginning of a new era.

17. Ocean Racing

This *Gipsy Moth* was an eight-ton boat, twenty-four feet on the waterline, carrying 540 feet of sail. Francis changed her rig from sloop to cutter, and redesigned her interior for ocean racing when she would have to carry a crew of five. She was an extravagance that gave him great pleasure.

In 1954 Giles experienced his first sail across the Channel, firmly hooked into a small life-line which was, in those days, an innovation. Sheila, an enthusiastic sailor, who had gone in for this sport in the past, had to keep to her bunk on this particularly rough voyage, and Giles spent the night in the cockpit gamely fighting his seasickness.

A Roman Catholic friend had come with them, and when they reached Ostend after a fairly hideous night, he dressed himself tidily and climbed up the steep iron staircase to walk to Mass. Sheila decided she couldn't let her side down and that she must make off to the English Church. Francis and Giles admired all this praying and helped her to smarten up and climb the slippery high ladder. But they themselves remained on the boat being prayed for. 'It was a lovely service,' recorded Sheila. 'I was still cold and glad to kneel by the stove. When I spoke to the Chaplain he was impressed to hear I'd arrived in a small yacht.' He had reason to be. It was exceedingly stormy weather.

After this trip Giles enjoyed many weekend sails and Francis began to find him an amusing companion – a boy who could do things with him. When Mike Richey came aboard he considered Giles over-lively and not very keen on going to bed – traits which could hardly be considered unique. Later on, when he was allowed to bring a school friend, the grown-ups were amused to hear Giles's first directive: 'Now remember, *I* am the captain and *you* are an A.B. [able-bodied seaman].'

Francis liked experiment, and he thought the best way to learn about ocean racing was simply to enter his boat and have a try. After becoming a member of the Royal Ocean Racing Club, he entered for the North Sea Race, 220 miles from Harwich to Rotterdam round the North Sea. At the start he ran aground and lost his kedge anchor, and at the end found that he had arrived nearly last. As the other crew members had never been in any ocean race whatever, they did not mind. In fact, they thought it wonderful to get back at all. In Francis's next race, from Cowes to Corunna, the masthead snapped in the middle of the night and he found it difficult to get his boat safely to the Channel Islands with a tangle of shrouds, halyards and wires on the deck. But eventually *Gipsy Moth* sailed safely into St Peter Port where Sheila arrived to listen sympathetically to the sagas of disaster familiar to all wives of sailing men.

During his first season Francis sailed his boat 2510 miles and competed in three ocean races. In the following year, with Colonel Marston Tickell, an experienced star-turn ocean-racer, in the crew, he won the 220-miles race from Southsea to Harwich and was thrilled at this first victory. Every other boat had packed it in because of no wind. Only Francis and Tickell battled on, changing sail at every breath and enduring the slatting while the rest of the crew threatened to mutiny if not allowed to get back home to their jobs.

The way in which Marston Tickell could make a boat sail proved a revelation, and although now in his mid-fifties, Francis had completely retained his eagerness and his capacity to learn. What he had not retained was the physical resilience of his youth. The time was coming when he would have to pay for punishing himself so hard over the years. Even now he was overdoing things – keeping business accounts, tearing down to the boat, working on her himself to save money, and going in for all those tough ocean races. His nerves became edgy. Once in Cherbourg, Sheila fell, breaking a bone in her ankle and fainted with the pain. Francis thought she was dead and when she came round he was extremely cross, as people often are after being thoroughly shaken. She had not seen him quite like that before.

But whenever the weather turned really nasty, so that she and Giles said they couldn't bear another moment, he would relent. One summer, at the end of the race from England to San Sebastian and on to Belle Isle, Sheila and Giles travelled out to meet *Gipsy Moth*. Bad weather made all the boats late. When *Gipsy Moth* turned up

Francis had to let his crew return to England immediately, leaving him only one first-class hand, the well-known Stormy Nicol, and Sheila and Giles to help him sail on. After a day's rest they set off, despite the weather forecast, while a yachting friend gloomily remarked, 'You need your head seen to sailing with a wife and child in weather like this.' But all went well and they reached port triumphant.

The first frightening intimation that something might be seriously wrong with Francis occurred after the Dinard Race of 1955. When all the crew had gone home, except Sheila, leaving him with *Gipsy Moth* at St Malo, he was suddenly crippled by what appeared to be a form of arthritis. Reluctantly, because of her basic belief in the powers of nature cure (which demand, however, 'complete rest'), Sheila called in the local doctor. He examined the ashen-faced Francis, racked with pain, murmured a slight understatement, '*Monsieur est très fatigué*', and gave him butazoliden pills. Francis was exceedingly highly strung and these pills put him into a kind of delirium. Terrified at his symptoms, Sheila banished all drugs and instead presented him with the most tempting dishes the local restaurant could produce. Tim and Katie Heywood, whose boat *Isolda* lay nearby, came over to help her. They tried to persuade Francis to renounce the idea of sailing back to England. Under concerted pressure, Francis, looking as Katie said 'gaunt and drawn as Gandhi', gave in. Tim, who was remaining in St Malo, swore he would keep an eye on *Gipsy Moth*. 'And if necessary I'll get some chaps to sail her back to England for you.' These promises soothed Francis and he agreed to go. Tim could hardly believe his ears when, as Francis was led tottering to the steamer, he called back, 'Awfully good of you to look after her, but it's only for a few days because I must get her back to prepare for the Fastnet.' 'Of course, of course,' said Tim, and turning to his wife he added, 'Ye Gods – one has to humour a man as sick as that, but what an idea – the Fastnet indeed!'

But Francis meant it. No sooner had his wife got him back to London and tucked him up in bed than he announced himself cured. To the amazement of the Heywoods and the St Malo harbour master Monsieur Chichester reappeared to sail his boat back to England. 'She needs a quick refit,' he said. Ten days later *Gipsy Moth* set off in the Fastnet, toughest of all ocean races, with her dauntless skipper at the helm. Actually, she did rather well and just missed winning the A class, but the six-day Atlantic buffeting knocked the stuffing out of Francis. All through the race he had to be helped from his bunk to the cockpit, and it was with difficulty that he wedged himself steady while working out navigation at the chart table. His crew were horrified at the way in which he drove himself.

After this he *had* to rest. Two doctors diagnosed chronic arthritis. Sheila stoutly refused to call anything 'chronic' that had only just flared up, and when he started orthodox treatment their friend Dr Gordon Latto quizzed him. 'Ask your fellow patients how long they have been at that and then ask yourself why it should cure *you*.' Francis had always accepted his wife's nature cure ideas in principle but he was impatient. He wanted to get well quickly and without letting up. Now sheer physical pain brought him to his knees. He went to the Nature Cure Clinic at Edstone, and by spring he considered himself fit and ready for another hard season of ocean racing. He got through this and through the English winter.

During the summer of 1957 he entered *Gipsy Moth* in one ocean race after another. Tim Heywood, riveted by Francis's personality and endurance, crewed for him in the race from England to the Hook of Holland, but Tim said afterwards that he'd been on tenterhooks all the time. First he feared that Francis could not stand the strain and would collapse physically, and then, as an experienced seaman, he could not help perceiving that *Gipsy Moth* was an old boat taking a very hard battering, and finally, as an orthodox skipper, he found Francis's habit of applying the principles and equipment of air navigation to marine pilotage absolutely hair-raising. 'How can checking by the stars help you to keep off sandbanks?' was Tim's plaintive cry.

After the race, when the rest of the crew had hurried off 'on urgent business' the two of them sailed *Gipsy Moth* back to England together, and as always when he was alone with a man, the originality of Francis's mind made every hour fascinating. Tim would describe these days:

We got so near sandbanks that there was thick sand in the water washing over the deck. But we only got badly 'had' once – and that was in a small port where the restaurant-owner welcomed us to his daughter's birthday-party. At the end of a hilarious evening, we discovered the bill for entertaining the entire village was on us! I had to leave Francis as 'hostage' while I walked, not too steadily, back to the boat to scrape together our last francs with which to pay.

'Don't tell Sheila,' said Francis. 'I mean, don't tell her that we were had for suckers.'

Tim never recounted the episode during Francis's lifetime.

Towards the end of this gruelling but happy summer, when *Gipsy*

Moth had just finished the English Channel Race, Francis literally jumped off her to board the crack American yacht *Figaro* which he had been asked to navigate for Bill Smith in a series of races. Very stormy weather blew up during the Fastnet and only twelve out of forty-five starters finished the course, but the magnificent *Figaro* rode so steadily compared to little *Gipsy Moth* that Francis hardly noticed the rough seas.

After this race, the owner allowed Sheila to sail back in *Figaro* from Plymouth to London. She revelled in such luxury and comfort. 'Do you think he knows where we are?' one of the American crew kept asking nervously whenever Francis lay down for a sleep. *That* aspect didn't worry her but 'the weather got progressively rougher and rougher until it was for me the most terrifying storm I had been in. All night we ran up the Channel under bare poles . . . Next morning when I woke up and looked out, "Goodness," I said to Francis, "how green the cliffs look." "Don't be silly, those are waves you're looking at." ' He enjoyed this sort of remark. A know-all Women's Lib crew would have been no use at all to Francis.

These were glorious sea days, but once ashore he never felt well and Sheila sensed a new battle. Their life had finally seemed to be panning out. The map business, although weighted with overdrafts, had grown, Giles liked his day school, they could afford a yacht, and now this – suddenly the iron-hard fibre of Francis was cracking. He could not, or would not, stop overdoing, but Sheila still kept him off drugs. She wrote: 'I had seen my mother, absolutely devastated by the effects of orthodox medicine, die in great pain, and I was determined the same thing should not happen to my husband.'

In St James's Place Sheila presided like Ceres bearing cornucopias of fruit and vegetables, and she *tried* to make him rest. The best way to encourage relaxation was to ask the famous boat designer Robert Clark to prepare blueprints for a new boat to be called *Gipsy Moth III*. They would all sit in the white drawing-room discussing the layout. Obviously, the idea of a world circumnavigation always lurked in the back of Francis's mind. He had never quite got over the break-up of his ambition to circumnavigate in a plane. This new boat was, therefore, designed with an iron keel which he thought might prove practical for bouncing off coral reefs in the Pacific. He kept his idea secret. He wanted to be the first and to do it alone.

The map business would now allow enough money to build this new boat of their own, but Francis wrote:

I had a nightmare fear of not being able to sell *Gipsy Moth II*, and of being landed with two yachts. It was all too much to bear. The trouble was that by the end of the Fastnet I was tired out. If only I had laid off everything for a week. I should have regained the strength to cope . . .

That was the wisdom of hindsight. At the time nothing would induce him to take a week off.

18. The Dreaded Word

Instead of resting, Francis drove himself hard all through the cold damp autumn. Eager to economize, he travelled down to the Beaulieu River every weekend, where he did odd jobs on the boat. There is no economy more false than the dispersion of health and Francis accelerated this process by himself removing old paint from the fore-castle floor with a strong chemical dissolvent. Kneeling in a crouched position while working, he felt the damp river-cold permeate his being, so he kept the forehatch closed. It was the kind of foolish thing people do when too tired to think. The smell of the chemical tickled his throat and a week or so later he developed a cough. Only then did he begin to wonder if the paint-remover fumes had burnt his lung lining. That was what it felt like, but he could be very obstinate. Coughing painfully, he travelled to Ireland with Robert Clark to look at *Gipsy Moth III* being built at Arklow. It was a chilling journey and he returned with a pain in his lung, which turned into pleurisy. Pneumonia followed. He needed a spell of deliberate in-activity, but time seemed precious. As he grew sicker he fretted feverishly and unreasonably about how much there was to *do*.

In early spring, a sailing acquaintance, who happened to be a doctor, took one look at him and said, 'Look here, you *must* have your lungs X-rayed.' This suggestion spread a pall of depression over Francis and he began to think he had never felt so ill. Like most people in England he was on the National Health Scheme. Was it the hours spent in the waiting-room which affected him? Or was it a purely physical trouble? A few days after the X-ray he returned to the chest hospital expecting to learn the verdict from the chief surgeon. Instead, he was, to his surprise, used for demonstration pur-poses in front of twelve student doctors. Francis heard them discuss his breathing while they examined his neck and finger nails. 'This is a typical case of an advanced CARCINOMA,' pronounced the head surgeon. Francis had no idea what the word meant, but he dragged himself gloomily home and told Sheila. She knew that carcinoma meant cancer, but she said nothing.

A few days later a bronchoscopy was carried out. Francis made the mistake of requesting no general anaesthetic. It proved an exceedingly disagreeable experience. Before leaving the hospital he cornered one of the surgeons whom he guessed might be particularly frank because he was an Australian, and wrung the diagnosis out of him. 'Cancer. We are making these examinations all the time and cannot possibly be mistaken . . . I not only saw it, but cut off a piece and sent it to the laboratory for examination . . . Your only possible hope is to remove that lung immediately.'

The anguish caused by the word 'cancer' is one which many thousands of families have known. It would be an intrusion into privacy of feeling to hammer out the reactions of Francis Chichester had he not himself been persuaded by that famous padre, the Reverend 'Tubby' Clayton of Toc H to recount his own story. He thought that others should know exactly what he went through.

When I emerged from the hospital it was a fine spring morning in April. As I walked along, the sun shone in my face. I heard the gay spring-song of birds. Young pale-green leaves were beginning to tint the trees. Life had never seemed more wonderful – a priceless, desirable thing to lose. My body seemed empty, my bones full of water. It was like a nightmare where I was in a bottomless space of loneliness, and I walked along slowly, wondering how long I had got before I was snuffed out from this lovely fresh spring of life.

On reaching home he steeled himself to the desolation of telling Sheila. To his surprise she said that she had known this ever since he used the term 'carcinoma'. She had talked it over with Gordon Latto, who would receive official reports as their family doctor.

'What are you going to do?' she asked.

'What can I do, but obey the experts?' he answered wearily.

On 9 April an operation for thoracotomy was advised by an eminent specialist after a second opinion. The report received by Dr Gordon Latto read:

Francis Chichester, age 57. There is no doubt that he has an advanced Carcinoma of the left upper lobe and I expect that it may well be inoperable. On bronchoscopy there is no evidence that it is yet inoperable, and I have no alternative but to advise thoracotomy. I hesitate to put undue pressure on him as his condition is clearly advanced.

Francis agreed to have the operation and was allotted a bed on the National Health Scheme. He told Sheila the operation was to take place in the following week and he did not want to waste money on a private room. She persuaded him to change his status to that of a paying patient in a small ward and then she brought her guns to bear.

It was a tricky moment. Here was a wife who believed that cancer could be cured by nature's forces and by prayer, pitting her instinct against the knives of the medical profession, with a husband half agreeing with her, but too sick to make decisions. Because she was so afraid for his sake, ordinary fear left her. 'How can you give in? It's wrong. I can see by your face that you will die if they cut your lung out. I won't have it.'

Francis murmured, 'The radiologist says that he is examining pictures all the time and can't be mistaken . . . the surgeon says he has not only seen the cancer but removed a piece of it . . . what can I do but agree to an operation?'

He acquiesced to her demand for a totally separate examination by another famous lung specialist, but the verdict proved identical. When five professional men had diagnosed carcinoma of the main left bronchus she still maintained the lung should not be removed. She did not wish to argue the technicalities of his disease but to cure it by different means – means she believed in so fervently that she would accept the very gravest responsibility.

On 15 April Francis packed up for hospital. On his way there he dropped in at the Royal Ocean Racing Club – he could not resist a farewell drink at the bar where he had so often sat with ocean-racing friends. As he entered the lobby his eyes happened to rest on the notice-board where a sheet of paper fluttered. It proposed a single-handed race across the Atlantic, and was signed by the famous 'Blondie' Hasler (Lieutenant-Colonel H. G. Hasler, the Marine Officer who led the canoe expedition up the Gironde during the war, depicted in the film *The Cockleshell Heroes*). Francis paused and sighed. What excitements life held; that would be a terrific race; if *only* he could enter!

Meanwhile Sheila knew the courage of desperation. 'The navigating instinct is a very tenuous affair,' her husband had said, and she was now navigating for his life. She felt certain Francis could not survive any operation, and she believed in the power of the human body to heal itself *if given the chance*. The basic theory of nature cure healing is that all ills have a cause and if the cause is eliminated the vital life force will do repairs (unless the vitality is so spent and the damage so heavy that it is time to die). Maybe the breakdown of harmony leading to a malignant growth had been caused by the stresses of Francis's early life. Maybe he had simply overworked and ill-treated his physical machine until a part of it packed up. Quite possibly the inhaling of paint dissolvent while in a crouching position had been the last straw to what his system could support. However that might be, she wanted him to live, and she did not believe that he could live one-lunged.

Francis crawled towards that chest hospital resigning himself, but, as he later admitted, ' . . . not so my wife; she was now in a fighting mood, and went into action'.

Sheila steeled herself for the most difficult task of her life. Praying as hard as she knew how, she requested an interview with the head surgeon. He rebuffed her, saying that he never interviewed relatives. She then asked for a paid consultation. Perhaps her determination aroused his curiosity.

The day came for me to see this great surgeon. I was scared to be opposing the decision of this very eminent man, but I could not change my destiny. I told him I felt the operation was unnecessary. He got very impatient with me and said, 'You are the most extraordinary woman and you're wasting time.' I said, 'I apologize, I realize you're a busy man.' (He'd just come out after one operation and was going back to do another.) Then he said, 'No, I mean *your husband's* time,' and went on to assure me that a lot of people lived quite safely with one lung.

She remained certain the operation would prove fatal.

Even apart from this fear, the idea of him without a lung seemed terrible to me, like cutting off a bird's wing. He had so liked flying and going out on the ocean.

She never saw the eminent surgeon again, nor did he send her a bill. Francis wrote:

I suppose that he, like me, had never met a woman like Sheila – someone who would carry the responsibility of refusing to allow an operation against overwhelming weight of medical opinion. As far as I was concerned, things moved slowly, and in somewhat of a dreamy blur. Hospital routine; dreadful nights, lying still hour after hour unable to sleep, sometimes choking and gasping for breath; not allowed to switch on a light because it would wake up other patients in the ward, patients coming in, having a lung removed, suffering bravely, leaving.

The laboratory report on the lung tissue came in 'Negative'. But Francis was given to understand that a negative report only meant that the malignant tumour was not at the moment active. He still ought to have his lung removed.

Sheila asked for another bronchoscopy. After this the surgeons agreed not to operate, but to try instead a course of antibiotics. Francis hated this and felt that it made his coughing worse. He thought, 'I'm damned if I'm going to be killed this way', and started hiding the pills.

Sheila visited him every day and she asked many people to pray for his recovery, Roman Catholics, Protestants, Christian Scientists.

I felt I was fighting a strange battle, but I kept steadily on my course. Every evening when I came out of the hospital I used to sit in St James's Park for a while. It was lovely there, and looking at the flowers and birds I longed for Francis to be well and share all this.

All through the month of May Francis lay in hospital too ill to speak. He dreaded the visits of friends and could but look at them silently, not daring to whisper in case it started a coughing attack. He could think of nothing except how to defer the feeling of being suffocated. His dread is revealed in the words: 'There came a time when I said that suffocation had caused me to die a thousand deaths.'

But he strengthened, and in late June Sheila drove him, still very ill, to Enton Hall, a nature cure clinic which had once been a Chichester family home. During his months here he suffered from asthma, which is a fear disease as well as a physical one, but eventually, after a very violent crisis during which Sheila sat up all night applying hot and cold compresses to enable him to breathe, he began to strengthen. When able to walk in the grounds he wrote: 'I loved the warm touch of the sun on my skin, the rising scent of the pine needles, the soothing green of juicy young curled-up bracken fronds.'

'You must get well. Think of your new boat,' urged Sheila. Eventually she dared, with some trepidation, to drive him back to their own house in London.

I was able to go home, to the only place where I wanted to be, to my room at the very top of the house, my cave, my kennel, where I could wrap a blanket round the remains of my shattered personality, and turn my face to the window. I could sleep only on one side, could breathe only propped on one elbow, but at least it was facing the window. My arm and shoulder joint began to change shape. . . . When I struggled for breath, sometimes oxygen, always at hand, seemed to help, and at other times it seemed useless.

Francis with his talent for survival was wondering if it might not be time to cease surviving – but Sheila felt that he could live, that he *must* live.

In the following spring he visited his mother and sister in Devonshire. This was a mistake. He became ill in their damp house and the local doctor when called immediately suggested lung cancer. When Francis heard this, he started to laugh. He was tired of that word. If that was all a doctor could say – the devil take him!

Incredibly resilient, piqued rather than depressed at the diagnosis, he travelled back to London in quite a merry frame of mind. Sheila suggested another X-ray. He hesitated. 'Supposing there is anything bad in it?' 'There won't be. I'm sure.'

At this moment she was busy seeing an excited Giles off with schoolboy friends for a holiday in France. He had just departed when Francis returned from his X-ray. 'I've got absolutely clear lungs. I want to go to France too. Anywhere in the Alpes Maritimes.' She did not hesitate, but dashed off to buy two tickets for the Blue Train.

They chose Vence. Sheila always believed that they were directed there in answer to the force of prayer. Soon after they arrived they went for a walk. Francis started one of his terrible breathless attacks. She led him back to the hotel a few steps at a time, sometimes letting him rest against a tree. This was a bitter ordeal. She had believed him completely well. At long last she now began to wonder – am *I* wrong? Can I stand much more of this? 'Yet at some deeper level I knew it was going to be all right.'

Francis asked for a cylinder of oxygen, but in France chemists cannot supply this without a doctor's order. Much as they both dreaded calling in a doctor, they had to. Neither of them knew that the doctor, Jean Mattei, who promptly sent his assistant over with a cylinder, was a lung specialist who had cured many patients with an almost supernatural touch. He was not a nature-cure practitioner, but he was not rigidly orthodox either. As sometimes happened, the oxygen had no effect and Francis continued to gasp for breath, and thought he was dying. Indeed, as the author can unfortunately attest, it is quite easy to *hope* you are dying during this kind of asthma! After a long night of it Sheila reached the end of her tether. She felt that the spasms were partly mentally induced – if you become sufficiently frightened of asthma, some part of your mind can throw a sort of fit, tighten the bronchial tubes and bring about what you fear most – suffocation. But how do you turn off the tap of mental terror?

In the morning Dr Jean Mattei came and gave Francis a long careful examination. His words astounded them. '*Ce n'est rien,* and if you follow my treatment you will be climbing up those mountains in three days' time.'

The tap turned. Five days later Francis slowly ascended the Baou Blanc. Mattei gave him vitamin injections and re-created the confidence in his body which a year of horrible suffering had destroyed.

Francis has recorded this April in Vence, and so has Sheila. He wrote:

What I regarded as a miraculous chain of events had started in London when I felt the urge to go to the South of France. There I reached a doctor who had been considered one of the cleverest lung physicians in Paris before he settled in Vence; also I had fetched up in a town which had been considered a health resort, with a magic quality of air for lungs, since the time of the Romans. How did this thing come about? Sheila said that the doctor gave me back confidence, that my illness was already on its last legs. For myself, I think that some part of my body had ceased to function, that the doctor correctly diagnosed what this was, and supplied the deficiency. To me he was a wonderful man; short, nuggety, fit, with terrific energy exuding strength and activity.

Sheila's version ran:

I believe myself that life is a long road and that you're helped along it by different people; if you are lucky enough and courageous enough to stick to the middle of this road and not be sidetracked, then help will come. To me Vence was almost like the end of a pilgrimage; I went into the Church there and thanked God in a big way for bringing us to this final place of cure. I felt that this recovery was very miraculous. Throughout I was controlled and directed by a power outside myself. I felt that these were holy matters and must be kept private, but this was not to be.

Francis would write a detailed account of that terrible period during which he suffered from lung cancer. It was April 1959 when Dr Mattei pronounced the shining words: '*Monsieur, ce n'est rien.*' Two months later Francis accepted an offer to navigate David Boyer's *Pym*, a fast eleven-tonner designed by Robert Clark, in the Cowes-Dinard Race, and in July he navigated the crack Italian yacht *Mait II* throughout the Cowes Week Races and then in the Fastnet Race. 'This was great fun, with eleven Italians (seven of them Olympic helmsmen); none of them could speak English, and I could not speak any Italian. We talked in slow French.'

People criticized Sheila for letting her husband sail in these ocean races, but none could imagine her joy as she saw the sails go up and knew that once again Francis was out there in his element – a bird with *both* wings.

19. First Transatlantic Race

After the Fastnet Race, Francis came to London and walked into the Royal Ocean Racing Club. There, on the notice-board, he saw 'Blondie' Hasler's proposal for a solo Atlantic race *still* pinned up. He could hardly believe it had stayed there, in exactly the same wording, after all he had undergone since the evening when he first read it – that the same little sheet of paper had remained there during all he had undergone since that bitter evening when he had dropped in on his way to hospital for what he truly expected to be a last drink on earth. Now, fifteen months later, after a summer spent successfully navigating for other people, he thought of his new boat, *Gipsy Moth III*, and little hopeful bells started to peal in his mind. 'Good God! I believe I can go in for this race!'

On a hot September day Sheila drove her husband and son from Dublin to Arklow where they launched *Gipsy Moth III*. After a brisk week of trials, they sailed her to England, and in October they took her over to France with two experienced yachtsmen. Then the new boat was laid up for the winter.

Meanwhile, 'Blondie' Hasler had received no encouragement whatever regarding his idea of a solo transatlantic race. But when 'Blondie' learned how keen Francis was to join in efforts to get the race going, he became a frequent visitor to 9 St James's Place, discussing his basic motive for the project – this was to cut down sailing chores and show what a man alone in a boat could do with self-steering gear and simplified rigging. Although the Press and yacht clubs were stalling, they worked out likely rules for entrants. Francis, with his extraordinary resilience, now became very healthy indeed! The cure which had been started in April by Doctor Mattei was completed in November by Colonel Hasler's proposition. Both men were certain that a race solo across the Atlantic was perfectly feasible for knowledgeable skippers, and a three-thousand-mile voyage plugging into the Westerlies was just the medicine for a man who had suffered lung trouble. Francis said it 'fired his imagination' and that always made him feel well.

When imagination is fired, Chichester lungs stay healed. Sheila could but rejoice that Francis would have the chance to battle close to nature in the way he loved. She wrote:

I was fascinated to think of the entrants starting from the same port at the same time for the same destination, testing themselves and their boats against the loneliness of the ocean. I saw immediately that this would be the cure, the final cure, for my husband, that he needed this kind of venture . . .

'Blondie' Hasler had spent three years trying to arouse interest in this race, but the idea frightened people off. Solo sailing was considered both dangerous and eccentric and few yacht owners could spare the time for five- or six-week Atlantic crossings.

Now things suddenly began to move. The *Observer* newspaper offered £250 to any yacht taking part for an option on its story and another £750 for the winner's story. Chris Brasher, the Sports Editor, who had been a famous runner and Olympic Gold Medallist, and could therefore understand a passionate approach to high endeavour, travelled down to Plymouth with Francis and 'Blondie' to see if they could persuade the Royal Western Yacht Club to supervise the start of the race. In the train on the way down, the men seriously discussed what they should do if *no one* would accept responsibility for anything to do with solo ocean sailing. 'Blondie' and Francis decided that they would race each other across the Atlantic anyway – the bet being half-a-crown.

But Francis possessed considerable powers of charm and persuasion. There was a lot of reluctance on the part of the Club sailing committee, but he knew just how to present a hair-raising project temptingly and soon enlisted his chairman friend, Colonel Jack Odling-Smee, on his side. The Royal Western Yacht Club agreed to see the contestants off in Plymouth and a group called the Slocum Society said it would attend to the American end.

This was the *first* single-handed transatlantic race and no other could ever have such glamour and such appeal. The race did not depend on money but on determination. No expensive boat took part. A handful of skippers resolved to test their skill and endurance, to see if they could do it, that was all.

The starting date was fixed as 11 June 1960. 'Blondie' Hasler was, of course, the first entrant with his Chinese-junk rig, which he considered the easiest and most practical single-handed rig in existence. Dr Lewis entered his *Cardinal Virtue*, and Val Howells entered *Éira*.

Francis would have liked two seasons rather than ten weeks for trials with his new yacht, but this was not possible. *Gipsy Moth III*, thirteen tons and thirty-nine feet seven inches overall, was much bigger than his previous boat, and he had to get the feel of her and learn the disadvantages of handling a larger yacht alone, but 'she was staunchly built and gave me confidence. She seemed so powerful that I felt at first like a small boy astride a tall, strong, broad-backed horse which could not stop.'

Some self-steering device would, of course, be essential for lone sailors racing each other for five or six weeks at a stretch. Power-operated self-steering gear was prohibited by the rules of the race – the gear used must derive its power from the wind, or from the water flowing past the boat.

Vane gears of various kinds had been used on model yachts since before World War II, but had not appeared on full-sized yachts until 1955. Self-steering techniques were still in their infancy with various pioneers experimenting with different systems. Among these pioneers 'Blondie' Hasler was outstanding. A good vane gear will steer the boat on any point of sailing thus allowing a solo skipper time off to navigate, cook, eat and sleep. When, in March, Francis returned from Vence, where he went for his regular yearly lung check by Jean Mattei, he set about devising his own vane gear, based on the simple system used in model yachts. In this, a large wind vane turns the boat's main rudder directly. Every Sunday morning he took a bus to Kensington Gardens to watch the model yachts being sailed across the Round Pond. In his mind's eye he saw *Gipsy Moth* speeding across the Atlantic in exactly the same way. The wind vane which Francis designed would always weathercock into wind. In fact, it was a mast which could rotate in a socket at the stern of the yacht, with a flat sail instead of a metal vane. When the boat was sailing as she should, the vane could be locked to the tiller. If the yacht altered its course, the vane would be moved round with the yacht, and the wind would press on the side of it. This would pull on the tiller until the yacht had been steered back on to its original heading. Model yacht books decreed that the area of the vane must be four and a half times that of the rudder, so Francis designed a vane sail of forty-five square feet (an enormous area). It was, of course, very difficult to make all the parts strong enough to stand up to gale-force winds without being too heavy to weathercock easily. When the vane gear was finally fitted on, beautiful *Gipsy Moth III* looked very ugly, but no sooner had Francis crossed the bar at the entrance to the Beaulieu River and headed her across the Solent and locked the vane to the tiller, than his boat started tearing through the water, sailing herself entirely, while keeping a dead straight wake. Francis would write:

That was one of the most thrilling moments of my life. Gradually I found out that 'Miranda', as I christened the self-steering device, required just as much skill to get the best out of her as does setting the sails of a yacht in a keen race. Also it gave me the same pleasure to succeed.

One night he wrote in his log:

I have not enjoyed myself so much since I was preparing to fly out alone to Australia in 1929. I was thinking the old query, 'Is fate too strong for man's self will? Am I so happy because I am doing the sort of thing I was destined for?' How I enjoyed it – no, that's not right because I hated a lot of it, always scared stiff – my flying. No, I should say *how it satisfied me*.

This was Francis Chichester at the age of fifty-nine, a man possessing a veneer of health and a schoolboy's *joie de vivre*. Even the novelty of Press and television interviews struck him as 'great sport'. Sheila sailed down to Plymouth on *Gipsy Moth*, and on the night before the race commenced, when Giles appeared, they intended a quiet family dinner at a Greek restaurant; it started that way but ended as a not exactly non-alcoholic party of seventy, headed by the *Observer* staff, Lindley Abbatt and Chris Brasher who had worked for the venture through thick and thin, assuring their hesitant Editor-in-Chief that he need not fear being torn to pieces by rival newspapers for luring the flower of fearless yachtsmen to their doom by offering monetary reward.

Next morning the four boats entered for this romantic solo race left the tidal dock and jockeyed about waiting for the starting gun. Apart from Hasler's *Jester* and Chichester's *Gipsy Moth*, only Dr David Lewis in *Cardinal Virtue* and Val Howells in *Eira* actually sailed on 11 June. They were followed several days later by a gallant fifth, the Frenchman Jean Lacombe in *Cap Horn*, who had just arrived in Plymouth and could not get ready in time.

The instructions for this race were short and simple:

LEAVE THE MELAMPUS BUOY TO STARBOARD AND
THENCE BY ANY ROUTE TO THE AMBROSE LIGHT
VESSEL, NEW YORK

The Reverend 'Tubby' Clayton had given Sheila prayer cards mentioning all participants. She distributed these among friends and every single night each of the five skippers was remembered in the prayers of a wide variety of people.

Soon after leaving, *Cardinal Virtue* broke her mast and returned to Plymouth where the Mashford brothers worked hard for three days and got her to sea again. Meanwhile, *Jester, Éira* and *Gipsy Moth* vanished into Atlantic mist. Francis had the biggest boat, which gave him an advantage in waterline length, but soon he began to think the weight of sails and gear too much for him to handle alone and he envied his rivals the comparative ease of changing sail on their smaller vessels. Reefing the mainsail, lowering it and hoisting the trysail took an hour or more of hard struggle and when really rough weather came he wished he had a nine-tonner for this particular venture.

Gipsy Moth III had been dry as a bone in normal seas, but she let a lot of water in through her seams during the very heavy weather into which they immediately ran. Francis found all his clothing wet and he did not get the chance to dry it for thirty-seven days, except for an occasional vest tied round a saucepan of hot water. Despite the Aladdin stove which kept bravely going through every storm, he was often cold, and at other times sweating heavily inside his oilskins when he had to deal with the 380-square-foot mainsail and heavy eighteen-foot boom.

Hardly a health cruise one might think, but a man's body is made to endure wet and cold and to sweat. What man's system is *not* made to withstand is financial worry, petrol fumes and lack of exercise. Francis Chichester, who had painfully steeled himself to survive the long, gasping hospital nights, the cramped sleeping on one side, now found himself between sea and sky, not tense and apprehensive as he had been in flying days, but cradled on the deep, roughly cradled, flung around the cabin, bruised, thrown out of his bunk by waves that made him fear the yacht had crashed into a steamer – but he was a living animal again with air pouring into his lungs, knowing hunger and aching fatigue and the wild exaltation of conquering natural elements. Jubilantly he was able to record that on one occasion he sailed at eight and a half knots for two hours. '*Gipsy Moth* was going so fast that it was hard to stand up. She was like a horse flying over fallen logs on rough ground.' Everything amused him, especially the whim of answering a steamer's fog-horn with the correct toots on his own little motor-horn.

On 17 June, when six days out, the fog lifted and Francis got a sun-fix with his sextant. He found that his dead-reckoning was only fifteen miles out – no more accurate result could have been expected with a crew of good helmsmen. He always worked out the dead-reckoning carefully but he could only guess what course 'Miranda' had been steering while he slept.

After two weeks *Gipsy Moth III* had travelled 1264 miles from Plymouth in a straight line, then she ran into a serious storm. The ex-invalid spent over five hours on deck lashing down gear, including the mainsail boom. He wrote:

It was only after I had finished that I became aware of the appalling up-roar, with a high-pitched shriek or screams dominating. I reckoned that the wind was now 80 m.p.h. (I still think of winds above 60 m.p.h. in terms of m.p.h. instead of knots because of getting used to the speeds of my seaplane propeller slipstream in m.p.h.).

During his third week of battling against the Westerlies, Francis grew ever more light of heart. Things which would have irritated him ashore, such as spilling his tea, made him laugh out loud. Rain, fog, gales, squalls and turbulent seas under grey skies suited his spirit. He felt that out here in the pounding ocean he understood the true values of life. The meals he cooked for himself tasted absolutely delicious, and his noggins of whisky like nectar. All his senses sharpened. He felt with his whole being the changing character of the sea, the colours of the sea, the rhythms of the sea and wind, even the differences between light and darkness were a joy.

This summer the Atlantic proved unusually foggy. According to the log, *Gipsy Moth III* sailed through 1430 miles of fog and the mist grew worse over the Grand Banks, where Francis dreaded hitting a trawler or an iceberg.

He was closing the coast of Nova Scotia when one of those inner warnings, which saved him from disaster on several occasions in his life, rang out like a bell. He had reckoned on enough sea room to allow him a couple of hours' sleep. Just as he dropped off a noise in the rigging woke him, but as he lay in the darkness thinking over the boat's position, there seemed absolutely no reason to change tack so he tried to get back to sleep. However, the rigging sang shriller; instead of lulling him as it often did, there seemed to be warning in the note. At last he rose up, went on deck, and for no reason that his mind could give, he put about and sailed away from the coast on the other tack. When he returned to his bunk the sound of warning seemed to have died away, the boat no longer called to him. He slept for five hours.

Next morning, on comparing his charts, he felt a cold tremor go down his spine. When changing from one chart sheet to another, he had not noticed that the new scale was less than half that of the old. He had been not twenty miles off the coast but eight. Had he slept for two hours on the original tack, he would have wrecked his boat. He was saved because a voice had sung to him through the rigging.

On 8 July, after twenty-seven days of vainly trying to make a radio telephone call, Francis suddenly got through and was able to send messages to Chris Brasher and Sheila.

July 16, the thirty-seventh day of the race, was the first completely fine day, and that night Francis perceived bright stars instead of heavy blackness. He was now approaching the Nantucket Shoals which need most careful navigation. He would, in forty days, have changed sails 118 times and he was getting tired.

Sheila had never doubted the successful outcome of this race – not only was she sure that Francis would arrive safely, but that the others would also. Such was her confidence that she had crossed the Atlantic by steamer and was calmly waiting in New York for days before any news came in. 'Blondie' Hasler had once been sighted by the *Queen Mary* far to the north of *Gipsy Moth III* (in fact, he had, at the end of the third week, sailed farther in a straight line from Plymouth than Francis). But now the Atlantic seemed extremely empty of yachts.

Rumours concerning the 'mad cap racers' aroused a flicker of interest in the American newspapers, but the journalists as a whole did not know quite what to make of it. Maybe if the five boats were *never* seen again there would be a story, but for the moment nothing sensational was happening.

Francis had reckoned on reaching New York by 18 July. On the 17th, the U.S. coastguards reported him off Nantucket. Sheila hired a fishing boat and went out, but no *Gipsy Moth* appeared. She returned to her hotel and the rumours of 'five missing yachts' began to develop a certain public appeal. The phone never stopped ringing and messages kept being pushed under her door.

Chris Brasher arrived from London to cover the story for the *Observer*, and stayed in the same hotel. He was much amused at the scene when a tough reporter out for a 'worried wife reaction' tried interviewing Sheila in the lift. 'What are you going to do while waiting Mrs Chichester?'

'Well, actually, I'm going to have my hair styled.'

On 20 July, Chris hired a plane and flew out towards Nantucket, looking for the little recognizable sail, but the trip proved fruitless.

Sheila was just waking up at eight next morning when the phone rang. It was Chris. 'It's Eureka! We've found him.' He'd been out again in a plane and definitely contacted *Gipsy Moth*. Sheila rushed off to her fishing boat and out they chugged to the Ambrose Light Vessel. Still no sign. Then suddenly Francis's voice sounded clear on the radio telephone giving his course, and within twenty minutes a little white sail appeared on the horizon.

Meanwhile, the skipper was tidying the cabin littered with objects broken in the storms he'd passed through, and sprucing himself up for arrival. At 5.30 he saw the fishing boat with 'Sheila very smart in her scarf hat waving'. Suddenly there were launches and photographers all around.

'What news of the others?' he called out.

'You are first,' someone shouted.

The words were honey sweet, and how good was the first sip of champagne from the bottle which Sheila carried determinedly on board. Francis had got to be fortified for questioning by Press, Quarantine and Customs.

It was long after midnight when they reached their hotel room. Chris Brasher had ordered a delicious supper to be wheeled in on a trolley. Too sleepy to talk they lay down on their beds trying to pick at various dishes while Chris scribbled out the story he must telephone to his paper at 3 a.m. He asked a few questions, then aware of silence in the room, he looked up. Sheila's head was nodding. 'I thank God for the return of his health – he looks so well – not for winning the race,' was all she could say. Francis was fast asleep. Chris collected the soup plates and wheeled the trolley out.

Tell about it?

How could Francis talk of forty days of thunderous seas, thick fogs, flogging sails, gybes, jammed wet ropes, nerve-racking tiller adjustments, clampings that slipped, broachings-to, wind-vane breakage and spinnaker poles doing unutterable things – all these momentous incidents would be picked from the log and written up for *Alone Across the Atlantic* in language comprehensible to fellow mariners.

It had been a splendid cure.

20. Laurel Wreaths

'Blondie' Hasler came in eight days later and Dr Lewis arrived seven days after this. Val Howells, who had made a great sweep to the south, took sixty-three days, and Jean Lacombe, who had started five days late in his tiny *Cap Horn*, sailed for seventy days, arriving on 24 August. Each yachtsman was given a stirring welcome. Everyone felt so happy that all five had got across safely. It seemed to prove that lone sailors are very careful – more so perhaps than when sustained by other crew members – and there is no inducement to show off!

While waiting for the other boats to arrive, Francis and Sheila visited Mrs Dick du Pont, a splendid old lady born a Chichester who lived at Cape Cod. Her son, Felix, fetched them in his private plane – an outing which rather frightened Sheila, unused to the sensation of flying 'in and out of the skyscrapers of New York City'.

American hospitality proved dazing. When the du Ponts gave a celebration dinner, Francis insisted, despite the heat-wave, on wearing his old green velvet smoking jacket which had crossed the Atlantic in *Gipsy Moth*'s small cupboard.

Sheila wished to sail back to England with her husband – her first long ocean passage. Intense heat made the refitting and re-victualling fairly exhausting, for *Gipsy Moth* was lying in City Island and they had no awning or ice box. While they lived aboard, the special flag presented to each single-handed sailor by the City of New York, hung at the mast-head. What a relief it was to see it begin to flutter in the evening breeze. In fact, they could not wait for the cool open ocean, and with the Westerlies behind them they could expect a fast passage home. They left New York on 24 August and were soon enjoying a lazy happy existence helped by the perfect behaviour of 'Miranda', the vane-steering. By day they could sunbathe and at night sit silently in the cockpit with the silvery sails billowing out and the boat sighing her way over a moonlit sea.

The weather worsened as they reached the Azores, and once a steamer seemed to be about to run them down. 'Where are you bound?' came through a megaphone. 'Horta,' Sheila shouted back.

'Short of water. We'll give you water.' The great bows loomed frighteningly near.

'NO. NO. We are making for HORTA!'

On 17 September Francis celebrated his birthday with a bottle of wine. A day later they sighted the Azores, and after a very uncomfortable night spent hove-to outside the harbour, they beat in to Horta against a strong head-wind.

During the fortnight they had to spend in harbour doing repairs, the one luxury they craved was a hot bath, but no such thing was available, for all the island pipes had cracked during a recent earthquake. They left the Azores on 3 October and reached Plymouth fifteen days later, riding through what Francis called 'impressive seas, magnificent and monumental, but not malicious'.

Off Ushant their radio picked up the chimes of Big Ben and curiously the sound jarred them, for it broke into a special world which had been all their own. There is always something sad about the end of a long ocean passage, even when the sailors are longing to get home.

When they reached Plymouth it was to find that they had to beat in to the harbour against a force eight head-wind. Then just as they finally picked up a mooring a BBC television team arrived and asked them to go out and sail in again, explaining, 'We didn't get a picture of you entering.'

That winter passed happily, and in the spring Prince Philip presented five well-deserved prizes to the gallant contestants of the first Transatlantic Race.

When he was at home, Francis had to attend to the expanding map business which he ran with his efficient staff of two – Joy Weeks managed the production side and Monica Cooper now remained in charge of sales. Sheila wrote a guide book called *London Woman* which gave pertinent information to any woman visiting the city for the day, or week or month for that matter. The maps of this feminine publication were designed as Francis's fighter pilot maps had been, to catch the eye with big clear drawings of monuments and landmarks that made for easy gyration to high-brow museums or bargain basements.

For Francis, the months he had to spend in London attending to his business were now full of interest. His inquiring mind never ceased to play with new possibilities and new theories. His contributions to navigational thought were considerable. 'Blondie' Hasler had related his dismay when, during the transatlantic race, his chronometer broke down. Francis enjoyed digesting such problems. He worked out the alternative methods by which it is possible for a man to determine his position on the face of the globe. Eventually, with the diffidence which always impressed fellows of the Royal Geographic Society and gentlemen of that ilk, he presented a paper to the Institute of Navigation entitled *An elegant variant of the lunar distance method of determining longitude at sea without reference to Greenwich Mean Time.* His audience, learned in the ways of stars and planets, assimilated all this with rapture. And even the most un-navigational reader must admit a euphonious charm in the title – which leads the imagination on to hope that elegant variants may decorate all our idle hours.

Michael Richey, the Executive Secretary of the Institute of Navigation, has sought to elucidate for the author the point at which a brilliant navigator becomes a great navigator. The delicate distinction seems to lie in this – after all mathematical calculation has been made, when pressed by unforeseen danger, when no further logical deduction is possible, there is a split second in which a decision has to be taken. The great navigator, under stress, reaching a point where no more sums can help him, will choose the right line of action. He could no more explain this extra instinct which guides when technical aids end than a homing pigeon, given a vocabulary of say fifty words, could describe how he knows where to go. This trait, in addition to the genius's infinite capacity for taking pains, is what makes a *great navigator*. Francis Chichester was the greatest of our century and to win the regard of men qualified to understand was balm to him. Egotistical and unreasonable might be the verdict of many. Tempestuous and ambitious he certainly was, especially when struggling to produce a book – but the appreciation of the Institute of Navigation gave him serenity, and its members considered him as humble as he was entrancing.

21. *Gipsy Moth III* Goes Again

Francis had intended to spend the next summer sailing *Gipsy Moth III* in ocean races, but he fell and bruised his back in the area of that old air-crash injury. An attack of hepatitis followed, but he thought he could navigate *Stormvogel*, a big seventy-five-foot light-displacement yacht belonging to Caes Brynzeel, during Cowes Week Races and in the Fastnet. After the hepatitis Francis found himself unable to tuck into the rich food provided by *Stormvogel's* Dutch owner, but he learned much about the 'hard-driving racing mentality' of serious ocean racing.

Ordinary yacht-racing did not in fact deeply appeal to Francis. He hankered less to compete than to try new things. Forty days had seemed to him a very slow passage across the Atlantic and he felt certain that he could break his own record. He had thought up a number of ways to make the gear-handling easier and the yacht faster. Now he asked the famous John Illingworth, most successful of ocean racers, to redesign *Gipsy Moth's* mast and sail plan.

As a result, by the spring of 1962, *Gipsy Moth III* had a shorter mast made of metal (fifty-three instead of fifty-five feet), and the following changes:

A smaller mainsail which would balance the headsails better, and be easier to handle. The heavy main boom which had caused so much trouble was cut down from eighteen feet to fourteen feet, and the lethal runners which had seemed animated by a mad lust to brain me were eliminated. The headsails were bigger, to compensate for the smaller mainsail, and the sloop rig was changed to cutter rig.

All he now needed was financial aid. It was towards Christmas

1961 that he met John Anderson, Assistant Editor of the *Guardian*, a sailing man who was particularly interested in what triggered off men to seek high adventure. Anderson had reviewed *Alone Across the Atlantic* and Francis thought that the writer of this review showed uncanny perception of the true values and spiritual issues involved in solo racing across an ocean. After he had presented the annual prizes at the sailing club of which Anderson was vice-commodore, Francis offered him the story of a new Atlantic crossing in which he would be out to beat his own record. Anderson accepted it and an interesting friendship formed. The *Guardian* wanted a daily report to be transmitted by a new type of Marconi radio telephone and the General Post Office seemed anxious to help, wanting to find out *how* far across the ocean a small boat could keep contact.

All this resulted in much hard work and the alteration of *Gipsy Moth*'s interior. Like most mariners Francis found that preparations wearied him more than being buffeted at sea.

Place had to be found for four heavy banks of accumulators in acid-proof boxes, with Atlantic-proof tops; also for a special charging motor, which might seem light to them, but was heavy to me; and for a radio telephone of half a man's weight, which had to be high above the water line. All this weight would put the stern down, increase the rolling movement and decrease the sailing power, but the brilliant technical bandits were merciless to *Gipsy Moth*. My chart table and navigating department had to be partially wrecked to make room for the telephone. There followed trouble with the transmitting aerials, trouble with the earthing arrangements, trouble with the electrolytic action, trouble with noxious fumes from the batteries being charged. Fortunately, Marconis were keen that the R/T should transmit, and the G.P.O. men determined that it should be received.

The regular transmission of reports on this trip was in fact a fascinating important experiment in wireless communication.

On 1 June 1962 *Gipsy Moth III* set off from Plymouth to race herself across the Atlantic. Francis felt that nothing could quite equal the romance of sailing an ocean for the first time, but now he was tackling the Atlantic in a different way, with his yacht in first-class racing trim. He planned a more northerly course than that he had taken in 1960. For a time the weather remained marvellous; he could enjoy sunlit days with the boat tearing along under full sail, then came the usual weeks of gales and jib trouble and halyards fouling the forestays, added to which the charging motor seized up and he had to convert the main engine to do the charging – a nasty task.

A racing pigeon landing on the boat became a dominating interest.

As Pidge made ceaseless messes he had to be banished to a little tent in the cockpit, and, although apparently feeling queasy, he would pick at certain carefully prepared meals. After a week Pidge actually cooed. Every morning Francis diligently fed and watered him before trimming the sails and getting the ship back onto her proper heading. It became a curious, rather worrying, relationship. When Pidge's number was transmitted to London, he was identified as a well-bred French bird racing from the Channel Islands to Preston in Lancashire. The Press wanted to send a plane out to drop boxes of pigeon food on the yacht as a stunt. 'What! Risk hitting Francis with boxes of bird food! Certainly not,' said Sheila. Pidge occasionally flew off, circling the boat, but he always alighted again. 'Go on, fly home,' Francis would say, but he seemed to have lost his bearings and always came back. Then one rough day he took off astern and landed in the water a few feet away. Francis tried frantically to save him, throwing out canvas, trying to grab his wings and finally picking him out of the water by hand. 'I felt cut up as I held his soaking body; I felt responsible for him, and somehow his mean crabbed nature and his dreadful habits made me feel worse.' He wrapped the thin little creature in a warm cloth and tried artificial respiration, but to no avail. 'It was the breakdown in communication between a human being and an animal which was so distressing. If only he could have trusted me . . .' Such a breakdown often happens between humans – when it happens between man and bird it is easier to analyse.

During the three-day gale which sealed Pidge's fate, the yacht not only made no progress, she was actually driven back twenty miles. Then the skies changed and on 24 June Francis wrote in his log: 'This is the sailing that sailors' dreams are made of, across the mysterious Grand Banks smooth as the Solent with water gliding along the hull gurgling and rumbling.'

When alone, he felt twice as efficient, and twice as sensitive to excitement, fear, and pleasure. His senses grew acute and the colours of the sky and sea seemed more vivid. Exultation filled him and the feel of the spray and the wind became a delight.

On 2 July, Sheila, flying to New York by jet, was able to recognize the tiny sail of *Gipsy Moth* nearing Nantucket, and at midnight on 4 July, Francis sailed into New York harbour, having knocked nearly seven days off his previous record. There were Independence Day fireworks going off on Coney Island as if to applaud the yacht sailing into New York harbour 'looking just like a big white moth'. Telegrams of congratulation arrived from all over the world and next morning *Gipsy Moth* was proceeding up East River when the *Queen*

Elizabeth passed by. The liner saluted the little boat with three blasts, 'and that was one of the great moments of a lifetime', said Francis.

Next day there had to be a Press conference, and Sheila was asked to read through the script of some of the American reporters. In her forthright way she proceeded to give them stick for missing the point of this voyage, which demonstrated for the first time the quality of the Marconi Kestrel set whereby for over two thousand miles a tiny boat had been able to speak direct to an office in London. 'But that was an *English* set, ma'am', was one reporter's brush-off. Later on Sheila read through all the papers with disgust. They made no mention of the daily direct phone call across the ocean.

Giles, who had now passed his sixteenth birthday, flew out to join his parents and to sail home with them. Sheila would write: 'I'd been rather frightened Francis might get tough with Giles and send him out on the foredeck, but there I was quite wrong, for he was splendid with our son.'

In 1963 Francis published his autobiography *The Lonely Sea and the Sky*. It was a long book, but even so it could not contain half the teeming ideas which he wished to weave into it. John Anderson, who had pressed him to place some record of his life on paper, helped to tighten it up, but added nothing except an introduction which began, 'We know nothing of the boyhood of Ulysses and it has always seemed to me a great loss that he did not write the story of his early life after he had got back from his travels. Perhaps he could not . . .' But this Ulysses could and did. In thanking John Anderson for helping him to cut his material Francis explained, 'I wrote far too much, for one reason. Little voyages have been sweet to me – on a bicycle, on a horse, on foot, skis or skates, but there is no room for bicycles in a biography.' To Francis everything held interest, nothing was dull. So passionate was his approach to each excursion in life that he could not forbear to describe each small discovery, each golden morn, nor could he desist from expressing his loathing for school life which to him, though not to many others, was deadening to the spirit. Francis Chichester, on the surface an unemotional, conventional Englishman, secretly suffered from a most unusual exuberance and sense of urgency. There was wonder in every flower and bird. Literary friends had to advise – sometimes to his chagrin – omitting the surprises on bicycle rides while retaining surprises over the Tasman Sea! *The Lonely Sea and the Sky* became a bestseller.

The winter months in London now provided blissful hours of boat planning. Francis would spend the long evenings working out modifications to increase *Gipsy Moth*'s speed so that she must surely win the second Transatlantic Race in 1964. (Once every four years was enough for the organizers!) And in that spring Francis wrote cockily, 'What is more, I shall take my green velvet smoking jacket again, hoping that my new handling methods will be efficient enough for me to dine in style one night while keeping *Gipsy Moth* racing at her full speed.'

But she did not win the second Transatlantic Race. It was, in fact, a very different kind of race. Instead of five small boats there were fifteen entrants, eleven were British, two French, one Danish and one Australian. *Gipsy Moth III* came second, beaten by the great French sailor Eric Tabarly whose *Penduick II* was specially built to compete in this race. And a new nationalistic note crept in when the newspaper *Paris Jour* wrote about Tabarly: 'Thanks to him it is the French flag which triumphs in the longest and most spectacular race on the ocean which the Anglo-Saxons consider their special domain.'

The Anglo-Saxons who had for years ignored 'Blondie' Hasler's efforts to get such a race going felt snubbed. Chichester was English, Chichester should certainly have won again.

Among those who thought that Francis ought to have had a better yacht for what seemed to have developed into an important international race, was his cousin Lord Dulverton, a patriotic Englishman whose family had founded Wills's Tobacco. Although usually referred to in the Press as a 'magnate', the second Lord Dulverton's interests did not lie in finance, but in backing imaginative projects. Having founded the first College of Adult Education in Africa twenty years before such colleges were thought of, and planted trees over 12 000 acres of wasteland in Scotland long before these projects were demanded by the nation, he now devoted his energies to a charitable trust which ran youth training schemes. Under his auspices a sailing centre owning a standing top-gallant schooner of 380 tons, which could take young men on adventure training cruises, was created on Loch Eil in Scotland. Sensing what his cousin must feel when his own boat was outclassed, Tony Dulverton impulsively telephoned to Sheila: 'What a shame Francis only had his same old boat when the French were backing their chap all out. If British industry won't do anything for Francis, then I jolly well will.'

Sheila was thrilled. It had been all they could do to pay for that 'same old boat' and her refittings. Lord Dulverton's next words were adamant: 'He's got to have a proper fast boat for the next race and I want you to tell him that I will provide it!'

Lord Dulverton's mother had been a Chichester (the daughter of Sir Edward, the ninth Baronet of Youlston), so he naturally felt a certain pride in family achievements, but his real motive lay in the desire to back something worth while, when his extraordinary cousin was attempting more than he could afford.

Sheila flew to America and there told Francis the news. He received it thoughtfully. Twice he had sailed the Atlantic alone in *Gipsy Moth III*, and now there was little more he could do with her except go back to ordinary ocean races. Then he spoke for the first time of the project he had long been nursing. He had always had the urge to do something different from other people, something nobody else had ever thought of. 'I want to try a very fast sail right round the world alone.' As he poured forth this plan Sheila felt as if a rush of fresh air filled the room. This would be fulfilment for Francis. This would finally mend him.

Giles, who was now eighteen, sailed home with his father. Their relationship had grown with Giles's stature. Francis had never been good with small children. He could not properly enjoy the companionship of his son until Giles had become strong and capable of reasonable discussion and able to *do* things with him. When they reached England Francis gratefully accepted Lord Dulverton's offer to build this new boat which could compete in trans-ocean races with the best, *or* sail around the world. A magnificent yacht suitable for any spectacular deed in the hands of a great navigator was what his cousin visualized. There was only one sad side. *Gipsy Moth III*, the brave little boat in which Francis had regained his health, and Sheila and Giles had sailed the Atlantic, must be sold. It was impossible to say good-bye to her without a twinge.

But Francis was less sentimental over such things than his wife and son. The longings of his youth had for some years been reawakening. That plane crash in Japan had seemed to end the possibility of world circumnavigation, and for a long time, through marriage and war and physical suffering, he had half-forgotten his burning aim when he set out from Australia in 1931. 'But as the years passed this urge to circle the world alone lay dormant in me, like a gorse seed which will lie in the earth for fifty years until the soil is stirred to admit some air or light, and the seed suddenly burgeons.'

The world for most of us seems a mat beneath our feet – for some a globe to be circled – for a few a globe to be circled alone. What Fate had not allowed Francis to do in the air he would accomplish on the sea.

22. The Building of
Gipsy Moth IV

Francis had already discussed a possible new boat with John Illingworth, who had redesigned *Gipsy Moth III*'s mast for her second transatlantic crossing. Lord Dulverton wished the world-famous firm of Camper & Nicholson to build the yacht, but he agreed that John Illingworth and Angus Primrose should produce the drawings for this unique craft. No one had ever before attempted to design a very fast boat, which could be handled by one man alone in the world's most terrible seas. So the experienced John Illingworth faced a difficult order. The boat had to be long enough to obtain speed, and light enough to be driven at that speed by the amount of sail which a man of sixty would be able to handle.

At the first meeting of builders and designers, Lord Dulverton stressed the importance of perfection in every detail, regardless of expense. This rare order had such an intoxicating effect on those present that the ultimate possibilities of cost if changes were made during construction were not foreseen. Although Camper & Nicholson could not immediately quote a definite price, they worked out what they genuinely believed to be an approximate estimate and in the euphoria resultant on discussions concerning the exciting project, Lord Dulverton accepted the adjective *approximate* as meaning exactly that. Francis, who had always had to scrimp and save, asked to pay a two and a half per cent share in the yacht. His cousin accepted this, but later he refused to cash Francis's cheque. He intended to pay for this marvellous new boat himself.

The yacht which John Illingworth designed was to be of light displacement, fifty-four feet overall and thirty-nine and a half feet on the waterline. The theoretical maximum speed of a boat depends on her waterline length. The length of *Gipsy Moth IV* would ensure that she was very fast indeed. Illingworth had a great reputation for designing light-displacement boats which were very fast to windward. His own racing yacht *Myth of Malham* had created a revolution of thought in the designing world. One might add that many fast-to-windward boats sail on their ear, and this uncomfortable likelihood does not seem to have been sufficiently envisaged or discussed. The hull would be cold-moulded. This new idea in construction – entailing the creation of a mould over which six thin skins of laminated plywood would be glued, making a total thickness of seven-eighths of an inch – would result in wonderful strength, but the immense work involved made it difficult for a firm to cost accurately before they were very experienced in the method.

The usual arguments cropped up. Francis insisted on 'Blondie' Hasler's self-steering gear which had brought three boats in the last Transatlantic Race safely across. John Illingworth favoured a heavier version for this exceptionally fast boat, and a prototype 'B.P.' gear, larger and more powerful than anything previously known was fitted straight off the drawing board. Hasler's invention had been well tried in Atlantic storms, but naturally no one had inaugurated trials in the Roaring Forties. Despite an eventual breakage, it was to prove a technical triumph.

Over a year went by with Francis making weekly visits to Portsmouth. He would insist on walking from St James's Place to Waterloo to catch an 8 a.m. train, with Sheila panting at his side. When they returned in the evening she would be exhausted, he resilient. Francis never noticed when other people grew tired.

The months of boat-building passed, lightened by reading sea sagas and preparing an anthology of dramatic passages about the southern ocean which was to be called *Along the Clipper Way*, and dedicated to Tony Dulverton.

Francis felt extremely emotional about the sea and he liked to build up a mood. During this tense London period he avoided discussing his project, partly because he feared someone else might try to sail the old clipper routes before he was ready, and partly because he still had the feeling, inherited from early flying days, that 'disclosing a particularly difficult objective was to invite failure'.

The construction of every newly designed boat entails a tremendous amount of worry. Inevitably alterations from the original drawings accrue and the constant need for decisions is very hard on the nervous systems of those involved. Because she was such an important, expensive boat, *Gipsy Moth IV* caused even more brainstorms and sleepless nights than most. The things that went wrong have been recorded in detail. Francis sometimes wished that he had just sold his Number Three and built his Number Four on the same lines with modifications. The result would have been a cheaper boat, certainly less fast, but one which he knew, and with those faults he had diagnosed over the years, carefully eliminated. He began to fuss about the wisdom of attempting this immense undertaking with a new yacht in the experimental stage.

My old *Gipsy Moth III* would have done well enough for the voyage, except for some constructional features. First of all, I wanted a flush deck, to give easy passage to breaking waves without risk to deck hamper, secondly, I thought I should have a stronger cabin or doghouse . . . Another feature of *Gipsy Moth III* that I wanted to change was the single-plank hull to one of laminated plywood only seven-eighths inch thick, but immensely strong . . . I also wanted a watertight bulkhead forward . . . which would give the boat a good chance of survival if she had a head-on collision with an iceberg.

The interior of Number Three to which Francis was so well accustomed after his six Atlantic crossings, had been perfect for him. Wishing to have the same lay-out, he asked for measurements of the galley, bunks, settees, tables, etc., to be made before she was stripped, laid up and sold. Everything must be exactly as in the previous boat. Unfortunately, the man in charge lost these drawings before the time came to build cabin fittings in Number Four, and a new layout had to be devised, imperfectly, from memory. Such episodes made Francis literally ill.

Building started in December 1964 and the new *Gipsy* was launched in March 1966. When Sheila threw the champagne bottle it did not break. Francis minded this but she scorned superstitions and omens. Then the hull appeared to Francis to have stuck and he rushed forward himself to push her into the water. Finally, after these horrid exertions, *Gypsy Moth IV* sat on the surface looking strangely high. She was, in fact, a brand new design, a light-displacement boat produced for a most extraordinary voyage, nothing like her had ever been commissioned before and all new boats need months of discussion and adjustment. These months were simply not available. Most yachting experts, including Francis's friend Commander Erroll Bruce, thought the boat a masterpiece in that so many of the drawing-board guesses came right.

During her first trials with John Illingworth and 'Blondie' Hasler on board, it became obvious that *Gipsy Moth IV* was much too lightly ballasted. They decided to add 2400 lb of lead to her keel to lessen the tendency to heel over in light winds. This meant that the boat must be returned to the slip while chunks of wood were sawn out of the keel and molten lead poured in. This operation took up a precious month which should have been spent on sailing trials. Francis grew sour and testy as delays increased, and extremely agitated when he discovered this fast new boat to be much harder to manoeuvre than his old one. He had determined to sail to Sydney in a hundred days, but now he felt that speed had been obtained at too high a price – she was too long and too light and too short in the keel for true running. The last straw occurred when she also proved too expensive.

On the night before his big Press conference of 22 March, when Francis was resting at home, the telephone rang. 'Don't answer it,' pleaded Sheila, but he reached out drowsily for the receiver. It was Tony Dulverton to say that the cost of the new boat had come to nearly three times the original estimate. Could Francis find the last £12 000 himself? 'Oh God,' he said to Sheila.

How could it happen? How *could* a boat so far exceed its original estimate? Well, with alterations – and there had been very numerous ones – and escalating costs – this can happen. It is even more likely to occur when the design and method of construction are new. Camper & Nicolson had not, perhaps, stressed sufficiently their own inability to foresee costs, and because Francis had been refused any financial stake he had not thought it necessary to supervise the accounts.

Next day, while Francis faced his Press conference, Sheila lay in bed fretting. As so often happens in time of crisis, she had suffered an accident; pulling up her window curtain as she had hundreds of times before, the brass knob flew out and injured an eye rather seriously. She knew that Francis was getting rather overwrought. Just as he had once held his plane together with glue and determination, now he must hold the physical fibres of his being together. The lack of communication between him and Tony and the builders and designers now seemed incomprehensible. How bitterly Francis regretted not having closely watched the accounts.

And there was still so much to attend to. As he had contracted to send twice-weekly radio accounts of the voyage for the *Sunday Times* and the *Guardian*, an expensive super Marconi Kestrel set must be installed and radio contacts organized in different countries. John Anderson proved enthusiastic and encouraging during this difficult time. 'You aren't just interested in sailing as seamen are – what you love is aero-dynamics,' Anderson would cajole. 'You don't think of your boat as a house, but as a kite.'

Homecoming. A glass of champagne with Sheila and Giles after the
second solo transatlantic race, 1964

Left Gipsy Moth II off Cowes

Right Gipsy Moth IV in a typical stance

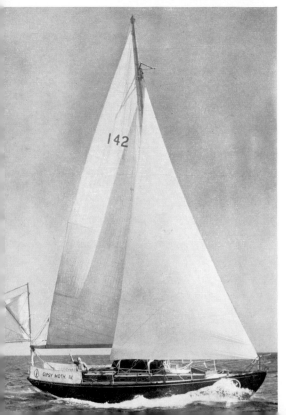

Gipsy Moth III winning the first solo transatlantic race (1960) under full sail as she approaches Ambrose Lightship

Gipsy Moth IV on the round the world voyage (1967).
Above leaving Sydney Harbour to a tumultuous send-off.

Right rounding the Cape Horn.

The ceremony in the grounds of the Royal Naval College, Greenwich, when the Queen knighted Francis after his round-the-world voyage. She dubbed him with the sword which had been used to knight Sir Francis Drake.

The newly knighted Sir Francis stands on the balcony of the Mansion House to receive the welcome of the City of London.

Francis returns from his last voyage happy, with Giles (in overcoat) and eager hands.

Gipsy Moth V sails away

Francis had to agree. He *was* different to most seamen and to most sportsmen. He had tried to express himself in *Alone Across the Atlantic*.

'I know now I don't do a thing nearly as well when with someone. It makes me think I was cut out for solo jobs, and any attempt to diverge from that lot only makes me half a person. It looks as if the only way to be happy is to do fully what you are destined for.'

And to get around the world in the arms of the wind, harnessing the forces of the air was this man's destiny. The pressures of arrangements that now had to be made overwhelmed him. With the responsibility of radio transmission to those newspapers which held him under contract, added to the search for financial sponsorship, Francis began to wonder if he would survive long enough to escape onto the ocean.

There was just too much to do, and to cap it all, he fell on an armoured glass skylight in the deck of his new boat and severely damaged a leg. The summer months of 1966 which ought to have been devoted to deep sea trials were instead spent making arrangements on shore. Several yacht chandlers rallied round eager to provide ropes and accessories free of charge and Colonel Whitbread of the Whitbread Breweries, and the International Wool Secretariat offered generous sponsorship, so did Shell Oil who had backed Francis in his old flying days. But the strain of it all affected Francis's health.

Francis Chichester would be much criticized for publishing his lamentations concerning all these troubles with *Gipsy Moth IV*. The facts of the matter are that he rejoiced when his cousin offered to give him a new boat in which to win fame, that neither he nor Lord Dulverton realized that a builder's estimate can more than double itself when a completely novel form of construction is used, that for various reasons he had no time for proper trials and that when he got into great storms several aspects of the boat's design did not suit him. Her great length and narrow beam caused her to heel right over and when sailing hard she tended to gripe (charge up into the wind). Although two years had gone into the project, Francis was now short of time and money and energy. Misunderstandings abounded and his leg hurt like hell and it was nearly time to sail.

Illingworth had designed a very, very fast boat suitable for long ocean races. No designer could assess how difficult she might be for a man alone to manage in the extraordinary conditions of Antarctic seas.

23. Off

Francis Chichester had always been a romantic. Picturesque detail appealed to him. He loved his home in a very special way. It was his nest, his 'kennel', the place in which he had come back to life. He was a tremendous walker, and it had been his intention to walk from 9 St James's Place to *Gipsy Moth IV* lying at Tower Pier where the clippers used to unload. Then he would sail her down the Thames and on to Plymouth with his family as crew. From Plymouth he would set out alone around the world following the old clipper route and making only one stop – in Australia. Having returned to England after reaching Plymouth via the Horn, he wished to sail his boat up to the Tower of London, walk ashore and *walk* back home through London streets. This is what he *wanted* to do. However, his injured leg would not permit him to follow up this fancy for a pedestrian start.

On 12 August 1966, with Giles and Commander Erroll Bruce as crew, Francis sailed the new boat from Camper & Nicholson's yard to London, where his old friend, 'Tubby' Clayton, held a service of blessing on board, and read Francis's favourite psalm.

He gathereth the waters of the sea together. And layeth them up as in a treasure house. Thy way is in the sea. And thy path is the great waters. They that go down to the sea in ships and occupy their business in the great waters, these men see the work of the Lord and His wonders in the deep.

Then *Gipsy Moth IV* departed, sailing past the famous old clipper ship *Cutty Sark*, and on down to Plymouth for a hundred last-minute jobs to be done. Erroll Bruce, who had been watching Francis closely, wondered that a man in his physical state could consider himself fit for such an adventure without even having time for proper trials. But Sheila wanted him to get off. Apart from the leg injury he did not appear to her to be unwell. The sea was his best nurse. He would recover out there, away from mundane worries, in the wild solitude.

On reaching Plymouth they learnt that unexpected disaster had befallen Alec Rose, another Englishman who also intended to sail round the world. When on 29 June Rose had written to Francis:

How are you? I envy you your advanced state of preparedness. I'm in chaos . . . When I first decided to go on this trip to 'keep you company' I didn't consider a race. However the press with their flair for building things up thought otherwise, and I must say it stimulates interest . . . As you mentioned when I telephoned you – I ought to start early in August if I have *Lively Lady* ready and I had formed my plans on this basis. Although it would add to the attraction to start together I feel I ought not to leave as late as you can do.

Would you be agreeable then for me to start earlier and to sail under some form of handicap rules, such as R.O.R.C. do . . .

Francis had answered:

5.7.66: Dear Alec. I have been thinking about this race business. On April 23 before you thought of joining in I announced my intention of racing against the average clipper's time round the world. This was all planned long ago and cannot be changed. I think a race could be good sport and provide interest as you say. However, I am dead against handicapping: as indeed I was in the second Singlehanded Race. It defeats the whole object of singlehanded endeavour.

Francis had for so long cherished the notion of pitting himself against the great clipper ships of the past that he could not change his intent. Alec Rose had therefore sailed off from Portsmouth on his own on 17 August. Damaged by a storm, he had put in to Plymouth for repairs, set out again, was rammed by a steamer, and returned to Plymouth for fresh repairs. There his yacht had just been blown off her cradle and still further damaged. Francis had refused to work in with plans for a handicap race against a much older boat, but he was genuinely sympathetic at such a run of bad luck, and he immensely admired, as everyone else did, Alec Rose's pluck and determination to effect repairs for the third time and sail a year later.

On 27 August, with Sheila and Giles, he sailed *Gipsy IV* to the Royal Western Yacht Club's race-starting line. Sid Mashford of Mashford's yard followed in a launch to take off Sheila and Giles. At 11 o'clock Jack Odling-Smee fired a gun to mark his departure and then Francis found himself alone in the long, fast, bucketing boat with 14 000 miles of ocean ahead. When the masts disappeared on the horizon, Sheila relaxed. To her Francis was off on 'a great spiritual adventure, a sort of pilgrimage'.

Francis was so tired that even before he lost sight of England he had to roll into his bunk for a quick nap, and risk a collision in the shipping lanes. Then for seven grim days he felt seasick, but on 4 September he enjoyed a real sleep, the first good sleep, it seemed, for months. After that he felt happy. At least he never had to worry about his position. He carried a fine assortment of navigational instruments on board, some of them of considerable refinement, and he enjoyed testing his skill. When he reached the lee of Madeira, several squalls struck hard and he realized again how frightening it could be when this very fast, very light boat met really rough weather, but the effort needed to control her and to keep alive, had a therapeutic effect, and when he reached warm seas the pain of his bruised leg eased.

One midnight *Gipsy Moth* suffered a violent shock and Francis thought he must have hit a whale, but the dark sea revealed nothing. On 17 September he enjoyed the best sixty-fifth birthday a man could wish for. He started it off with a fresh-water wash. Then came the opening of birthday presents. Sheila had chosen for him a pair of luxurious silk pyjamas. 'I shed a tear to think of her kindness and love, and all the happiness we have had together since 1937.' Then he unpacked a bottle of wine from Monica Cooper and other members of the map-making firm. He drank that for lunch. In the evening he celebrated by opening a bottle of champagne in the cockpit, and wearing full evening rig – smart new trousers, black shoes and that famous old green velvet smoking jacket which he had carried six times across the Atlantic. This was the first time he had actually worn it on board. And through it all *Gipsy Moth IV* travelled southwards at seven knots.

This must be one of the greatest nights of my life – right in the middle of this wonderful venture – just passed by 100 miles the longest six-day run by any singlehander that I know of, and a great feeling of love and goodwill towards my family and friends . . . People keep at me about my age. I suppose they think I think I can beat age. I am not that foolish. Nobody, I am sure, can be more aware than I am that my time is limited. I don't think I can escape ageing, but why beef about it? Our only purpose in life, if we are able to say such a thing, is to put up the best performance we can – in anything – and only in doing so lies the satisfaction of living.

'*In anything*', he said, and he meant just that. It is the effort that counts, the perfection of individual performance. Success lay in pitting yourself and in not failing through weakness or boredom. A worthwhile aim must be found but what is more worth while than the balancing of kindness and courage in ordinary life? His own equilibrium he had discovered in ways unlike those of other men, he had needed colour and danger and to achieve the exceptional. Fate had woven unusual stress into his existence. He had *had* to try to do things differently, but he was only beginning to realize the true value of achievement – it was self-knowledge. This was the gift brought to him by the years, and as a pain-killer he could divert himself with the game of breaking records – the clipper ship records and his own records.

In the meantime, pounding through the South Atlantic, he had little time to philosophize. As *Gipsy Moth IV* had sailed without proper trials, it was surprising that so many of the design guesses came right. But, like a thoroughbred, she was not easy to handle and Francis had not had very much experience of the thoroughbred type of boat. She was exceedingly lively, and tender and heeled right over in the slightest breeze which worried him greatly. However, he was still getting to know his boat; she had faults which only these seas could show up – a habit of hobby-horsing if sailed close to the wind and a tendency to edge-up into the wind on her own. She was so much bigger than the slower, more stable *Gipsy Moth III*, and Francis found himself getting exhausted by the numerous sail changes necessary whenever winds grew suddenly lighter or harder. *Gipsy Moth IV* carried ten different sails and a morning's log entries could run like this:

06.05 Port pole and sail down and pole housed.
06.27 Mizzen staysail down.
06.27 Gybed.
06.43 Mizzen staysail hoisted for opposite gybe.
07.05 Big genny rigged on starboard side dropped. Five or six hanks off the stay. Changed sheet to port-rigged genny and hoisted that.
07.47 Starboard spinnaker pole rigged and sail rehanked. Sail hoisted O.K. but difficulty with self-steering.
08.07 Mizzen staysail dropped and rehoisted because of twisted tack pennant.
08.10 Gybing completed.

Then it was time for breakfast!

Not until Francis had been five weeks at sea did he begin to feel really well and hungry. As an *hors d'œuvre* before each meal he could now add fresh flying fish which landed on deck in just the required quantities.

During October he had trouble with the radio telephone and had to ask Cape Town to seek top advice from England. This eventually arrived in the form of instructions which took an hour for the operator to read and Francis had to try to listen while sailing his boat. He dreaded mechanical jobs when alone on the ocean; sea and wind he could battle with, even hate and then obtain a kind of elation – generators were quite a different matter.

By 11 October Francis was over half-way – 7300 miles from Plymouth and 6570 miles from Sydney. With marvellous satisfaction he pulled out his charts for the Indian Ocean and from now on *Gipsy Moth* was borne along in the Roaring Forties – those great westerly winds of the Southern Ocean. 'When all the sails were trimmed *Gipsy Moth* was on a close reach and went beautifully . . . The ship sailed as if she were satisfied – to me this is like being on a good horse, riding fast, but within her strength.'

When the wind went up to fifty-five knots he hoped that she would run down wind under bare poles but this *Gipsy Moth IV* would not do, turning broadside on to the waves. Francis raged. 'I had never even considered that such a thing could happen! *Gipsy Moth III* had steered easily down wind under bare poles or even with the wind on the quarter.' He forgot that this boat, designed essentially for speed, had been given no fair trials. The air grew icy cold, yet the water felt warm when it sluiced over the deck. In the log he noted even more acrimoniously his boat's tendency to whip around and lie broadside to the waves. (It was broaching-to which had sent many great clippers to the ocean bottom. If their masts went under and their sails submerged, a great sailing ship soon foundered.) Francis feared for his self-steering gear and felt that with her short forefoot, his boat had rather little grip on the water. Also because the laminated hull and doghouse were flexible, while the deck remained rigid, many leaks sprang up.

Then, in the midst of one storm, while forcing himself to eat a mint-cake, Francis broke off a tooth. No moment can be called *convenient* for tooth-breaking, but this one seemed particularly tiresome. He waited for calm weather before attempting to cement it back on with a do-it-yourself dentist outfit!

The Roaring Forties did not behave as they should. They roared in bursts only and blew from the wrong directions! Francis had expected them to blow from the west as the books said – fierce, but *steady*. 'That with unreason was just what they were not – it seemed to luff and puff, luff and puff all the time.'

A strange feeling of spiritual loneliness which he had never experienced in the North Atlantic crept over him. 'This Southern Ocean was totally different; the seas were fierce, vicious and frightening . . . The incessant squalls had one unexpected quality – often the sun would continue to shine brightly while the wind whipped the sea to fury.'

Francis had hoped to reach Sydney in one hundred days, the average of the clippers, but when huge seas fractured the steel frame of the self-steering gear, he knew this to be impossible, and decided dolefully, to make for Fremantle.

His radio still worked and Sheila's liner the *Oriana* was now approaching Fremantle. He had a radio call arranged. In fact, they had ambitiously planned a possible sighting! When Francis contacted the radio operator, Sheila was beside him. 'I'm going to Fremantle,' she heard him say. Then silence. Knowing that Francis had set his heart on Sydney she wondered what on earth had gone wrong.

All that night Francis worked at the broken self-steering and eventually, by dint of experimenting and changing over the storm sails to balance the pull on the tiller, he managed to improvise a new method which worked. Surprised and pleased with his own ingenuity, he tried to contact the *Oriana* to say that he was making for Sydney after all. The radio transmitted so faintly that he could not be sure if his voice had been heard. But the radio operator got the message and next morning Sheila found a slip of paper under her cabin door – 'It's all right. He's going on.'

Now that Francis was only 2800 miles from Sydney he grew light-hearted. From the start he had feared that the self-steering gear might break – the worst had happened and been overcome. The new arrangement was working.

Then demands for radio-telephone news started to rattle him. There was always a kind of peace in battling against the sea's violence. Now that peace must end. Ahead lay the pressures of land life, interviews and the fuss of finance. Repairs and alterations were needed. Everything cost money.

The sea birds still soothed him with their beauty, soaring and balancing exquisitely on air eddies in their swirling world. And one night Francis had the fantastic experience of seeing two albatrosses – probably courting – sitting on the water facing each other with great wings raised in a curved V. And from one of them arose the unbelievable human shriek which has on rare occasions been recorded by frightened sailors in darkness around the Horn.

24. Sydney

Sometimes in a head-on gale Francis felt that the pounding could drive him mad. But as he approached Sydney and sensed the tumult awaiting, he felt no, only people drove him mad. The raging sea contained its own bliss, its own sedation.

As he sailed through the shipping lanes south of Australia, where rocks and islands demanded constant careful navigation, Francis's inward tensions increased. He longed to reach port and yet he dreaded it.

On 7 December, while ghosting along in little wind, he heard the unlovely chug of a diesel motor, and peeped out of the cabin to see a boat-load of journalists and cameramen. He refused to be photographed before shaving and tidying himself up. There was something very irritating about being caught by pressmen days before he expected them. A journalist whom he had once met drew near in a rubber dinghy and handed him a bottle of whisky. This act before clearance fussed Francis because it breached Australian Customs' regulations. Then a motor launch approached so close that it hit *Gipsy Moth*'s stern, and Francis hurt his elbow trying to prevent worse damage. 'Wander off,' he remarked – using a shorter verb. After this unfortunate encounter, the journalist on board who was making his scoop reported Francis Chichester's first direct words to a human being after three months alone at sea as 'You bloody Sunday driver'. Not correct but amusing.

Just when it would have been convenient to press on, winds dropped. On 10 December, *Gipsy Moth* lay becalmed 102 miles from Sydney, and it was not until 12 December that, after much hard tacking, Francis entered Sydney Heads completing a voyage of 105 days 20 hours. As *Gipsy Moth* lowered sails, an excited fleet of boats raced out to cheer him into harbour – and the first family member to greet him was his son George, who had been in Australia for twenty years. Then another launch drove alongside and Sheila and Giles scrambled aboard.

The awaiting welcome proved even more marvellous than he had imagined, and the exhausting Press interviews worse. Within ten minutes of tying up and stepping ashore, he had to give a Press conference for over ninety news outlets. Such was his fatigue that he found it very difficult to answer questions coherently. Sheila tried to protect him, but she herself had been worn out by a Press barrage while awaiting his arrival. The telephone in her hotel bedroom had never stopped ringing, yet amidst the pandemonium she had enjoyed a very happy time with George and his new bride. Giles met his half-brother for the first time on the night before their father arrived. It was a wonderfully romantic family reunion.

Francis had always loved Sydney; it was for him a special city – after Peking the most exciting in the world. His first visit had been an unsuccessful juvenile amorous excursion, but in 1930 when he arrived in his *Gipsy Moth* plane from England he had revelled in the breeze of applause. And then never would he forget the warm-hearted Sydney crowds cheering him after that flight over the Tasman Sea. Sydney naturally threw caps in the air for originality, audaciousness and everything that Francis stood for. He felt Australian enthusiasm burn him like wine – but he desperately needed rest. At the big Press and television conferences he wilted under the strain. 'It is difficult not to lose the thread,' he pleaded, and there was a moment's hush as the questioners realized they were intruding into an extraordinary, almost psychic adventure – one in which a man had to make delicate mental adjustment.

A fast refit was essential if he intended to round the Horn in February, the warmest month, and he was thankful to avail himself of the offers of the Royal Sydney Yacht Squadron. Warwick Hood and Alan Payne, two well-known yacht designers, tried to dissuade Francis from sailing *Gipsy Moth IV* across the treacherous Tasman Sea where so many yachts had been lost. Then, realizing the hopelessness of changing his intention, they set about advising alterations and improvements. The short keel was extended and the weight of gear concentrated amidships to keep the ends more buoyant. The loads on the main-mast shrouds were changed to lessen the danger of the mast breaking in a knock-down, and the Squadron's yard-manager, Jim Perry, himself slaved to stop the leaks, which had occurred along the joins between the deck and the coach-house and hull, the deck being rigid while the hull moved flexibly on impact with the sea. The sails were carried off to be repaired, anti-chafe patches being sewn on, and the self-steering gear mended with stainless steel plates which made it stronger though unfortunately heavier. There seemed an immense amount to do, but, as Erroll Bruce pertinently remarked, 'One can get this sort of damage after a single season's ocean racing!' Michael Richey would epitomize the situation:

That Sir Francis Chichester lost his wager with the clipper ships is a matter of no significance. He has now sailed far greater distances, at much higher average speeds than any other single-handed sailor. Whatever modifications proved necessary in Australia, *Gipsy Moth IV*'s performance characterizes her as outstanding in design and construction. Such a voyage, too, would have been quite impossible without an effective system of self-steering on all points of sailing. Hasler's 'Pendulum' gear, in which the direction of the apparent wind is used to govern alterations of rudder angle by the stronger hydraulic force of the boat's movement, has achieved a fundamental breakthrough.

By now it was midsummer and extremely hot, but everyone who could help *Gipsy Moth IV* worked flat out right through the Christmas holiday. Giles, with a willing team of girl-friends, unloaded remaining stores so that work could continue uninterrupted. Meanwhile, Sheila started listing, replenishing and trying to get Francis rested. What worried her was the tempo of life inseparable from an enthusiastic warm welcome. Hard exercise and long hours of sleep were what Francis needed; unending entertaining and feasting was what he got. He loved Sydney immensely, but all those strong, vital Australians could not realize that silence had become a necessity during which he tuned up his own batteries. As the welcome and hospitality showed no signs of terminating, he had to risk hurting people's feelings. The deluge of invitations had to be refused if he was to survive the month. Even young Giles had more than he could take of 'good times'. Then, to Francis's amazement and disgust, an English Press campaign arose insisting that he should cease to tempt Fate and end his voyage in Sydney. The famous Captain Alan Villiers, who had sailed big ships round the Horn, wrote to the *Guardian*:

I see that the redoubtable Francis Chichester plans to sail homewards by way of the Horn, as one would expect. But I hope that this time he will not drive himself single-handed against some record of 'average' made by the clipper ships . . . In my opinion no self-steering device can be really satisfactory over the 6000 mile run from Sydney towards the Horn. Sailors learned long ago that the price of survival there is constant vigilance and expert helmsmanship, with equally constant attention to the set of sails . . .

Francis was feeling rotten, overtired and unable to get the long walks he craved, but he remained absolutely determined to sail on. And his vanity had been injured by uncomplimentary photographs taken as he arrived! One showed him hugging Giles and it looked as if he clung to him for support, another taken from high up showed him with Giles holding his arm to prevent the usual after-sea lurching and because his leg was hurting. These most unflattering photographs received wide publicity and Francis was piqued. After all, he'd sailed 14 000 miles, and had had no rest while beating up into Sydney – he had never thought of himself as a handsome man, but to be caught from the wrong angle in an unlucky stance, after two sleepless nights at sea, made the publicity seem intolerable. Tony Dulverton was so shocked by these photographs that he cabled Francis not to press on. He thought that Francis might feel he *ought* to sail home because so much had been spent on the boat. While appreciating this concern, Francis telegraphed blithely that he was off. And that was that.

He had been assessing the dangers of the Horn for three years. Now was not the moment to stop – especially as the voyage out had produced the 'trials' his boat so sorely needed. Amidst all this, Sheila fluttered with fresh stores and Press hand-outs. Francis wrote: 'I do not believe that there is any other woman in the world who could have stood up against this steady sniping from doom-forecasters . . .' But for Sheila, who had seen her husband really suffer, this was just a very strenuous, very interesting time, and she thought the applause *must* be good for Francis as long as she could save him from incessantly attending lavish functions.

An article in the *Sun* on 12 January suggested somewhat cheekily that 'with such a monstrously small yacht' Francis Chichester was 'asking a little too much of God'. As the Deity does not communicate with the Sunday Press, Sheila had to answer back. 'You don't *ask* anything of God. That is not prayer. You offer up the person you pray for, you hold them with your own strength and love.' The *Sun* fell silent.

Soon after Christmas Giles had to return to his university, and Francis felt a twinge when he saw his son going off – might it be the last time he would see him? The male Chichesters had not got Sheila's absolute assurance.

Many thousands of letters poured in; several thousands came from children alone, and these Francis wished to be individually acknow-ledged.

Under a new contract made with the *Sunday Times*, he would give his positions twice a week via various radio transmitting stations, so that readers of the newspaper could plot his course and share his circumnavigation with thousands of people.

Just before Francis sailed Sheila fell, tearing a ligament in her foot. She was unable to walk for several days and had to be lifted onto the yacht to supervise the stowing of stores, but the Press generously re-frained from photographing her in this state.

Francis liked to choose a definite date for sailing and stick to it. He had decided on the morning of Sunday, 29 January. On the Friday, when they were trying to get an early night and had gone to bed at 10 p.m., the telephone rang. Sheila, half-asleep, murmured, 'Don't answer it.' But Francis picked up the receiver. The voice of Sir Charles Johnson, the British Commissioner, came through. 'Whatever's happened?' asked Sheila. 'He says I've been knighted,' said Francis, blinking. 'Knighted?' 'Yes, that's what he said.' 'But one can't just go back to sleep.' 'One can, and one must.'

At 3 a.m. the telephone rang again. It was the night porter with a message from the London *Daily Mirror* who had obtained the news early. After the second awakening, they simply could not return to slumber. It was pitch dark still, but the porter gladly brought tea, and they got up to sort some of the gifts people had sent, and then Francis started signing the autograph books which had piled up. Two hours later the morning papers arrived carrying the news and friends began to telephone. They went down to *Gipsy Moth* in a tumult of congratulations. There, the Governor-General, Lord Casey, brought a telegram from the Queen.

That night, Francis's last on land, Sheila insisted that his rest remain unbroken. Alan Payne was worrying about the fastenings of the forward hatch, which he still did not consider strong enough, but there was no time to reinforce it further. Weather reports came in forecasting a tropical cyclone east of Sydney and Max Hinchliffe advised Francis to escape it by sailing southwards fast. However, it was a fine sunny morning when *Gipsy Moth IV* slipped her moorings and slid off past a fleet of cheering boats to Sydney Heads. Alan Payne, Warwick Hood, Max Hinchliffe and Hugh Eaton acted as crew, while Francis acknowledged the tumultuous shouts and cheers and Sheila took the helm. It was blowing fairly rough and after the sail went up it was no easy matter for her to climb from *Gipsy Moth* onto the return launch. Francis watched her vanishing and felt desperately sorry for her. He knew that she would have to face a barrage of remonstrances – 'How *could* you let him go?' People would think her a heartless wife. But he understood her quality. 'Sheila and I parted as if for a day. She has an uncanny foresight in spiritual matters, and had no doubt but that we should meet again; I must confess that I wondered rather sadly if we would, as I sailed away from the fleet.'

25. Around the Horn

Within twenty-four hours of leaving Sydney *Gipsy Moth IV* ran into a storm, a real Tasman terror – 'the white breakers showed in the blackness like monstrous beasts charging down on the yacht'. Francis was unready. Feeling seasick as he always did during his first week at sea, he had deferred making final storm lashings and on that Monday night he rolled into his bunk for some fitful sleep. Then it was that *Gipsy Moth* met an unusually huge wave. Later on Francis would recall the moment in detail:

I think I was awake when the boat began to roll over. If not, I woke immediately she started to do so. Perhaps when the wave hit her I woke. As she started rolling I said to myself, 'Over she goes!' I was not frightened, but intensely alert and curious. Then a lot of crashing and banging started, and my head and shoulders were being bombarded with crockery and cutlery and bottles. I had an oppressive feeling of the boat being on top of me. I wondered if she would roll over completely and what the damage would be; but she came up quietly the same side that she had gone down. I reached up and put the boat's light on. It worked, giving me a curious feeling of something normal in a world of utter chaos. I have only a confused idea of what I did for the next hour or so. I had an absolutely hopeless feeling when I looked at the pile of jumbled up food and gear . . . The cabin was two feet deep all along with hundreds of tins, bottles, tools, shackles, blocks, sextant, and oddments. Every settee locker, the whole starboard bunk, and the three starboard drop lockers had all emptied out . . .

Water was pouring in through the heavy forehatch which had swung open when the boat went over. A piece of the cockpit side had been torn away and one big sail had been washed overboard. But when he looked out, he saw with joy that mast and rigging remained intact.

Everything in the cabin had been hurled out of place and water slushed loudly in the bilges. He was glad to find the radio still worked, and soon after midnight, two and a quarter hours after the knock-down, Francis managed to contact Sydney on the distress frequency. He made a factual report, said that he did not need assistance and asked that his wife should not be given the news till morning.

The radio operator of a P. & O. liner S.S. *Himalaya*, which was caught in the same kind of giant seas overheard Francis talking to Sydney and took a recording. The captain considered going to his aid, but the words 'I do not require assistance' deterred him. Then he remarked, 'Well, Chichester can keep the bloody Tasman!' After the radio contact, Francis removed the cutlery from his soaking wet bunk and fell into heavy sleep for a few hours.

All next day the gale roared on while he stared dismally around at the damage. He had to admit: 'Let's face it, I was frightened.' At regular intervals he drove himself to work at the pump, stopping for a rest after every two hundred strokes. All the floorboards had flown through the air and fallen deep into the bilges along with plates, tins of food and tools. It was almost fascinating to track the flight of one bottle of Irish whiskey which had jumped from its hole in the wine locker, made a deep indent on the ceiling and turned into hundreds of small glass splinters all over the boat, while leaving cork and neck sitting demurely intact. That night Francis again obtained radio contact and was able to talk to Sheila. 'I told her that I had spares on board for most things, and that I should be able to tidy up. I drew strength from her.' Those who have, even in a minor way, met bad weather in sailing boats, been deluged with seawater and bruised by buffeting, will be able to reconstruct in their imagination the tasks that confronted Francis Chichester when at the very start of a three-month lone voyage his carefully stowed boat turned over. For days he would be mending, improvising, looking for lost tools, inventing methods to hold lids on lockers, and fishing up crockery from the bilges with a six-foot pole.

On 4 February he was only 100 miles from Lord Howe Island where he had spent those happy weeks in the long ago re-building his plane *Gipsy Moth I*. Nostalgic memories swept through his mind. And on 9 February Norfolk Island sent a radio message, 'We feel as if you belong a little to us because the memory is with many Norfolk Islanders of how in 1931 you brought to them their first aircraft visitor.' Then, he belonged to the air, now he belonged to the sea, but really, and most of all, Francis Chichester belonged to people.

He sought adventure as a loner, but it was human contact he craved – emotional contact, not necessarily presence.

On 25 February, his and Sheila's thirtieth wedding anniversary, he wrote in his log: 'I wish I was at home with my darling and feel sad to be away from her . . . I am drinking a toast to Sheila in the delicious Montrachet she brought out from England and left on board for me . . . I did what is supposed to be un-British, shed a tear.'

The gales blew on, carrying him 1115 miles in seven days. Sometimes the great seas looked like valleys, sometimes like moving hills. All down the Southern Ocean *Gipsy Moth* tore with an albatross for playmate, and alone in this empty world one man worked hard. She was indeed a demanding boat. As many as twelve different sails might have to be hoisted or dropped within twenty-four hours. But wild exuberance filled Francis as he neared Cape Horn. This was his real target, the dreaded Horn where Atlantic and Pacific Oceans meet in terrible embrace as the westerly winds collide with cyclones rolling off the Andes. It was icy cold and yet the big breaking seas showed up dazzling white with phosphorescence, and seething bow waves shone in brilliance. Checking and re-checking his navigation, Francis made towards the island rock which is the Horn. To his surprise, and, indeed, irritation, he sighted a patrol ship H.M.S. *Protector*, which made radio contact. Little did he guess that a number of seasick journalists and photographers were struggling around the heaving decks. The wind rose to forty knots and *Gipsy Moth* broached-to. As Francis went to the cockpit to free the self-steering, he looked around and 'there was the Horn, quite plain to see. It stood up out of the sea like a black ice-cream cone.'

When he was sailing seven and a half miles south of the Horn, a small yellow plane appeared and waggled its wings in salute. Francis, busy with the gear and feeling seasick in the tumultuous waves, waved back and cursed it. He knew enough about flying to be aghast at such temerity. It looked as if the bouncing plane, a battered little Piper Apache, might crash into the sea, and he did not relish the idea of trying to rescue the occupants. Puzzled and horrified, Francis stared up into the blackening, cloud-tossed sky. He recognized brilliant flying. The pilot was a man of his own calibre – but what risks he was taking!

What Francis could not know was that the little machine contained two men from the BBC and Murray Sayle of the *Sunday Times*, all terrified, but determined to get a 'scoop' on 'Chichester rounding the Horn'! When Fuenzalida, the intrepid Chilean pilot (who earned his living as a fish-spotter and frequently crash-landed in these parts) waggled his wings, the passengers truly believed the plane was breaking up and their last hour had come. Murray Sayle, jubilant at having reached the position, which Francis had radioed to him alone, would write:

As I flew by Cape Horn, its grey pyramid could be seen lashed by heavy seas . . . South of the Horn the waves were driving eastward in long ridges of white and grey-green. Overhead were black driving clouds driven by the gale and a mile or two ahead the clouds were joined to the sea by rain in a black, impenetrable barrier towards the south and the pole . . . Then I picked out the salt-grimed hull of *Gipsy Moth* lurching forward as the seas passed under her . . . It was a flight I am not anxious to repeat, but the sight of *Gipsy Moth* ploughing bravely through this wilderness of rain and sea was well worth it.

What Sayle did *not* write until much later was a description of thirty-odd rival reporters and cameramen who had been waiting for weeks in Punta Arenas where every available aircraft had been chartered and each time a plane took off all the others followed thinking the leader must have a fix on Chichester's position. With Francis's transmission to go on, Sayle and his friends beat the bunch. They employed the star pilot and were ready to risk their lives gleefully. Sayle's photograph was sent to London by wireless photo machine, reaching *The Times* at 2.20 a.m., and appeared on the front page for breakfast.

Meanwhile back in the roaring ocean off the Horn, H.M.S. *Protector* had disappeared and Francis, feeling strangely forlorn, decided that it was horribly disconcerting to glimpse a ship. 'It emphasizes the isolation, because it makes one realize the impossibility of being helped.'

He had intended to try photographing the mountainous seas, but could not face it. 'Photography seems so paltry beside the tremendous display of force by nature.' As *Gipsy Moth* sped on her new home course, with only the storm jib set, Francis saw the impossibility of any attempt to lie ahull. There was far more power in this sea than in the one that had capsized him. *Gipsy Moth* must just keep running before the wind. Then, with a thump of joy, he realized that he had left the Pacific and was in the Atlantic heading north for the Equator and for England. It was a strange moment – he had won a private race with the sun by passing the Horn at 16·07 G.M.T. on 20 March. The sun was still 15·275 miles south of the Line. This pleased him, but as a health cruise things were not too good. Due perhaps to stove fumes, he felt headachy and could neither eat nor sleep. What the exhilaration of rounding the Horn had done to him, Francis was unable to express in his log. He felt he could not describe the changes which this lone sea battle had on that part of him which, not entirely concerned with gear, food and survival, the Greeks would have called his Θυμός.

Once the fear of sailing on a lee shore ended, he could relax while making for the Falkland Islands. Clear starry skies and sunny days became more frequent although the winds still blew bitter cold from the South Pole. On 25 March, sailing northwards, he crossed the 50th parallel and was back in the Forties. He had crossed the 50th parallel when sailing southwards in the Pacific on 12 March. That made thirteen days out of the Roaring Forties down in the Wholly Abominable Fifties. Now the wide South Atlantic spread its glittering and ever-warming waters before the little boat. By 26 March he was half-way – 7637 miles from Sydney, 7637 to Plymouth. The wonder of the sea took hold of him afresh and he begged the *Sunday Times* to 'stop questioning and interviewing me, which poisons the romantic attraction of this voyage – I do not want to hurt your feelings, but hope you can sympathize with my state of mind.'

On 11 April, which was Sheila's birthday (and she felt this to be more than a coincidence) Francis completed his circumnavigation of the globe, crossing his outward-bound track in the South Atlantic. The old ambition was fulfilled – the ambition he had had as a young man setting off from New Zealand to fly alone around the world.

On 24 April he crossed the Equator. And then it was to be a fast run for home.

26. *Gipsy Moth IV* Gets Home

Meanwhile, back in England, Sheila underwent what she considered a rough time. She was not anxious about Francis, but ceaseless Press questions frayed her nerves. 'You all seem to *want* me to worry,' she expostulated. She began to fear that his great spiritual adventure was being turned into a publicity stunt. Of course Francis needed money – the unexpected final costs of *Gipsy Moth IV* had rattled him severely – but he never intended his exploits to be just money-making stunts. Now, as interest in the outcome of his voyage increased, pressure was brought on Sheila to employ a professional publicity agent who could 'build up a fortune'. She tried to assess what this might involve. As Francis became a figure of world-wide attention the staff in the map business simply could not cope, and she thought there might exist reasonable plans which would not ruin the spirit of her husband's voyage, but the arguments bewildered her.

Giles was at Oxford University, out of this feverish debate. Incessant important decisions had to be made, and she feared making them. Turning to a friend who was both businessman and lay-reader, she asked his advice about financial sponsorship. He answered: 'You've got a clear course here. Either you do go in for this very vast publicity or you pull away from it and do your best to damp it down. It's your choice.' Sheila decided to dampen. 'These terrific business propositions which were afoot were something we couldn't handle, even if we wanted to, without engaging a much bigger staff, and transforming the whole enterprise into something quite different.'

Few of Sheila's friends realized that she was trying to stop the blaze of publicity rather than foment it. This adventure had now inflamed world imagination and as *Gipsy Moth IV* crept northwards into home waters a crescendo of excitement arose. 9 St James's Place was besieged by reporters, Monica Cooper and the office staff

187

were swamped by enquiries, and the telephone never stopped ringing. The fact that Francis was delicate, sixty-five years old and had to wear thick spectacles added appeal. He made headlines for weeks, and as *Gipsy Moth* approached Plymouth the world's Press prepared for a field day. The first photograph of his boat on its way home could be sold for thousands.

Francis had agreed to give his story to the *Sunday Times* and *The Times* only – he did not guess the extent to which other newspapers might spy on him. Nor did he yet know of the journalists who had wangled their way onto H.M.S. *Protector* at the Horn. Sheila, who had remained calm during the months of danger, now became alarmed. She guessed that once Francis sailed within range of the Azores he might be chased by rival newspapermen in aeroplanes, and as this whole voyage was still partly intended – strange as it may sound – to be a health-restorer, it would be too bad if the pressures of being pestered at sea should make the skipper ill. When the *Sunday Times* suggested sending out a motor yacht, the *Sea Huntress*, with photographers, Sheila hotly remonstrated. This would be the last thing her husband wanted. But the paper contacted Francis by radio telephone and persuaded him to agree. They never mentioned the fact that a BBC film unit would also be aboard. Sheila described the situation:

I was distracted about the whole thing . . . the intrusion of his privacy, the danger that he could be run down, for you can't keep watch all the time when you're sailing single-handed. I pictured them chasing him along when he was tired. He had got trouble with his arm, and as long ago as 1962, when I discussed the question with him, we'd agreed that sending a dispatch to a newspaper is a very different thing from being interviewed when you are at sea. You are very vulnerable and when everybody is listening it can be acutely embarrassing.

All during this time plans had to be made behind the scenes with the Queen's Press Officer, Sir Richard Colville, concerning the moment at which Her Majesty should bestow the accolade on Francis. As *Gipsy Moth* had sailed from Tower Pier in London and intended to return there, it was decided that the ceremony should take place at Greenwich rather than at Plymouth. The City of London wished to give Francis a public welcome – the first accorded to a private individual since Lord Nelson. Sheila enjoyed visiting the Thames by launch with the Chief Harbour Master of the Port of London to work out the details 'artistically', and she tried not to worry about Francis being hounded in the Western Approaches.

There was enough to rejoice about, enough to give thanks for – if only she could protect him from the terrifying force of the welcome lying ahead.

On 7 May *Gipsy Moth* was hailed by a big ship. Francis recorded the impact.

To my disgust, I found that this first contact with people was making me tremble, but it reminded me that three months' solitude is strong medicine. One may behave as usual, but for a while one's feelings are changed. The beauty and magic of nature is as if seen under a magnifying glass and life seems lived to the full . . . I felt that in some ways I should be sorry when the voyage come to an end.

It was 18 May when the *Sea Huntress* discovered *Gipsy Moth* and gave Francis a bad night because he had to keep an eye on her throughout the hours of darkness instead of sleeping. He was weary by now and very annoyed at being put out of routine. Also it meant he had to delay gybing onto another tack because he dreaded being photographed in action in case his injured knee and elbow made him appear unworkmanlike. For the last few hundred miles he just wanted to be left alone. But having with much difficulty found *Gipsy Moth* the *Sea Huntress* stuck around. While the BBC cameramen took a film of him swinging around awkwardly trying to save his leg and not realizing he was in camera range, Francis, more forgivably, tried to photograph a dolphin scratching its back on the stern.

On 25 May Francis was fast asleep in his bunk when two R.A.F. planes started to buzz *Gipsy Moth*. He lay doggo for a bit, then thinking perhaps it was mean to hide below after all the trouble they must have had to find his little boat, he replied by hoisting a burgee and the White Ensign.

Now that he was nearly home and could race along in perfect sailing weather with blue seas and just the right wind, different moods assailed Francis. He became aware of himself as part of this vast creation of sea and sky, aware of the sun and stars as near things, as helpers. Within the delicate structure of the boat he moved and thought, and within the yet more delicate structure of his body he suffered pain and knew joy. He was also aware that for the first time in over three months, he could put away fear. He started to analyse how different a creature he had become. Certainly he must be different from all those waiting humans. Could they imagine a man who had deliberately to force himself to eat to keep alive and to sleep whenever lack of tasks permitted? Because all nights were broken by the need to attend to sails or gear, sleep had become a discipline, to be snatched at every possible moment. And now he dreaded the readjustment lying ahead. Soon he would have to talk to people again, not just give himself orders and keep his mind concentrated on the feel of the wind.

When 210 miles from Plymouth *Gipsy Moth* became almost completely becalmed. Television vessels turned up but with kindness remained at a discreet distance. On 28 May Francis counted thirteen ships, including five naval vessels, escorting him. *Gipsy Moth* crept along for there was hardly any wind. Being dog-tired and aware of many watchful eyes, he had hesitated to expend energy on poling out a big sail to increase speed. At three in the afternoon the great aircraft carrier, H.M.S. *Eagle*, passed close by and the crew lining her deck gave a ceremonial three cheers to *Gipsy Moth IV*. Francis dipped his ensign in salute and his heart fluttered. Beside him in the cockpit sat a shadow self – the unloved boy of nineteen, full of longing, who had taken passage from this harbour all those years ago. How *he* would have thrilled to see himself now – this was the grist of which young men's dreams are made – this is what they plan to make happen.

Two Cornishmen had procured the last existing models of ancient Gipsy Moth planes, and were endeavouring to take to the air. One of them rose successfully and Francis could hardly believe his eyes when he saw a replica of that precious little plane flying over the Sound waggling its wings in greeting.

Meanwhile the Royal Western Yacht Club struggled to cope with the dramas of timing. Three large senior police officers arrived at the Club to explain that all Plymouth streets were blocked with traffic and the Hoe black with people. Colonel Odling-Smee was discussing the problem when Francis suddenly came through loud and clear on the blower: 'Completely becalmed off the Lizard. Cannot make it today.' The police officers expostulated, 'We can't possibly send the crowds away. Half the county police have been called in to help as it is.' Jack Odling-Smee relayed this to Francis, assured him that a good breeze was blowing at Plymouth and begged him to try to press on. 'All right, Jack,' he said, 'what is the latest time you can accept me?' 'Nine o'clock.' 'Right. I'll have a go.' Up went every sail that could be set.

The excitement spread like spontaneous combustion. Half a million people had trooped into the city, keeping their children up long after bedtime so that they might remember this night when they stood on Plymouth Hoe watching a little boat sail into the wide harbour. Lord Dulverton had arrived at the Royal Western Yacht

Club and was greeted by a harassed steward who had no idea he was anything to do with *Gipsy Moth*. 'Good day, m'Lord – have you got a boat?' Tony Dulverton hesitated: 'Well – er – no – well, as a matter of fact, another chap is sailing her today!'

While Sheila hurried around making arrangements for friends who kept turning up, the Dulvertons went out to the breakwater with Jack Odling-Smee, who was to fire the gun as Francis passed so that the multitudes could know. Fearing that one of the Club finishing guns would not be loud enough he took two and his son brought a shot gun. They would let off the lot. Geoffrey Goodwin had arrived from New Zealand. Nigel Tangye, watching from the shore, remembered the Francis of early flying days and exclaimed, 'Never was there such a glittering day – everything glittering – sea and shore and memories.'

It happened to be a most beautiful Sunday evening, and the sun was just setting when *Gipsy Moth* appeared surrounded by a fleet of boats. Just before nine o'clock she passed the breakwater, guns sounded and the beacon on Drake's Island lit up to signal Francis Chichester's safe return.

It was a magnificent moment in time. Francis tried to savour it to the full, to keep his receiving memory clear. He steered towards the Yacht Club steps, called for sea room and rounded up into the wind and quietly picked up the special mooring. The Commander-in-Chief of Plymouth approached on his launch with Sheila and Giles. They climbed aboard *Gipsy Moth* and looked at each other bewildered.

'It's strange, but I don't feel anything at all,' said Francis.

'One can't,' said Sheila. 'There's too much to feel.'

27. Aftermath

It was not possible to sit down in *Gipsy Moth,* just trying to take it in, when the Lord Mayor and the Queen's Harbour Master were waiting, and a Press conference had to be faced. They stared at each other and gulped a mouthful of champagne. Sheila saw what mattered most to her – he looked well, thin but well. They searched for necessities to take ashore. Suddenly, Francis couldn't remember where things were – he who at sea knew every object in every corner of his boat. Sheila looked frantically for pyjamas and razor. People wondered why they did not appear. Fireworks and bonfires were going off all round the harbour. After a week of smooth weather, Francis was able to step off and mount the stone steps fairly steady on his legs. There stood the Lord Mayor in his red robes and feathered hat for the official greeting. Francis registered the feathered hat and the fireworks, but not much else. They walked through hurrahing crowds to an awaiting official Rolls-Royce. Francis and Sheila sat on the back seat. Giles sat in front. Dusk had fallen. Slowly the car advanced through thronged streets to the Town Hall. More champagne. Then the Press conference. Francis had not spoken to a fellow-human except by radio for three months. He tried to answer questions coherently but showed the effort it caused him, although he seemed far fitter than when he had reached Sydney. This was partly due to the last weeks of fast enjoyable sailing in the North Atlantic. Some questions he could answer without hesitation.

I don't feel different, I don't think. You have a certain kind of nature and you must fulfil that . . . Did I think I'd had it when she capsized? Well, I was curious – wondering what would happen – all that Southern Ocean is dangerous for a small boat – of the last nine yachts to round the Horn six capsized – fast sailing in the Trades is great sport – the Atlantic is more friendly than the Southern Ocean – I wasn't held up in the Doldrums – and I like the French name for the North East Trades. They call them *les alizés*. They carried me along – Am I more sane than before leaving Sydney? [Francis laughed] Well, what do *you* think!

Because of the late hour the reporters kept rushing away to telephone their stories to morning editions. By the time they reached Astor House (Nancy Astor's old home which she bequeathed to Plymouth) Francis felt himself loosening up. It was long after midnight when Giles showed his father to his room.

Two days later came the Thanksgiving Service. The Chichester family walked in procession through ever-cheering crowds to the church. Then they went on to the Guildhall and the Town Hall to be greeted by a fanfare of trumpets.

It was difficult to take it all in. The Lord Mayor's speech was so charming that Sheila could not resist congratulating him. 'Well, I spent all day preparing it,' he explained modestly. That night they attended a dinner party for forty people. Next day the Flag Officer of the Royal Western Yacht Club gave a champagne lunch in a country house – Francis never ceased shaking hands with friends who had travelled long distances to greet him.

And so it went on for a week. Then the warning bell rang. He had, after all, once suffered from something the doctors called lung cancer, the hardships of the ocean seemed to act as a preservative, but beneath that weather-beaten exterior Francis remained a frail machine, fuelled by exuberance and determination. People could tire him more than the great seas around the Horn.

The Chichesters had visited Mashford's yard for a moving welcome among old friends and Francis enjoyed this. But on returning to *Gipsy Moth* he lay down half-fainting in his bunk. 'I've simply got to escape.' Sheila took him ashore and they drove to the promontory overlooking Plymouth and sat alone trying to enjoy a sandwich lunch. But Francis looked ashen. She begged him not to attend the dinner which the Commander-in-Chief was giving in his honour that night, but he insisted: 'Such an honour! I couldn't let them down.' When they got back to the hotel she managed to borrow a thermometer without arousing suspicion – the Press were just waiting to write up some episode such as this. He had no fever, only a rapid pulse.

Alas, that night Francis had to leave the dinner table, murmuring that he would be all right after a lie down. Sheila put as good a face on it as she could, and crept from the room after coffee. She found Francis lying unconscious on the floor, beside the bed on which he had been resting. Yet the doctor who hurried to him could find nothing radically amiss. Sheila accepted the responsibility of driving him back to the hotel instead of to hospital. Two naval orderlies arrived to help her; they were so sweet and so eager that her leaden heart lightened. This sort of kindness gave strength.

Tests failed to reveal anything wrong except 'extreme fatigue', and Francis's temperature, blood pressure and heart proved normal, so the doctors could but suggest a blood transfusion. This was against Sheila's nature cure beliefs, but the pressures on her were heavy. A day later the hospital announced, 'Good news – just a duodenal ulcer.' This was supposed to be accepted as a jolly diagnosis. Sheila telephoned to Buckingham Palace where her tale met with sympathy. The Queen would meet them at Greenwich on 7 July instead of on 13 June.

Although Francis shared – in a lesser degree – Sheila's fear of conventional medical treatment, he loved this naval hospital. Amidst people he liked he was sure he would simply *become well*. He did not know that the doctors feared that he might have again developed some form of cancer. They let him read their detailed medical report, which included one paragraph which greatly amused him.

The fact remains that apart from emphysema and bronchitis the lungs are at the present moment free from any disease. If Sir Francis had been in the Navy he would have been invalided out on this account. On the other hand, had he been seen as a civilian his doctor would probably have recommended him to take a long sea voyage!

While in hospital Francis glanced through some of the thousands of messages and letters which had arrived. Among those from children, which he always read with pleasure, were two which particularly made him smile. One began: 'Dear Lady Chichester, I am 9 years old and have taken a great interest in Sir Francis' voyage. I think he has been a very brave man. I hope the Queen will make him a Lord when he gets back . . .' And another dated 30 June was addressed to the medical staff: 'Dear Doctors, My mother says I shouldn't write this but please don't let Sir Francis die. He is a great and brave man and we are sorry he is ill . . .'

By Sunday, 2 July, Francis was strong enough to board *Gipsy Moth* with his wife and son and Commander Erroll Bruce, whose presence aboard enabled them to relax during the voyage from Plymouth to London. They left harbour as quietly as possible with a small boat escort and spent five nights on the way. At Newhaven the Harbour Master had physically to rescue Francis from hordes of autograph hunters. From Dover came a greeting from the Warden of the Cinque Ports, and a crowd of Press boats, but *Gipsy Moth* crept away to a place where the old clipper ships used to tie up, and spent a night of perfect peace.

Then the Chichesters found a surprisingly quiet anchorage near the mouth of the Thames. Here they could remain unmolested before the long day spent sailing up the river. It was the fairest of summer days when *Gipsy Moth* sedately returned to London after her great experience. Many thousands of people were waiting on the banks in brilliant sunshine. The passage up the Thames had been carefully planned. Timing arrangements had to be co-ordinated with the tides and Sir Richard Colville, the Palace Press Officer, had discussed with Sheila what she was to wear when accompanying Francis to receive the accolade in Greenwich Palace. As she would have spent several days crewing from Plymouth it was considered quite suitable to step ashore in her trouser suit.

As *Gipsy Moth* sailed along towards Tilbury, all the ships hooted in salute and a great roar arose from the crowded river banks. It was such a spectacle. Such a welcome. Erroll called down the hatch to Francis, who was resting: 'You must not miss this, it's all for you!' He got up and laughed with excitement at the terrific Southend gun salute. Here the Mayor came out in his launch to present two silver cups – one for Francis and one for a good wife!

The training ship *Worcester* entertained them to lunch while waiting for the tide to allow them up river, and Sheila, watching anxiously, thought that Francis looked well. He had this extraordinary resilience, he could reach the snapping point and go right back to high-geared normal. Sir Richard Colville arrived to announce a change of plan. The Queen now wished to bestow the accolade in public. *Gipsy Moth* would spend the night at a prepared mooring off Woolwich and was to reach Greenwich at 10.25 in the morning. Then, instead of going to Greenwich Palace for a private ceremony, Francis would kneel before the Queen in public, and he and his lady would be presented at the Watergate. The change of Palace procedure did not entail any alterations of attire.

After a quiet night they made an early start for Greenwich. *Gipsy Moth* arrived spot on and drew up trimly alongside the special pontoon put out for her. A red carpet had been laid and the pontoon was lined by the Queen's Watermen magnificently clad in scarlet and gold. This Tudor grandeur made the boat look extraordinarily small and fragile. Francis, Sheila and Giles crossed the pontoon feeling slightly shaky after five days at sea.

The Queen, in a white dress, was standing with her husband at the head of the steps. The sword to be used was that with which Queen Elizabeth I had knighted Francis Drake after his historic circumnavigation in the *Golden Hind*. England possesses all the props! Francis knelt and was touched on the shoulder.

The Queen and Prince Philip then wished to see over *Gipsy Moth*. As they returned along the carpeted pontoon, fresh roars and cheers arose from the spectators. Her Majesty turned smiling to Francis: 'You wave. It's your day.' Unexpectedly, she then invited the Chichesters to walk back to the Naval College for a chat – and here of course the Press scored a bull's-eye. Had Sheila attended her husband's investiture turning cartwheels in a sequined circus outfit she could hardly have been given bigger, more critical headlines. As Buckingham Palace had decreed that trousers would be proper attire for a crew-member wife when stepping off a yacht, it does seem odd that *quite* so much excitement should have arisen.

In the bright sunshine Francis and Sheila returned to *Gipsy Moth* and drove her on slowly to Tower Pier where the Lord Mayor of London waited. It was lunch hour and the streets were absolutely packed as they drove through the City of London in a white Rolls-Royce flanked by policemen on white horses. Londoners appreciate this kind of show, and Francis seemed to revive in the general excitement.

On the Mansion House balcony in view of five thousand cheering people, the Lord Mayor presented him with a plaque, and then came an official banquet. After this, in the golden afternoon, the Chichesters returned to 9 St James's Place. Neighbours had hung the whole street with flags, the front door opened and Francis knew that he was truly home.

28. More Laurels

In August Francis was invited to Geneva to present to the city Museum the Rolex watch which had given him navigational fixes around the world. Sheila accompanied him and hoped that he might obtain some rest in the Alpine air. Asked to go to Survretta House in St Moritz as guests of the Swiss Government, they took the valley train and stepped out at the station to find themselves met by a coach and attendant horn-blowers. Music and wild acclaim accompanied them everywhere. Francis only wished he was more robust and fully able to enjoy this enthusiasm.

After receiving the Polona Trophy at San Remo, he had to face a huge celebration dinner. Sheila watched him trying not to wilt. It was impossible to explain his fatigue to people eager to fête him.

They escaped to Vence, their favourite haunt, and here they were now the guests of the famous Hotel Domaine St Martin. Francis undertook long mountain walks, but privacy proved impossible. When he pulled off his shirt to sunbathe in the mountains an unseen cameraman stalked up behind a boulder and the photo appeared in a London daily. Bernard Moitessier visited them and expressed horror at such pressure and lack of privacy. Francis's asthma recommenced.

They only just managed to get back for the festivities arranged for *Gipsy Moth IV* at Beaulieu. On Francis's sixty-sixth birthday, 17 September 1967, he took *Gipsy Moth IV* up the lovely Beaulieu River to the mooring given him by Lord Montagu of Beaulieu and presented the charts of his circumnavigation to the Bucklers Hard Maritime Museum. As night fell the Soho Concertante played Handel's Water Music. *Gipsy Moth IV* was floodlit and a fireworks display skittered overhead. Again the crowds got their money's worth. Francis, with a temperature of 101, looked on somewhat quizzically. He could *not* be fond of this yacht; although a brilliant performer, she had been so difficult to handle. He forgot the demands he had made on her and thought only of her faults and of how she had heeled over and sailed at an uncomfortable angle at speed. Eventually, after she had been on display at the London Boat Show, Lord Dulverton formally presented *Gipsy Moth IV* to the City of London. Entrusted to the Cutty Sark Society, she was put on view beside that famous old clipper at Greenwich where thousands of people could visit her each year. It was a happy ending and Tony Dulverton could feel his original impulse had ended in a splendidly worthwhile result. But Francis continued to glance at this boat with a slightly sardonic expression – as if she was a race-horse who had won the Derby but kicked!

As Francis got his strength back he agreed to speak at various functions and the lashing seas of the Horn seemed to have washed shyness away from him – or at least the kind of shyness which strikes people down when addressing crowds. Francis was still shy when he met new people, but in December he gave a lecture on the circum-navigation to nearly three thousand in the Festival Hall, and far from showing any timidity, Francis let his extraordinary magnetic quality flow easily out to the public. He took immense pains when preparing any lecture, but this could not explain the absolute confidence with which an unpractised orator could captivate a large audience. He had known the intoxication of high adventure, and he found he could share it. Sir Paul Davie wrote to Sheila: '. . . one could hardly keep one's seat. The manner of it was so skilful that as a connoisseur of public speaking (which I claim to be), I could hardly attend to the matter for savouring the manner.'

Very few people realized how meticulous Francis was when working out a lecture. He would spend three or four days in careful preparation – then he appeared absolutely spontaneous. But he could not do it often. To Monica Cooper he confided: 'When I have known a great experience such as sailing an ocean that experience is wrapped up inside me. Every time I talk about it it loses something. The original magic fades.'

Several months had, of course, to be dedicated to compiling a book. Francis had for some years employed a great friend, George Greenfield, as literary agent to arrange newspaper and publishing contracts. Their discussions usually took place over an excellent dinner and a bottle of carefully chosen wine. Greenfield noted with amusement how easily Francis could swing from the Spartan to the Sybarite taste. He never ate or drank very much, but he liked both food and wine to be of the very best when in civilized candle-lit surroundings. And he could display an unexpected toughness in financial deals. In fact, Greenfield was eventually forced to remark: 'What a literary agent *you* would have made!'

Now, while Sheila talked of 'resting', George Greenfield astringently reminded his client that large sales would depend entirely on getting this story into print while it remained fresh in the public mind. Francis ranted and raved about having to rush the script out for a deadline, but after all those impecunious years 'big lolly' was a real bait, and he got down to the task seriously. To write a book fast plays on an author's nerves at the best of times. The calm, decisive sailorman became quite different in these circumstances. Greenfield says that Francis, like the late Sam Goldwyn, was one of the few men who can 'run amok while sitting down'. And sometimes his agent wondered if Francis was driven by masochistic or sadistic impulses when he took up a pen. Although ready to flog himself to death, he seemed equally ready to flog everyone within reach as well.

The construction of this detailed sailing saga for early publication reduced more than one adviser to nervous prostration. 'And,' adds George Greenfield, 'I suspect he rather enjoyed doing this.'

Gipsy Moth Circles the World naturally proved a bestseller. Unwisely, Francis revealed every fault in the boat's performance and the fact that he criticized her design aroused much criticism of himself. By tradition, sportsmen must never blame their golf clubs, tennis racquets, football boots or other gear, much less their horses, and a yacht is nearly a horse. Francis not only wrote up from his log every storm, sail change, hot toddy and temper fit, but also the things which went wrong with the boat. He did not sufficiently stress the fact that he had left in a hurry, without giving her the chance for proper trials – without, in fact, having tried her out in anything like the conditions he would find in real ocean storms. As a result, a great deal of bitterness arose in yachting circles. Francis was always extremely outspoken and while his criticisms of gear and design might have been deemed fair enough in yachting magazines, the enormous publicity they received through being printed in a bestseller upset people. He was puzzled at the antagonism created by his scathing comments on the keel, buoyancy, and heeling tendencies.

However, several happy events occurred during this period. There was a touching visit to Barnstaple. Bill Wilkey, M.B.E., the gardener's son, who had once played with Master Francis at the Rectory, had, as in the fairy-tale, become Mayor of Barnstaple, and knew the pleasure of offering Sir Francis and his lady the honour of the freedom of the city. 'I did love your father,' Francis said thoughtfully, as he fingered the scroll of freedom. 'If only he could see us both today!'

Sad news arrived from Australia. George had died only a year after making a very happy marriage. He had struggled hard against asthma, and built up his life in his own way. A long letter full of plans had just reached Sheila and she felt glad that he had found her to depend on in days when she had no child of her own, and that through her he had learned not to recoil from his dynamic father.

The Chichester relationship, now that they had been married thirty years, was one which some members of the rising generation looked on with curiosity. How was it that two people could continue liking each other? How did this cement of devotion last when most human beings bored each other stiff after a year? 'Well, we were mature when we married,' said Sheila. The anguish of past illness she preferred not to talk about, nor did she wish to discuss her present incessant fight to keep Francis alive with every discipline of prayer she knew.

During 1967 and 1968 Francis *had* to take care of himself. He went to the south of France each spring to see Dr Mattei who would throw his arms around him and hug Francis prior to checking that old lung. It seemed to be holding up, but Francis's inner system had been strained by his own fantastic determination. He ate well but carefully, omitting meat. Luckily, he liked Sheila's nut-cutlets and fresh salads, and yet more luckily, vintage wines were part of the cure. Having grown interested in health he published a booklet on the yoga type of exercises he used to allay asthma and to get fit before voyages. He could climb twenty miles a day in the mountains behind Vence while Sheila, who herself considered ten miles sufficient, would follow with sandwiches and meet him at some rendezvous.

Friends wondered if Chichester would now rest content. Surely he had had his fill of aero-dynamics. Sometimes he spoke of the pleasures of just wandering around in a boat with Sheila, trying new anchorages, new ports, new wines. For the time being ordinary life seemed to suffice. He would wake like an ordinary man in his London bedroom, breakfast and walk in Green Park or over to St James's where he could watch the birds on the ponds and never tell them of greater fellows he had seen – albatrosses of eight-foot wingspan! Then came the map office, and hundreds of letters and telephone calls concerning charity or yachting functions. All yachting books were sent to him for comment or review, and he always took enormous pains with these. In 1967 Constance Babington-Smith's *Life of Amy Johnson* appeared and his review copy with meticulous notes in Francis's handwriting survives. He had liked and admired Amy – a dedicated pilot and a brave girl. The unhappy seven-year love affair which drove her to flying touched him. He marked a phrase which he thought evocative – a perfect description of those early flying days – 'The dew was still on the whole idea of flight.' 'Generous, warm-hearted, full-blooded', he wrote at the back of the book. 'I knew most of the women pilots except Amelia Earhart. If happily married Amy would have achieved nothing.'

Yacht clubs were constantly asking him to attend dinners, present prizes or judge events, and these invitations he dealt with dutifully. Some fifty English yacht clubs invited him to become an honorary member, but he only wanted to accept if he could do something useful for them. The one invitation for which he hoped did not arrive. When Alec Rose returned from *his* successful round-the-world voyage, Francis thought the welcoming committee would ask him down to Portsmouth to see *Lively Lady* sail in, but they did not do so and such is the price of fame that he could not possibly go on his own. 'Maddening not to feel free to just travel down and add my cheers to the rest but I daren't . . . it could look as if I was trying to steal his thunder.' Francis stayed in London and watched the arrival on television.

When the Yacht Club de France paid Francis the honour of making him *membre d'honneur*, he and Sheila went to Paris and stayed in the British Embassy. On St Valentine's Day Francis wandered out shopping on the rue de Rivoli, excited as a schoolboy contemplating extravagances. He bought a red velvet heart-shaped box filled with *very* expensive chocolates and meant to be used as a jewel casket afterwards. On the accompanying card he wrote for Sheila:

> *A Ma Valentine*
> *Aujourd'hui je t'aime*
> *Plus que Hier,*
> *Moins que Demain.*

Later on, the Chichesters were dining at the British Embassy when the Duke and Duchess of Windsor were present. Francis had not spoken to H.R.H. since the presentation of the Johnston Memorial Trophy for his Tasman Sea flight over thirty years before. While they sat together after dinner, Sheila told the Duke how sympathetic they had recently felt when watching a film of his youth. 'What you must have suffered, sir, as a boy with those terrible crowds pressing on you while you shook hands till your arm had to go into a sling. The pressure of crowds *is* terrifying, as Francis has learnt in the last years.'

The Duke of Windsor looked at her wistfully and said, 'But *he* had achieved something.' Suddenly Sheila saw his loneliness.

The long solitary months at sea actually improved Francis's power to converse. His most unusual mind and his great humour made him a sought-after dinner companion. That he liked solitude did not mean he did not like people. He did like people, he just couldn't be bothered with small talk. New viewpoints intrigued him, and he would snatch at opportunities to expound original solutions concerning almost any problem.

On one occasion, when attending a rather grand dinner given to celebrate the election of a new Commodore, he found the proceedings somewhat long drawn out. Turning to the Commodore's excited wife, he congratulated her on her husband's election, adding casually, 'Of course, you know that the Commodore's wife has to lie with all the club members.' It amused him to see her eyes grow indignantly round and her jaw drop in that split moment before disbelief.

Giles had now left Oxford and was able to join the family firm, so Number 9 was filled up with young people, as well as salt-encrusted mariners. Giles sometimes wondered about his father's early life – he noticed how attractive 'the old man' was to his own girl-friends. Was this just because he was famous? Giles thought not – the incredible suspicion entered his mind, and was then substantiated, that his father had sex-appeal. But Francis gave his son no leads beyond an admonition to be discreet – always *very very* discreet.

As for that 'pain', that mysterious 'thing' – not his lung, and presumably not really an ulcer – which often plagued him – what was it? His bad leg, due to the injury, was understandable. His elbow had healed. But the tension-pain that could strike him like a thunderbolt – that pain which never hit him on the ocean – what caused it? How could a man live with it?

After Christmas 1967 the Chichesters travelled to New Zealand in a cargo boat. A fleet of small craft came out to welcome them. Later they stayed in Wellington where Francis enjoyed looking at the shop-window decorations which depicted stormy sea scenes in which the waves were capped with *cotton wool*! Francis attended to what remained of his timber business and signed hundreds of books. He told Geoffrey Goodwin that he envied his 'robust health' but not his lack of ambition. Geoffrey found him, despite the lectures and speeches he had given – and given well – just as shy of new people as in the old days. He still could not break the ice easily with strangers, especially those who mentioned his 'fame'. 'I won't go to the club with you unless you *promise* not to introduce me to anyone,' he said.

Geoffrey found this very difficult. Every New Zealander wanted to meet the man who had been their 'Chich'.

Early in 1968, the *Daily Express* announced that it was sponsoring a former submarine captain to sail round the world non-stop alone in a four-and-a-half-ton boat. The author's husband, Commander Bill King, thought he would finally get six years of underwater patrols out of his system by this surface adventure. His boat *Galway Blazer II* was novel in design, whale-backed and with a Chinese-junk rig. Before she could be launched the *Sunday Times* went further than the *Daily Express*, announcing that it was going to sponsor a round-the-world solo *race* for any boat ready to set sail from England before 31 October. The first boat to sail round the world non-stop would be given a golden globe and the fastest boat £5000. These prizes triggered off many hopeful contestants, several of whom were reduced to nervous prostration in endeavouring to get ready in time.

Francis, in New Zealand, received a phone-call asking him to accept the position of Chairman of the Committee of this race. As sometimes happens when a person is caught by the long-distance telephone, he accepted the responsibility of chairmanship without insisting on conditions. When he began to think it over, he felt that the same strict rules which had governed the solo transatlantic races should be enforced. These rules were designed to prevent the ill-equipped or insufficiently prepared from setting out in a mad burst of enthusiasm.

When Francis returned to England he grumbled about the loose wording of the rules, but he was not very well and felt it late to lay down the law on right and proper inspections. As a result he was to suffer much distress during the next eight months.

During the summer of 1968 nine boats actually sailed in this race, at least two of which were unready and improperly equipped. Francis deemed it unseamanlike to allow the pressure of publicity to tempt men to risk their lives in ill-prepared-for adventure and fretted at his own inability to insist that each boat should be vetted by a knowledge-able committee before departure. Having spoken his mind Francis decided that it could not help matters if he now resigned the chairmanship.

When the race closed on 31 October, two unready boats sailed away with a jumble of unstored food and gear on deck and many important items missing. Of these the Italian Carozzo turned in to Portugal with duodenal ulcers due to nerve strain, and the Press jubilantly published photographs of what they called his 'agony'. The other man, Donald Crowhurst, who had wept all through the last night because he knew he was not ready, but then could not bear to let down those who were sponsoring him, was to find a far more tragic ending. Chay Blyth and John Ridgeway, who had rowed the Atlantic together, had their boats broken up by storms and were forced to turn in for repairs. A freak, out-of-season hurricane in the area of Tristan da Cunha smashed up the boat of Louis Fougeron who had to land in bad shape. The same hurricane capsized Bill King's *Galway Blazer II*, 1000 miles south-west of Cape Town and her masts broke in the pressure of water as she righted herself. It looked as if Bernard Moitessier, the magnificent French yachtsman, must surely complete the voyage fastest, but having rounded the Horn he felt unable to face the burst of publicity which he knew awaited and he sailed calmly away out of the race, passing the Cape of Good Hope a second time and making for the South Seas, where he settled.

At the time Moitessier made this decision (so understandable to Francis), the Chichesters happened to be in Paris and were witness to the amazement, disappointment and fury of the French sailing world that *their* chap scorned to win!

By spring of 1969, only three contestants remained at sea – Robin Knox Johnston, who alone would complete the voyage, Nigel Tetley, whose trimaran would sink off the Azores when in a desperate effort to increase speed against his supposed rival, Donald Crowhurst, he put up too much canvas, and that mysterious Crowhurst himself whose curious radio signals had been filling Sheila, so accustomed to being at the receiving end, with apprehension. Francis worried himself sick, but there was nothing he could do now. Nigel Tetley, who kept afloat in his rubber dinghy until sighted by the American Air Force, had gone sadly back to England without the boat which was his only home, when his opponent Crowhurst's yacht was discovered abandoned with two different log-books aboard. Out of his mind from strain, financial worry and the misery of letting others down, Crowhurst had, during months alone in the Atlantic, played with the idea of pretending to get his boat around the world. In the end death had taken him. Kind death.

The anguish of Crowhurst's expectant waiting family gave plenty of scope for journalistic enterprise. Clare Crowhurst, his wife, stood it bravely and wrote at that time to this author, 'My poor darling put it into words "Man is not happy unless he is trying" and now the thing which helps me most is the fact that he was free to try.'

Francis was sensitive to the pressures that drove other men, and he could imagine what Donald Crowhurst had endured while his mind lost balance. Although he enjoyed giving an enthusiastic welcome to

Robin Knox Johnston on his arrival home, he suffered painfully over the whole affair. Had he not been far away, when asked to accept the chairmanship, and tired and busy when he returned, he would have imposed strict rules. Tetley might still have his boat and Crowhurst his life. He felt responsible and depression hit him.

29. Old Wolf of the Sea

While the last three contestants in the Round-the-World Race were approaching the finish, Francis had enjoyed two months' rest in Portugal. During this period he seemed to be experiencing a sudden, surprising burst of health.

On the patio of a lovely villa, he amused himself drawing blueprints for a new boat – and while he was at this, peace reigned. Sheila sat beside him in the sunshine watching his intent, happy expression while he sketched sails that would be easy to handle, and she thought her own dream might be approaching – the dream she had always had, of sailing with him through the isles of Greece. She did not know that he was working out a new lone venture. He had always promised to take her to Greece – to sail gently from island to island, to find time to explore the white hill villages. But the old fever still burned. Francis was wondering what he could pit himself against next.

On his last lap up through the North Atlantic he had made the fastest-ever single-handed run. The long, slim *Gipsy Moth IV* had covered 1408 miles in eight days averaging 176 miles a day. Had she been less sensitive he believed he might have sailed her yet faster. Turning this over in his mind Francis devised an entertaining project. He had enough money now; he would build this new boat steadier of hull, and see if he could make a sustained run of 1000 miles at 200 miles a day. Why not? What a perfect challenge for the sunset years.

He knew exactly the type of hull required – one based on the fifty-seven-foot *Sir Thomas Lipton*, winner of the third single-handed Transatlantic Race. She had been designed by Robert Clark, the creator of that pet *Gipsy Moth III*, and Francis decided to go to him for a new fast, true-running boat.

Talks began. Clark drew out a sail plan on the back of an envelope.

To make for easier handling for a man alone, he would divide the sail area. In the 'staysail ketch rig' he sketched there was no big mainsail, but a staysail setting between the two masts from the top of the mizzen mast to the foot of the main mast. Blueprints were drawn up and contracts signed. The building of *Gipsy Moth V* started at Crosshaven boatyard in Cork early in 1970 and she was launched at the end of June. Rather like a big dinghy, fifty-seven feet overall and forty-one feet eight inches on the waterline, she was twenty-nine tons Thames measurement. There came the usual trouble fitting an engine. Sailing boats don't like engines – and engines don't seem to like sailing boats; they make themselves awkward. A fairly powerful motor was essential, both for the Beaulieu River, where Lord Montagu had given them about the loveliest anchorage in Britain, and to charge the batteries for the Marconi Kestrel radio telephone which Francis must carry if he was going to communicate. There were comic moments: the line-up of engine and propeller proved erratic; every now and again when put into reverse the boat went forward and vice versa. One morning when Francis was trying to reach his mooring on the river, this happened, and he ran onto a sandbank. Pressmen always kept an eye on him and within minutes a reporter had spotted 'Chichester stranded' and was joyfully ringing up the Harbour Master for details to phone to his paper. Sweating and chuckling, Francis got her off before photographers and interviewers could arrive.

When his boat was ready, Francis went into a happy huddle with wind charts. What pleasure it was for him trying to work out what great winds of the world could give him the best chance of sailing 200 miles a day for five consecutive days. He chose the January North-East Trades of the North Atlantic and planned to try one 1000-mile run down to the Equator and another from the Equator northwards in the tracks of his previous fast run. But he said nothing to anyone, not even to Sheila or Giles.

On 14 August 1970 he sailed for Majorca for Mediterranean trials with Christopher Doll, a television photographer, intent on making a TV film of the new *Gipsy Moth*. Francis remained aghast at Doll's pluck as he climbed the rigging for good shots while being violently seasick. Sheila joined them at Gibraltar and assured Doll, who had never been on a long ocean cruise, that they were not going to starve to death when winds fell light off the coast of Majorca.

Giles joined them at Palma to sail back alone with his father on the homeward trials, when it was hoped to test *Gipsy Moth V*'s speed in the same winds that had given *Gipsy IV* her speed burst, but the south-westerlies did not blow. Furious at being unable to get the wind behind them, they had to sail close-hauled against nose-enders for 1600 miles. Owing to the season, every time they turned a corner of Spain or Portugal the wind changed direction and continued to head *Gipsy Moth*, so the whole object of this voyage was lost. They did not get back to Beaulieu River until 22 October, which allowed only six weeks in which to refit, effect modifications and take on stores. Francis's many 'fans' provided tribute of preserved foodstuff – honeycombs in polythene wrapping, fresh brown eggs encased in isinglass. All had to be placed in the allotted storage space and labelled for easy finding. In the midst of these preparations Francis was begged to fly to Sicily for a presentation ceremony. Sheila forced him to rest for two days in Taormina and there he revealed to her the length of his projected voyage – four or five months alone in the Atlantic. After that, maybe, they could discover the Greek isles together!

Remunerative as his adventures were now proving, he had been sorely strained by the fatigue of having to attend the many functions for which his presence was ceaselessly requested. Feelings were hurt if he refused invitations. On top of this he had to sign many thousands of books – at least he swore they were thousands – some at his publisher's behest, some for charity and many for friends. The only way to escape from all this was to get off to sea.

When Francis confided his intention of trying to beat his own record over 1000 miles to his literary agent, George Greenfield said: 'Look, why not try an even longer *fast* sail between two definite fixed points? Try for the 1000-mile record, but it would be even more dramatic to run from point to point to give a little more practical interest to what might otherwise seem an almost intellectual approach to single-handed sailing.' With schoolboy eagerness, Francis returned to his charts. If only he could find a 4000-mile strip of open ocean he could attempt to sail it in twenty days. Getting out callipers he pored over ocean charts, measuring runs, but the Atlantic is not 4000 miles across at any point. He could not sleep with excitement. Then, one night, he jumped out of bed, crying, 'I've got it!' and hurried to his charts.

If he backed up the estuary of Bissau in Portuguese Guinea and sailed straight across westward to the little port of San Juan del Norte in Nicaragua, it would approximate 4000 miles. This was the longest straight line that could be worked out anywhere, and the winds should, on the whole, blow from the east, giving him a good chance to race all the way over.

Now he became frantic to be off. In order to get stores stowed quickly, Sheila lived on board *Gipsy Moth* while gangs of technicians and carpenters worked around her. As it was exceedingly cold she became most anxious for starting day – to get Francis into a better climate and herself back to her heated house.

Finally, on 12 December, taking Giles and young David Pierce as crew, Francis sailed *Gipsy Moth V* down to Plymouth. They were nearly sunk by a Panama-registered steamer on the way, and Francis trembled when he saw the great bows just miss the cabin where Giles lay sleeping.

On 18 December Francis set sail alone for Bissau. Once again he was outside Plymouth on what for him, though not for anyone else, could be called a 'health trip'. But the cold wintry weather took the gilt off this start. Then, three days out, the wind freshened and he was able to experiment with different sail trimmings and sail settings. The boat responded thrillingly and tore through the water at high speed, but the radio refused to work and this was a real worry because he had undertaken to report to the BBC during the speed run. He tried in vain to communicate on Christmas Day. All the way down to Africa he experimented with new settings for his sails. Hard gales blew and there were the usual battles on deck while *Gipsy Moth* tore along under bare poles and Francis grappled with gear. Sometimes when the boat's stern flicked in the air he found himself looking down on a big sea thirty feet below. It was a strange sensation. On 27 and 28 December a near hurricane did a deal of damage and badly bent the headsail booms which were constructed of light alloy. These booms were lashed to the deck until the time came for them to be used holding out headsails in the great speed dash. One might think of them as the bones of folded wings. When *Gipsy Moth V* really got going she could carry six sails and tear along like an angry swan.

Francis reached the Geba estuary by 7 January to find Christopher Doll and a TV team waiting. At Bissau, up the river, *Gipsy Moth* anchored and the Portuguese Vice-Governor, who happened to be the local naval commodore, offered to get all repairs done. The damaged booms and the BBC cine camera were taken off to the naval workshops to be dismantled. Eventually Francis would curse himself for not getting these headsail booms strengthened by inserting bamboo poles inside the hollow metal. They remained far too light for his purpose and would not stand up to the strain when the speed dash came.

After it had been overhauled Francis succeeded in getting through on the radio telephone to London to give the promised Press reports and talk to Sheila. That night he slept ten hours without moving. He knew that a difficult start lay ahead tacking down the breezeless Geba estuary, but only by going up river to Bissau could he have stretched out a 4000-mile course. Worried about lack of wind he might be, but deep inside himself Francis felt happy – once again he was off to pit himself against the elements, to try his capacities as lone sailor and aero-dynamicist.

On 12 January 1971 Francis started his sail down river from Bissau. This proved slower than he had expected. It took him twenty-one sleepless hours of tacking to cover fifty-three miles and reach the open sea. This frustrating beginning meant that he would now have to average 206 miles a day for nineteen days to achieve the longer of his targets. He began to think it would have been wiser to listen to Sheila who had wanted him to be content to start at the mouth of the Estuary. There wasn't sufficient open ocean to make the other record feasible. As a farewell present in Africa he had been given a bunch of green bananas which he hung in the cabin cupboard. From this bower suddenly emerged a large spider with upraised claws – a tarantula or of that ilk. Francis stalked him with a flit-gun, but instead of dropping dead in the lethal spray, the spider merely scowled and danced away through inaccessible nooks and crannies. For a time Francis watched dark corners nervously, then accepted the stowaway.

Soon he reached the North-East Trades, wonderfully beautiful with clear starlit nights and flying fish jumping onto the deck. But the wind did not play up. He wrote in his log: 'It is difficult to sleep because it is so exciting and gripping trying to get the most speed possible. I believe that with this rig and five knots more wind *Gipsy Moth* could whizz along.'

By the time he had covered 2000 miles of ocean, and could expect winds to increase, he saw that to reach his target he would be needing to average 216 miles a day. He began to over-drive *Gipsy Moth* and was reaching nine and a half knots through seething cascades when the two spinnaker booms broke leaving sails flogging about. It took him four hours to straighten out the mess. To obtain a record after this hold-up, *Gipsy Moth* would have to cover the impossible distance of 232 miles for each remaining day. Obviously *this* project was going to fail – and the expected north-east winds remained entirely easterly, which further delayed him. But at night he knew bliss; he could sit naked in the cockpit, cooling off in the balmy airs and write: 'I gave myself over to the romantic pleasure of sliding fast through the seas into the night in my slim powerful craft.'

Naturally, Francis was not nearly as strong as he had been as a young man, but he had learned to use his limbs with cunning, and he could confidently steel himself to effect repairs high up the mast in a rough sea.

One day the keel caught on a queer dragging mass that proved to be neither shark nor sea-serpent. Francis had to drop sails while he hooked the object on board. It was a sixty-foot-long fishing net in which a large turtle had become entangled! He cut the creature free and popped him overboard to swim back 2500 miles to Africa – if the mood took him! He thought it an interesting coincidence from the turtle's point of view – to have been found by the only small boat for a thousand miles and rescued by a vegetarian.

When only six days of the twenty were left, Francis knew he could not possibly complete the 4000-mile run in the time he had set himself, but he *had* attained his original ambition – he had sailed over 1000 miles in five consecutive days. The broken booms had cost him at least twenty-four hours.

Then, because he did not want to go home just yet, and could not think of anything else to do – he started to work out possible areas where he could try to beat this record. 'It would not be such a favourable time of year as I originally planned, but I would at least have the sport.'

At the end of twenty days' sailing he had covered not 4000 miles, but 3536 miles. However, he did sail the 4000 miles in twenty-two days and that has remained a record up to 1975. By now he was in the middle of the Caribbean Sea, feeling claustrophobic amidst so many islands. Yearning for the safety and freedom of the wide Atlantic he sailed on to cross what he had mentally laid down as his finishing line at San Juan del Norte, and then turned away.

The British Ambassador came out on a large craft with the TV team, and gallantly made a speech of welcome from the pitching deck. Francis had intended to sail down to Panama for repairs but the Ambassador's companions pressed him to make for a place called El Bluff, sixty miles away which, they said, had an excellent harbour. When Captain Bartlett of a firm called Caribbean Marine got through by radio offering the facilities of his first-class trawler repair workshop, Francis swiftly altered course for this place with its unlikely name. Seldom had he felt so *free* to go where he chose; it was a wonderful sensation – if Nicaragua clamoured for him, in Nicaragua he would stay! He sailed all night, nervously enough along the dark coast, from which he kept hearing ominous sounds as of running rivers. On the morning of 5 February he reached El Bluff and for twelve days he revelled in the surprises of a new little world.

Once again the dauntless British Ambassador appeared to greet him, and by his side stood the Director-General of the Nicaraguan Tourist Board with a Nicaraguan flag for *Gipsy Moth*. Then, before Francis had time to utter his thanks, the Director proposed the immediate organization of an international yacht race over Francis's 4000-mile route, 'to bring tourists and prosperity to Nicaragua'!

In Captain Bartlett, the American manager of a shrimp-packing factory, which kept eighty-five trawlers in repair, Francis found a congenial crony. Amused by the unexpected visitor, Captain Bartlett, a bearded character with a repertoire of sea shanties, did much of the repair work himself in the trawler workshop.

It was all so odd and unexpected, this stop-off in a country he had chosen by chance on the Atlas. 'Old Wolf of the Sea', the Nicaraguans named him, and Francis found his fame was such that on one occasion five ambassadors arrived to lunch with him in Captain Bartlett's house! Eventually, he had to accede to a presidential request that he fly to the capital to receive a gold medal. When he reached Managua a great deal of rum appeared but no medal. Francis did not grouse, for he had been able to watch an active volcano from the plane. By 17 February *Gipsy Moth*, superbly refitted and re-victualled, was ready to depart. Where? Francis sought an excuse to go on sailing for a few more months. At sixty-eight he could earnestly write: 'I wanted more adventure, and above all I wanted to be free, as free as a wild sea bird like the stormy petrel, to sail where I liked as long as I liked in the great ocean.'

The sands of life were running down, but to the very end Francis thirsted for the joy of action – he would *not* be caged again by illness or pain. The wonderful surface of the earth must remain his playground to the end.

He thought that just for fun he might try a couple of speed runs to see if he could coax more out of *Gipsy Moth V*. He settled on one run down to the Equator and another straight up north. As he would be at sea on his wedding anniversary, he wrote in advance to Sheila:

At El Bluff   Bluefields, Nicaragua,
                                               3 a.m. 15 February 1971
My darling wife,
   Just a note to wish you well and congratulate you on surviving 34 years of marriage to me on the 25th. A remarkable achievement . . .

He knew what a difficult husband he could be.

After an unwise drinking party with the irrepressible hard-headed Captain Bartlett and his friends, Francis slipped away from El Bluff to meet a head-on swell. He felt seasick, sad at leaving jolly helpmates and lonely for Sheila, all at the same time. But he wasn't racing, he could do what he liked, sail as he chose. That was a new sensation in itself.

Ruminating on the pleasures of navigating by star-fix rather than sun-fix, he made northwards for one of the passages out into the open sea – the Muna Passage, or the Windward Passage, between Cuba and Haiti. He couldn't wait to get back into the Atlantic and had 1000 miles to go. He sailed cautiously through the Spanish Main, whose reefs had claimed so many galleons and treasure ships in the long ago.

Calm weather with slatting sails alternated with boisterous squalls, but he felt marvellously fit – maybe because he was doing just what he wanted. It is perfectly natural for high-strung men to become seriously ill when they have to do what they don't like to do. This is not imaginary illness, it is real. The French say, '*Il ne faut pas se faire du mauvais sang*', and how right that phrase is. As one gets older the blood turns to poison if one can't get one's own way!

On 21 February in the Gulf of Darien, Francis was charmed by the appearance of a large, handsome, he thought feminine, moth. And then less charmed by finding a giant flying-ant aboard (who succumbed to the flit-gun), and then not charmed at all by the re-emergence of Monsieur/Madame Tarantula, the spider who had sailed the Atlantic alive after being dowsed with insecticide; he/she had hidden during the long noisy refit in Nicaragua and was now darting from one crevice to another, holding two claws up menacingly and apparently enjoying the occasional shower-bath of poison. Francis gave up the chase, deeming it 'a survivor', and just hoped he would not put his hand on it in the dark.

Because of winds and currents, Francis decided against the Muna Passage and sailed instead between Cuba and Haiti. He was pounding hard on the wind for days after this, which drives most men to a state of utter exhaustion, but in some strange way he thrived on such hammering and slept wonderfully – far better than he ever did on land.

Once through the Windward Passage between Cuba and Haiti, he had to make his way through the Bahamas. He selected the Mayaguana Passage, as the safest for a loner. 'Considering there were not any great waves, the seas were the most violent I have ever seen. The wind had got up to forty knots and *Gipsy Moth* was thrown, bounced, slammed. It was exhilarating because she was going through it like a witch.' It was difficult navigation all through the islands and Francis felt a surge of relief when he got through into the open ocean. He had been unable to relax for a hundred hours and now he dropped into a heavy sleep, rocked indeed as if in a cradle by the wide islandless Atlantic – his favourite ocean he called it, and he knew them all intimately.

The word Francis Chichester chose to describe the continuation of this five-month voyage was 'ambling'. With a boyishly light heart he set off to scour the ocean for winds to suit his pleasure. On 2 March he wrote: 'I'm lying in my berth, relaxed. It seems an age since I could rest or let go the tension, or allow myself to have a deep sleep. I am sipping nectar.'

He was in no hurry. His desire lay in a leisurely sail eastwards for 2000 miles to a point in the Atlantic where he could turn to try a speed-dash down to the Equator. The sea put on her most dazzling blue-greens to delight him, and the winds blew kindly, while he busied himself with sail experiments and minor repairs. He found himself analysing the past.

On 11 March, at two in the morning, he wrote introspectively:

I do not know if all kinds of solitary living have the same effect. The solitary sea-life . . . makes me think and feel more than is comfortable for my peace of mind. I have dreadful attacks of remorse. My chief remorse is for unkind acts to friends in the past. Maybe something deeply wounding that I have said or done. Then I find myself stuck with such things for ever; they cannot be undone and the awful thing is that often they did not mean much to me, nor were even seriously believed, but were used as a cruel weapon to hurt . . . This sea life makes one so sympathetic with others in trouble with their conscience or unable to cope with the overwhelming difficulties of their life. I often think of Donald Crowhurst with great sympathy. For me, to be nine months alone without aim, project, objective, challenge, would mean exposing my soul far too much. I can understand it being damaged or destroyed by continuous considering of it, relentless probing of it. I can only stand a very little peep at it now and then. Thank God for activity of body and mind to keep me away from my soul.

He did not really want to slide out of his hard-hammered body into esoteric zones. It was enough to register what he wished he had *not* done in his life; he wished he had never been unkind, he wished he had not teased that unfortunate schoolmaster the moment he dared to do so, he wished he had been clear-minded enough to see what hurt others instead of only what hurt himself. But one cannot wipe out the past. What's done and is past help *should* be past grief – but who can discipline the fretting memory?

Then, Francis discovered that owing to a leaking pipe connection, he was short of fresh water. The lack was not serious, but almost as a diversion he decided to ration himself. On 16 March he reached the 40th meridian where he intended to turn south and stop this 'ambling', making instead an all-out effort to break his own record over 1000 miles. He began to feel excited, uneasy, reluctant. What a game this was! And all of his own devising.

But, as often happens in sailing ventures, the winds threw tantrums. Right in the middle of the Trades, where they were supposed to be steady, they either dropped or suddenly blew from a wrong quarter. Francis grew deflated as the possibility of breaking his own five-day record receded, and that old leg trouble, which had never quite left him since he fell on *Gipsy IV*, recurred.

On the Equator a considerable cloud-burst filled the water tanks and washed the bed linen and underwear hung in the cockpit, but that 'fast run to the Equator' could not take place. After a short pause for thought, and some mulling over charts and sailing directions, he turned northwards. On 26 March he logged at 14.20:

Tacked for home and loved ones (I hope) . . . I snapped a sight of the sun to get at least a longitude of the point of departure. These rain storms seem to last about four hours, which means if involved in this one, that I shall have no chance of a star-fix at nightfall. I could not get a single star this morning because of cloud and was lucky to catch Jupiter and afterwards to find Venus in a clear patch in the daylight.

The planets had been his only friends for long enough. Now he felt wistful and dreamed of his London home. How strange it would seem to be back in those crowded streets with the same bright orbs high above the trees of St James's Park and the same old sun setting unfixed over Buckingham Palace!

Gipsy Moth V was an immensely fast boat in heavy weather, but in light breezes her rig did not carry enough sail to drive her along. She couldn't seem to be cajoled over her record run of 1000 miles in five days. Francis was now concentrating not only on sailing over 200 miles a day, but on keeping his physique in order with breathing and bending exercises in his bunk. Unused muscles atrophy and he had really been at sea for a very long time.

Actually, Francis did once manage to sail over the 200 miles for three consecutive days. Then during the night of 4 April the boom of the running sail broke and he had to spend a nasty three hours on deck.

On 8 April he made a long entry in the log: 'Today has been a

lovely one, the most delightful of the voyage I think. Contrast is probably the key to it . . . suddenly I had no commitments, worries,
frustrations, and my feelings opened like a flower on a spring
morning.'

And the tarantula reappeared looking somewhat shrunken –
perhaps the long voyage was getting him down – or perhaps this was
not him but his wife! And then a baby tarantula sneaked out with
short dancing steps onto the chart table. After sailing thousands of
miles with these spiders, Francis could not help rather liking them.

On this last run northward, the radio telephone did not work
properly and he used up nearly all his fuel charging the batteries.
This left him short for lights and with the shipping lanes coming
closer he decided to turn in to Horta in the Azores, a place he had
loved, ever since stopping off there with Sheila.

He spent seven days at Horta, replenished fuel and left for
England on 30 April: '*Gipsy Moth* had a businesslike press-on gait,
with a slight roll to port, a gurgle of water along the hull as she
rolled back which gave a feeling of power and speed.' Cutting
through the blue seas he grew dreamy and sentimental. He was, in
fact, just swanning along in a romantic haze, when suddenly on 2
May *Gipsy Moth* ran into bad weather. 'The movement was horrible,
jumping, twisting, snatching and rolling.' Next day it grew worse.
Francis wrote: 'The true wind is now 241° 48 knots . . . Thank
Heaven I am not feeling seasick. I think I will skip my exercises this
morning though. I feel very weary and I did have a lot of exercise in
the past nine hours even if the wrong sort.'

The barometer continued to drop. At 17.42 the wind vane broke
and 'all hell broke loose'. He was thrown across the cockpit and
landed hard, bruising his back. For several hours he feared from the
pain that his kidney had split, but all functioned correctly.* Now the
cabin resembled a rubbish heap as waves battered the hull from side
to side. 'The sea was an impressive sight. The flying spray from the
whipped-off wave crests made a carpet six to ten feet deep covering
the ocean as far as one could see, like a layer of ragged sea-mist.'
Unable to sleep in such pounding, he lay wondering if it was a
mistake to let Gipsy Moth run down wind. He rose up to re-lash the
helm and again a great wave threw the boat violently over. As
Francis left the floor he hung on to the safety rope he had devised
above his bunk. Then he crept into the cockpit to disengage the
wind vane, and re-lash the helm, but the yacht refused to head up

* Recent X-rays had revealed that Francis possessed only one kidney – the other
may have atrophied due to a punch during early boxing days.

into the wind and continued to lie abeam to the tempestuous seas. He did not dare to lower the one remaining sail – the storm jib – for fear of completely losing control, nor for that matter, did he fancy creeping along a foredeck washed by colossal waves.

Returning to his bunk clad in full oilskins and wondering if another knock-down might occur, he reckoned that the safety rope holding him in would not function if it grew rougher, so he got up and hooked his life-harness onto the steel beam above him. He had just done this when, for the third time, the boat was lifted and thrown over on her side. 'I was aware of terrific forces and had a lonely feeling as I was being hurled into space.' He found himself lying on his back on the cabin ceiling looking up at the floor-boards which were falling around him revealing the bilges.

I was tumbling from the ceiling. I was seeing badly. I remember putting up my hand and noting that my spectacles had been knocked half off: I remember pushing them back and being surprised that they had survived. I think all this occurred while I was tumbling. Then I was lying partly on the piece of floor beside my bunk. I began to lose consciousness and made an effort to flop into the bunk before I passed out . . . My impression was that *Gipsy Moth* had been hurled with terrific force off the crest of a wave into the trough ahead.

When he came to he scrambled over the inner debris to force open the damaged hatch and see if the masts were still intact. They were, and to his amazement both paraffin lamps remained alight in the mizzen shrouds. The storm jib had been torn to ribbons which waved screaming in the wind. *Gipsy Moth* was sailing fast down wind under bare poles, her deck all banging broken gear, while the mizzen stays'l, half unfurled, flogged itself to death.

The seas remained terrific; he had seen waves like these around Cape Horn, but here they seemed shorter and steeper. He went below and lay down in his life-harness trying to think. Water was pouring into the bilges but in the dark he could not discover the leak. When it became a foot deep in the cabin he started to fill plastic bags with food for the rubber dinghy in case *Gipsy Moth* sank beneath him – but what hope of survival had a dinghy in this storm? He tried to radio an S.O.S. but the aerial had been badly damaged.

I could think of nothing else to do. I reckoned this was one of the tightest jams I had ever been in; I was dead beat with sheer fatigue, fear, tension and depression. Only a sleep could give me a chance of a clear brain to think up something to save me.

He looked at the rising water level and reckoned it would be several hours before reaching the top of the bunk. He tried the electric pumps; one hummed weakly but he dared not waste precious current if the pumps were not in perfect order; he started on the hand pump which immediately jammed. Francis reverted to the primitive method which could not go wrong. One bucket after another he filled in the swirling bilges, carried laboriously up to the cockpit and tipped over into the sea. After emptying thirty buckets he spied a hole in the deck and stopped it with his underpants over which he spread a square of towelling, and then, having no plywood handy, he cut a piece out of a plastic Tupperware box and tacked this firmly in place. It wasn't easy because the hole went right up to the toerail, and every few seconds the sea would wash over him. After emptying 127 buckets, it was seven in the evening of 5 May. He started to write his log. The capsize had occurred at two minutes to midnight on the previous day. The cabin clock, smashed by a bottle, had stopped dead amidst a decoration of embedded glass splinters.

At intervals Francis swallowed spoonfuls of honey – good for sea-sickness and strength-giving. He had, after the knock-down, only thought of saving his life. Now he began to hate the idea of allowing his beautiful boat to sink. He was damned if he would push off in that dinghy. All through the next day, while the storm continued, he staggered from job to job and *Gipsy Moth* did not seem lower in the water.

On 6 May he obtained a sun-shot and calculated he was 651 miles from Plymouth. He baled and baled. The bilges refilled, but this did not prove that leaks lay below the waterline, it could have been the result of pockets of water draining down. After the 200th bucket he tried to light the Aladdin heater. The wick took its flame and began to dry things.

His log narrative ran:

What change of fortune in a man's life. Two or three days ago I was as smug as can be with everything clean and tidy in the yacht . . . A few hours later I was collecting hurriedly the necessaries to keep me alive for a few weeks in a dinghy, thinking it only a matter of how long *Gipsy Moth* could stay afloat.

By midnight on 7 May, just three days after the knock-down, he knew triumphantly the yacht could not be holed below the water-line, and he might discard all thought of abandoning ship. With confidence he put out a little more sail and sipped a champagne cocktail – in all Francis Chichester's disasters, the odd bottle always survived.

On the night of 8 May, he obtained contact at the arranged hour by radio telephone and enjoyed a nine-minute talk to Sheila. He described the chaos on board, but took care not to frighten her. As the home port lay so near he contented himself with a little tidying up and the salvaging of soaked belongings from the unbelievable hiding places they had found when the boat lay over.

On Tuesday, 11 May, at three in the morning, Francis heard the Lizard siren moaning through the mist and knew that he had entered the main shipping lanes. The fog lifted after dawn and there lay England all bright in sunshine. At noon he was only twenty-four miles from Plymouth. In a light breeze he passed into the Sound that night and then came the reunion which a week ago he had feared might never happen. 'My beloveds, Sheila and Giles, came out to meet me in the Harbour Master's launch.' They stared with amazement at the shambles of the cabin, and realized it was miraculous that he had survived. Soon after midnight they were all eating scrambled eggs in the Royal Western Yacht Club. Francis had been away five months and had sailed 18 581 miles. He had fulfilled a smaller ambition and failed to fulfil the bigger one. He was full of fun. The esoteric pleasures of this voyage had agreed with him. He had indeed become what the Nicaraguans called him – an 'Old Wolf of the Sea'.

30. Shadows

For the Chichesters, life now assumed a different quality. Outwardly they appeared to be on the crest of the wave. Francis had made a small fortune doing what interested him most, and if he wished to take time off, there was nothing to stop him. After years of money difficulties the map business prospered. They owned a superb yacht for their personal pleasure and could keep it at what must be the most beautiful mooring in England. Sheila thought more about resuming her painting and Francis bullied her to work at it. Although he had been her 'job' for thirty-five years, and it had in truth been *his* needs which kept her from the easel, he always pressed people to *use* their talents. Tough as Francis was, he possessed an inbuilt artistic temperament – that is, he *felt* artistically. As a young man, he had yearned to be a novelist. The knack was denied him but the desire for self-expression remained. Certainly in his early years he had been as tormented and restless as any poet. Now, after battling against heavy odds and winning by the skin of his teeth on more than one occasion, he had attained a special sense which he wanted to hand on – it was the game that mattered, not the prize money. He would say this even after bewildering George Greenfield by his insistence on squeezing all the 'lolly' possible out of newspapers – in fact, Greenfield often had to tone down his client's ideas of what 'exclusive Chichester reports' were worth. Francis was a most complicated being, and many people who knew him well give absolutely contradictory descriptions of his character – kind, selfish, generous, grasping, demanding, thoughtful, unreasonable. 'A quiet, modest hero that we early fliers regarded with reverence,' says test pilot Nigel Tangye. 'Clever at backing into the limelight,' adds a witty nameless friend. 'Argumentative, even fractious – but he had the gift of friendship and then no bond could be of nobler metal,' writes Michael

Richey, a man of the same metal, and close to him. 'He'd work you to death, and then forget about you for months,' says a man closely involved in Francis's writing schemes. 'I knew him fairly well from 1942 in the sense that whenever we met, which was not often, it was as if we had only parted the week before,' states Sir Peter Bristow, now a judge in the Law Courts. 'Fundamentally, he didn't like people,' comments one who served him loyally for many years. But he *did* like people, insists this author, though he liked solitude with a passion rare in most men. 'Materialistic and egocentric,' murmurs another acquaintance, 'yet ready to charm the birds off the trees for his own ends.' This view was to be tempered with Francis's own final belief that 'Happiness lies in striving for perfection'. He *was* a perfectionist – a notably intemperate breed.

He could see things clearly now – to dig out truth and to encourage those on different roads – this was what really mattered when the burning ambitions, the competitiveness, the egotism of youth faded. Francis Chichester's own artistry was, for the public, somewhat difficult to analyse – a navigating genius is a genius along with the rest, but it was not this flair so much as physical endurance which caught world imagination and aroused so much acclaim. The crowds hailed him as an intrepid adventurer rather than as a man who caught at chords from sky and sea, a man who could defeat physical torment in the exaltation of danger.

All during that June and July of 1971, Sheila wanted him to rest in Portugal, where he had always felt particularly well. But Francis would not hear of it. He was absolutely determined to write another book – his *best* book. *The Romantic Challenge* would describe the five months in the Atlantic and mingle his studies of sailing technique and navigational theories with his own philosophy. The book was to begin – 'I love life . . .'. From that statement would stem all the rest – the reasons that had caused him to embark on all his extraordinary projects. The effort of writing this book, which was of vital personal importance to him, had a derogatory effect on his health. He drove himself so hard in the desire to find appropriate words, and became so wound up, that by August he was near collapse. After three weeks in King Edward VII's Hospital in London, he retired to Greyshott Hall, a health farm, and it was while swimming in the pool there that the deep burrowing pain near his spine intensified. The doctors were growing ominously suspicious, but he seemed able to surmount each physical crisis, and he never stopped making plans. When Lord Thomson of Fleet, owner of the *Sunday Times*, who was also at Greyshott Hall, scolded Francis for contemplating the Transatlantic

Race of the following year, he warned, 'You have *got* to take care of yourself. I shall tell my boys not to give you any money . . .'

'Oh, but you will,' replied Francis jauntily. 'You are bound to want my reports and I shall insist that John Anderson shall collaborate with me.'

Off and on, Francis tried to cure his ills on nature-cure regime, but he disregarded the basic nature-cure of *rest*. By his seventieth birthday, on 17 September 1971, he was falling back on pain-killers.

In October Dr Gordon Latto insisted that he undergo intensive tests at Reading Hospital. 'Something is poisoning your blood stream,' said Latto. Francis looked wistful, so the doctor added kindly, 'You will have a room with a tree outside – you can look at it to keep your heart up.'

The resulting diagnosis was cancer – not of the lung (that had never returned) but there was an inoperable malignant growth embedded deep down near the spine. It was cancer that was poisoning his blood stream and hurting him. Francis accepted the news quietly and asked Sheila to tell Giles. The doctors thought he might carry on for two years or so if he was careful. The iron determination to live adventurously to the end never flickered. He kept the first lines of his new book unaltered: 'I love life; this great, exciting, absorbing, puzzling, adventurous life.'

By November he had finished the book, putting more of himself into it than into any other. In his mind he was tranquil. The records he had broken were falling into their proper perspective – they represented a game he had had to play in order to satisfy himself. He had risked his life over and over again, and deliberately faced fear in order to achieve these records, and yet in themselves, what did they mean – just a list of things no other man had done?

Was it fame he had sought? Certainly fame and fortune had once sounded magical words. The resolve to endure and to conquer and to win had hardened in him when quite a child – and it had tightened during the failures of his courting days and turned into emotional resolution quite out of the ordinary when he was smashed up in his plane. Because then he had known real terror, terror of falling and of physical hurt, and of castration – that deep terror lying in the subconscious of all men. He had taken a very long time to recover from the crash. Its memory never quite left him. Boats might sink but at least they did not explode!

He had mellowed. The years with Sheila had untangled his prides. All the fame he had yearned for in youth had come his way. No English boy could hanker for more romantic honour than to be knighted by the Queen of England with the sword which had touched Drake's shoulder.

That last winter was eventful, if poignant. Mariners kept dropping in to St James's Place with their tales of adventure woeful or joyful, and those besotted by ocean racing hammered out new ideas in the William and Mary drawing-room, that room selected for its proportions long ago in an empty bombed-to-blazes city. Sheila's paintings hung on the walls, her vegetarian dinners appeared from the kitchen; there would be laughter and the pop of corks. Francis, with his fleeting whimsical smile, now could be a springboard for others. He had that blessed capacity of making people feel their red lights were about to turn green. And Giles, his son and companion, could roister off with young friends and roister back again. How different it was to his own youth in that Rectory.

After Christmas at home, they were to go to Vence to tell Dr Mattei of the diagnosis. 'I feel I must live on so as not to let Jean Mattei down,' said Francis.

Just before departing for the south of France, Francis had agreed to give an important lecture to the Royal Geographical Society. He went to Reading for a blood transfusion first. By now he accepted such medical boosts in the casual manner in which others might freshen themselves up with a Turkish bath. His diary reads: '29 December: Blood transfusion of 9 hours at Reading Hospital.' '30 December: Left Hospital 10 a.m. Lunch with Larry Kirwin and Co. Then R.G.S. boys.   Standing and talking for about 2 hours. Seemed quite O.K.'

On the following day he travelled with Sheila to Vence. Francis was strong enough to go out for a daily walk in the mountains, but his steps were heavy on the stairs afterwards. Sheila had never heard them heavy like that. It was sad to have to tell Dr Mattei that cancer was in him, and after a few days the blood transfusion caused a bad reaction. He terrified Sheila by saying, 'I believe the blood of some evil person has entered my veins.' At least she knew the power of prayer. They had only been a week at Vence when he woke in the middle of the night in terrible pain. The hotelier, a hefty retired boxer devoted to Francis, came in to see if he could help and his wife upset Sheila, while at the same time making her laugh. 'My husband used to get a pain like this and he would take up the chef's knife shouting, "I am going to cut myself open and take the pain out!" ' Mine host volunteered to act as a night nurse if they stayed on, but at this stage Sheila felt it was imperative to get back home. Francis rallied for the journey, and to her indignation announced that he

223

intended getting off the plane in Paris to discuss translations with his French publisher. 'You will get on that plane and stay on that plane,' expostulated his wife.

Although by now very ill, he still remained interested in the adventures of others. This was one of the aspects of his strange, generous, demanding character. When Bill King, who had sailed his five-ton *Galway Blazer II* to Australia, was holed and nearly sunk by the attack of a Pacific killer whale, Francis, who understood the impetus which drives lone sailors and also (perhaps surprisingly) the strain imposed on a waiting wife, wrote cunningly to the author: 'Let us devise some new project for Bill and take his mind off the Horn. Could we not bring him back for the Transatlantic Race next summer? It will be the race of the century.'

Francis thought, perhaps rightly, that this race which he had won when it seemed a novel and amazing venture with only five contestants in their own small boats, would eventually grow so important that it might defeat its original object by becoming an expensive international competition between designers and builders. While he could reckon on a few more months of life he was quite determined to sail in it himself, and again test *Gipsy Moth V*'s speed. He thought that he had never quite succeeded in getting the best out of her.

So when spring came he was off to the Beaulieu River, thinking out alterations which could make his boat, not so much faster, as easier to handle in stormy conditions. Due to her length and her light displacement, she was already *too* fast when sailing under bare poles in high seas.

By April Sheila was back at her old job of making lists, selecting, labelling and packing stores. It was a very important chore. The honey and dried fruits as well as fresh cress grown at sea could tempt an appetite failing through fatigue. Francis still liked to tease her and a letter of this period ends: '. . . I shall soon be as bad at getting out of the dinghy as you are!'

Giles, with a rowing friend, David Pierce, remained on board helping to pack, label and stow food for two Atlantic crossings. Francis's leg was swelling badly and his bones were growing tender. He had to visit Reading Hospital fairly often for blood transfusions and during the enforced few days' rest he could philosophise. From the hospital on 17 May he wrote to George Greenfield:

You were quite right – I must be happy with my little private challenge to make the voyage and forget my speed craze. Conrad [his surgeon] said this morning, 'If I said this voyage might kill you, would you still go?' I fancy he put it more strongly. You will guess my reply. I have been happy the past ten days afloat. One ruins life by taking it too seriously . . . By the way, I have been engrossed in *A Winter's Tale* this week; I reckon it is the true Will Shakespeare and he helps one to understand one's own life.

Despite Lord Thomson's insistence that his paper would not tempt Francis into going to sea again, the *Sunday Times had* asked him to report to them exclusively and Francis *had* agreed – provided that John Anderson could be his radio link. After John paid him a visit to discuss the contract, Francis wrote the following note:

I was so glad to meet you yesterday, but worried by your worries such as *Sunday Times* etc. We make an odd pair. I think because our worries are so different. I know I could go mad trying to fathom the depths of your thoughts and feelings – I say this because you must wonder at times why I only think and talk of myself when with you. My mental state is so simple by comparison, easy to understand, unworrying – I am writing as I listen to the first birdsong of dawn, because I forgot to bring up anything easy to read.

Worldly delights he never scorned. He insisted on taking Sheila out to dinner for her birthday, and he felt much honoured at being asked to become Commodore of the Royal Western Yacht Club – the first commodore since Winston Churchill.

There could only be time for minimum sailing trials, but *Gipsy Moth V* was ready to leave the Beaulieu River in early June. Francis thought of hurrying back to Reading for a last-minute transfusion, but Sheila begged him not to risk another bad reaction. Actually he seemed to be working with his former zest, but they could see how much it hurt to knock himself, and he seemed reluctant to say that he would definitely sail in the race.

Nevertheless, he tremendously enjoyed a few short sails in the Solent with his family crewing, and some of the old magic of preparation time returned.

On 1 June, Francis wrote to Gordon Latto:

Aboard *Gipsy Moth*
Bucklers Hard.

My dear Gordon. I have written to Conrad to say I would like, if he agrees, to forgo a visit to Reading on 11 June. The reason is that I have been seriously ill again after the last transfusion. A similar attack to the one I had in France after the transfusion at the end of December, except that it was not so severe and lasted only one week instead of two. However I was crippled and lay in my bunk avoiding the slightest movement possible for two days. This started four days after the transfusion and if it happened again in June it would coincide with my setting off from

Plymouth at sea and be most troublesome. Also, I have a week of boat handling and am very short of time. I shall be here till 8 June when I sail to Plymouth (D.V.). With very best wishes.

Francis

It was in good heart that he eventually set sail for Plymouth with Giles and Frank Tredery and Pat Russell – a keen young crew. Sheila watched the boat slip down the Beaulieu River, out into the Solent, and away westward past the Needles. Then she returned to London to deal with the pressures of publicity which were building up around the race.

On reaching Plymouth, Francis, being Commodore of the Royal Western Yacht Club, naturally had to take the chair at the big pre-race dinner. He was quite determined to fulfil his role in style, although every now and again he felt himself unable to stand.

For Sheila the turmoil of these last weeks had a dream-like quality. She found herself acting the part of an efficient wife while secretly her spirit quailed for Francis's sake. She was certain it would do him good – just to set out on the ocean again – having a try. But sometimes the violence of her own feelings choked her, knowing what she did about his increasing suffering.

When, as Commodore, he rose to his feet at the Yacht Club dinner to make his carefully prepared speech, she could hardly bear to keep her eyes on him. He was wearing a very smart new suit and spoke beautifully. The brave show cut her to the quick.

It cut several of his friends too, although they could not know what Sheila knew. At the briefing, before the race, Francis asked Michael Richey to sit next to him. Mike was sailing in *Jester*, the famous little junk-rigged boat in which 'Blondie' Hasler had crossed the Atlantic in the first race. Francis spoke to Mike about the handicapping (which he disliked), and also about the difficulty he was having in standing up. He was just foiling death.

Mike never saw him again. He writes: 'We both knew, I think, that there were sounder reasons than our difference in waterline length for not meeting in Newport. I for one was glad he was sailing out!'

The fourth Transatlantic Race started on 17 June 1972. Sheila and Giles sailed with Francis to the starting line and Giles hoisted the sails. Then, in his old manner Francis chivvied them away. 'Off you scuttle, you two – let me get on with it.' They scrambled into Mashford's launch and *Gipsy Moth V* in her rare beauty sailed away with the fleet of contenders. Sheila sat silently, while the sails disappeared into the Atlantic. People were all around her – talking, cheering, comforting. For a moment she wondered if she would crack, then she knew she wouldn't. He was doing what he wished and he was still capable of doing it magnificently. What was the alternative with a man like Francis? No – the sea and the sky were his medicine. Nothing else could do him any good at all.

31. The Last Race

These were the newspaper headlines of the week.

THE LONGEST, LONELIEST RACE
'TRANSATLANTIC SINGLE-HANDED'
'52 STARTERS IN 3000-MILE BATTLE'

Previous winners were 1960 – Francis Chichester – *Gipsy Moth III* – in 40 days; 1964 – Eric Tabarly – *Penduick II* – in 27 days; 1968 – Geoffrey Williams – *Sir Thomas Lipton* – in 26 days.

This year the favourite was the £115 000 French boat *Vendredi 13*, a 128-foot schooner with electric gadgets which made it just possible for a lone sailor to handle her. The form had certainly changed in twelve years. 'Blondie' Hasler thought wistfully of the struggle he had undergone to launch that first race when he and Francis and three others had scraped their pennies together to sail off in their own boats costing hundreds rather than thousands.

Francis, on whom the public were betting twelve to one, had signed an agreement, as he said he would, to report to the *Sunday Times* by radio and had insisted that John Anderson should be his link. At the very start of the race he suffered two nasty moments; one when he nearly collided with the French yacht *Wild Rocket*, and then when he took a chance on clearing Rame Head, the first headland west of Plymouth, without making an extra southward tack. He realized late that he was not going to make it, and had finally to gybe, catching a headsail around a stay. In his log he wrote: '. . . the mussels on those rocks must be frightened still!'

By the second day of the race unseasonable gales and bad visibility began to sort out the contestants. Two boats returned to Plymouth for repairs. Francis discovered that the violent tossing was more agonizing than he had expected. On the night of 19 June he wrote in his log: 'I only want to lie on my back sleeping or dozing without pain. So *Gipsy Moth* trundles along at 3 knots west or south-west.' Next day he tried to send a message on his radio. He had planned to take the southern route and although he liked to keep his course and positions secret, he was anxious to get through to John Anderson at the scheduled times. But although he could hear clearly he found the set dead for transmitting purposes. This is a very frequent occurrence with old sets at sea; it had happened to him before, indeed it is an experience known to most sailors. However well radio sets behave during tests in harbour, they are prone to pack up on the ocean and even skilled electrical mechanics cannot always induce an outgoing whisper. Francis was in no mood to spend hours tinkering. He felt rotten, but hoped to improve in the sea air. In his log he wrote:

June 20: Did more today. A.M. tried all visible fuses on Kestrel and found 2 power unit ones blown . . . P.M. studied all manuals and instructions but could get no help from them. Succeeded in clearing mizzen topping lift fouled around top insulator of backstay in spite of Syd [Mashford]'s attempts to prevent it happening. G.M. has only done 200 miles in a straight line from Plymouth and I am sorry for letting down my backers. I felt a little better today and may pick up health and strength to move faster in a few days' time.

On 21 June he logged:

6 a.m. forecast gales and 10 a.m. yes it was – hurrah, and when I hoisted the mizzen stays'l, it was not very difficult either . . . I hope tomorrow I shall feel up to tackling a jib . . . No 1 or No 2? As I have no chance in the race now I think I must aim for health, getting which points to No 2.

In other words he had determined to take things easy and keep to the smaller jib – No 2. His optimism did not last and the impossibility of getting any radio reports through to John Anderson worried him greatly.

While Frank Tredery, editor of *Blackwood's Magazine*, wrote to Sheila, 'He would not wish it but he dominates the race', Francis was scribbling:

I did get the receiver to work whether due to clearing the fouled aerial or finding the dead fuses, I don't know, but the transmitter remains useless . . . Perhaps if I niggle away I will be able to find the fault. I could hear Portishead calling me at intervals . . . A lovely night with moon shining on the sea and nice breeze.

While *Gipsy Moth* sped swiftly along he could still love life, but the touch of any hard edge hurt. On 22 June he wrote:

Gordon Latto was right saying I must lie down 10 min. every hour. I carry a cockpit half-mattress and it saves me from pressing bones against sharp edges and corners.

On 23 June he recorded dolefully:

Tonight 6 days out is transmitting night. I am not even going to try. It is too isolating to hear them calling me. I am sorry for poor John, the frustration must be rage-making; but he is so ingenious with his fertile brain etc. I shall be surprised if he does not turn it to some worthwhile advantage somehow. I suspect the fault is in the matching unit. A great plan not to change that No 2 jib for anything bigger . . . If I were a keen yachting type I would have that No 1 jib up right now . . . It is time to alter course and then straight across the Atlantic.

The gales which had driven several boats out of the race hurt Francis physically. To be in an Atlantic gale is rather like being knocked about in a boxing ring and every time his limbs hit hard wood he suffered excruciatingly. He could not rest at all.

Alone, out of view, out of radio contact, Francis sailed fast along the southern route he had chosen – but the song in his heart died as the pains grew upon him, increased and broke his hope of crossing the ocean. When, unable to concentrate, such was his torment, he took the strongest of the pain-killers prescribed by his doctor, it put him into a heavy sleep. Then to his consternation he awoke unable to judge how many hours had passed. One night? Two nights – or was it the same dusk? In a state of hallucination, without the sure ability to make accurate checks, the great navigator was beaten at last. Accepting the fact that he would not be able to finish this, his last race, without possibly endangering other craft on nearing America, Francis did the sensible thing. He turned for home. It was an honourable surrender.

If, as he got within closer range, he could raise radio contact, he intended to ask Giles and John Anderson to meet him and help watch-keep in the congested shipping lanes of the Western Approaches. This was a reasonable request that should not cause anxiety. All lone sailors dread the areas of heavy traffic when they cannot sleep and have to keep constant look-out.

Francis had had his try. Because of the jagged agony of striking his bones when it blew hard he couldn't do it. The logical thing was to swallow disappointment and turn back. It was rather bitter after covering 1000 miles, but with the wind behind him he might enjoy the sail.

Meanwhile the Press were getting precious little to write about. *Strongbow* sailed by Major Martin Minter-Kemp had been knocked down and strained the rigging without, however, snapping a mast. The French sailor Yves Olivaux in his little thirty-four-foot sloop *Aloa I* was reported to have broken his arm. All this did not represent enough excitement, so headlines began to stress 'Anxiety' over the continued radio silence of *Vendredi 13* and *Gipsy Moth V*. 'Fears for Sir Francis after Radio Silence'; 'Growing Concern over Chichester'; 'Sir Francis – is he in trouble?'

When nothing much was happening the name Chichester always made the public perk up. Giles, caught by journalists in St James's Street, merely said, 'My father looks on the sea as a kind of health cure. He believes he's fitter there than anywhere else . . . I am certain the reason for his silence is the radio. He has a Mark II Marconi which is not exactly new and it went wrong while he was using it on a transatlantic trip eighteen months ago.' Sheila remained quietly with a friend in Jersey. She knew that radio silence should not be taken to indicate 'missing' and hoped no searches would be made.

During all this Francis kept hearing Portishead Radio at the end of the weather forecasts asking him to make contact. And R.A.F. planes on their routine training flights, which now had the interest of trying to spot a specific live object, combed the sea in vain.

As things turned out, it was very unfortunate that on 27 June, after Francis had turned back, a merchant ship S.S. *Barrister* happened to sight *Gipsy Moth* half-way between the Azores and Land's End, and reported her position to Lloyd's. A Director of the Line courteously forwarded the Master's message to Sheila in Jersey.

Sir Francis came up from below when I blew a whistle. On approaching, he waved and proceeded to stern, apparently to retrim gear with no sign of distress. As I circled *Gipsy Moth* no verbal or radio contact was made but he obviously did not require assistance. Yacht looked in excellent condition with fore sail and after sail set and centre one furled heading to course approximately 200 true.

S.S. *Barrister* further reported that *Gipsy Moth* was heading towards America although she seemed lagging curiously far behind in the race.

The yacht was not sailing westwards. She only happened at the time to be making a tack which gave the appearance of so doing. On learning *Gipsy Moth*'s position, Giles thought it very extraordinary his father should have covered so short a distance, even if he had kept to a light rig.

After Francis's position had been revealed, it was easy for R.A.F. training planes to spot him. They immediately noticed that he was not sailing towards America but on a direct course for Plymouth. The contradictory reports gave rise to inch-high headlines: 'WHERE IS HE GOING?'; 'NEW RIDDLE'.

As hardly any radio messages were arriving from the other yachts, and the giant *Vendredi 13* kept complete silence, the Press had to blow up what grist came to their mill.

From now on Francis became the object of wild speculations. Every time he turned on the radio to get the shipping forecast he heard about himself. The fact that he had been seen to carry very little canvas caused the Press to report that *Gipsy Moth* was 'limping along' whereas Francis simply wished, now that he had abandoned the race, to sail as smoothly as possible and save his bones from getting knocked.

On the evening of 28 June a Nimrod jet dipped to 1000 feet enabling the crew to take photographs (in these Francis looked rather well!). The pilot's published statement read: 'We couldn't raise him on the radio so we decided to use lamp signals. We asked: "Are you O.K.?" A few minutes later he came back: "I have been ill." He passed that message twice. We asked Sir Francis if he wanted help. He signalled back: "I am O.K. No rescue!" '

On the following evening another Nimrod found him and flew around signalling in the dusk. In his log Francis noted: 'The trouble with solo yachts is one cannot watch with binoculars and then focus the signal lamp while all the time twisting and turning to follow the plane's circles. Finally I sent: "Wish son and Anderson could meet me in Channel." '

Unable to comprehend why his decision to opt out of the race should cause quite so much anxiety, Francis balanced himself on deck, flashing answers by Aldis lamp. As the swaying masts and cross trees kept blotting out letters, after an hour he closed down with: 'Weak and cold. Want rest', and went below.

Next day several newspapers carried headlines: 'Francis Chichester weak and cold', and Sheila in her Jersey retreat received a bewildering message that *Gipsy Moth* was approaching Brest. This she could not understand. Brest seemed an unlikely port. Her one hope was that no searches would be started. She never guessed the correct word was 'rest'.

And Francis never divined the results that this phrase flashed by

Aldis lamp and intended merely as a request to cease making him stand signalling on deck could have.*

When a French weather-ship *France II* stationed nearby, with a meteorological team on board, heard the Nimrod's radio suggestion that nearby ships might care to investigate *Gipsy Moth*'s situation, she steamed hurriedly to the position given and arrived around noon on Friday, 30 June. This was the last thing that Francis wanted. All yachtsmen fear the approach of big ships at sea. When the *France II* loomed up he hastened to signal: 'No aid needed. Thank you. Go away.'

The import of these words may not have been fully understood, but Francis thought they were, and having headed his yacht in the opposite direction, he went below for a snack and hot drink (he had not eaten for six hours). Fifteen minutes later a hoot brought him scrambling back into the cockpit where to his astonishment he saw the *France II* had chased after him and was only twenty yards away.

Automatically he wondered if there was time to disengage the self-steering gear, but according to sea rules power gives way to sail and in addition *France II* was the overtaking ship. Francis thought he must be safe.

But the weather-ship grew ever nearer. A man on the bridge kept shouting: 'I must know where you are going.' Then Francis realized with horror that the *France II* had changed course and was about to cross his bows. It was now too late to override the self-steering gear and make a corresponding change of course. In the next second the flanges of the big ship's ports were twanging *Gipsy Moth*'s shrouds as if playing a harp.

Francis gasped with dismay as he saw his mizzen mast bend over. Then a black-bearded Frenchman came over in a launch presumably for a chat. 'Do you want a doctor?' 'No, but *Gipsy Moth* does!' shouted Francis, pointing at his rigging. The man could not seem to take in the damage done. He stared and went back to the weather-ship. As if miffed, the *France II* steamed away leaving Francis to glower at his mast which snapped completely when the wind filled

---

* Later on Francis would himself recount the signalling episode.

The fast aeroplanes today are really very difficult to signal to, because they pass so quickly out of visual range. And when you are singlehanded on a yacht it is hard enough to signal to an aircraft anyway, because so many things distract your view from the cockpit. I tried signalling the Nimrod for about an hour and a quarter but I wasn't at all sure how much of my Morse they were receiving. This hour and a quarter of attempted signalling left me pretty exhausted, and I sent a message saying that I felt weak and cold. By this I meant I wanted to stop signalling and I hoped they would understand this and withdraw. I can see that that signal could be interpreted in rather a different way.

his sails. If *only* the radio transmitter worked, he could *beg* people not to rescue him, but there was no stopping them now. He still hoped that Giles and Anderson might get out to meet him in the Western Approaches, but he had underestimated the effects of his Morse communication. Thinking the *Sunday Times* might well procure a boat, he listened in to the BBC news and at 1800 on this Friday, 30 June, he heard that 'an assignment at sea' had been made for him. In his log he wrote that he was 'agog to know what form that would take'.

Meanwhile, on this very afternoon Giles, who had been a rowing man at Oxford, was trying to enjoy Henley Regatta, when he received an urgent request to find a phone box and call the *Sunday Times*. He already knew of his father's desire for aid in the shipping lanes and had been planning to discuss the idea with his mother that night. When, however, he contacted the newspaper it was to learn that H.M.S. *Salisbury*, a frigate returning to Plymouth from exercises, had been detailed to find *Gipsy Moth* and offer assistance if needed. Harold Evans, the editor of the *Sunday Times*, thought that Giles and John Anderson ought to fly out by helicopter to join in the 'rescue'. 'But what if he doesn't want us?' argued Giles. 'He is perfectly capable of sailing when he is sick. Other people might not be. But he is.'

'If he was my father, I'd go,' said Harold Evans. Giles thought 'the old man' might be very angry indeed if he appeared uninvited in the open ocean, but he had to make a snap decision. Emotional feelings made him agree to go against his logical judgement based on previous experience with his father. It was three in the afternoon. Within two hours he had driven to Northolt Airport. In the boot of his car he found old trousers and a pair of seaboots; donning these, but still in his university blazer, without even a toothbrush or razor, he boarded a special *Sunday Times* plane and was off to Culdrose R.A.F. station in Cornwall with John Anderson.

Before dark they were over 200 miles out at sea being winched down from helicopters onto the deck of H.M.S. *Salisbury* where a volunteer crew of three experienced yachtsmen from the aircraft-carrier *Ark Royal* were already eagerly waiting.

As it was fairly rough and sick-making, after discussing the form with the Captain, Giles lay down to rest, while John Anderson tucked in to a good naval dinner. At 3 a.m. the frigate sighted *Gipsy Moth* moving along at five knots. As the minimum speed which H.M.S. *Salisbury* could sustain for any length of time was eight knots, she had to make wide circles until dawn. Commander Robert McQueen treated the little boat with wonderful courtesy. 'We'll wait until the skipper wakes up,' he said. The sun had risen when Francis opened an eye and switched on his radio to hear: 'H.M.S. *Salisbury* has been diverted to stand by Sir Francis Chichester's *Gipsy Moth* and offer assistance.' Puzzled and intrigued, he scrambled on deck. And there she was – standing by a quarter of a mile away! How delicately the Captain manoeuvred around *Gipsy Moth* – from the deck it was easy to see that the little boat had been damaged, her mizzen mast was broken and the sails torn, although she continued to move along under short canvas. Commander McQueen brought his ship up carefully on the leeward side and used a loud hailer: 'Good morning, Sir Francis. Can we send a launch across to see how you are?'

'Yes, do,' replied the skipper, grateful at such display of considerate seamanship. So Giles pulled on John Anderson's spare oilskin trousers and went over in a rubber dinghy to explain things to 'the old man'. The volunteer crew of experienced yachtsmen, Commander Peter Martin, Chief Petty Officer Wiggy Bennett and Petty Officer Bob Nunn, followed. Francis liked them. He was certain that, even with a damaged mast and rigging he could have reached Plymouth alone but he said, 'I am very happy to have you aboard,' and he meant it.

Commander Martin went up the mainmast, a tricky assignment in that choppy sea, and cut through the triatic stay from which the broken-off top of the mizzen was now dangling. Anxious moments were suffered by all as the triatic was cut away for fear the released mast-end would fall and skewer the deck. Then to help her sailing and prevent the mainmast from breaking without the support of a backstay they rigged up two jury backstays using spare halliards fastened to cleats on the counter and winched up on the mainmast. It was quite a job.

By midday H.M.S. *Salisbury* had vanished towards England, and with a third sail up to relieve the strain on her mainmast *Gipsy Moth* was heading in a fair wind for Plymouth. Francis, delighted at having an efficient crew for the last 250 miles, retired to his bunk. 'So glad you're not cross I came out,' said Giles, 'I really couldn't help it – events swept me along – but of course it *is* fun being winched down from a helicopter onto the deck of a frigate . . . quite a new experience!' So there *was* a little fun intermingled in this sad story, and unusual diversion for the Navy and R.A.F. who had the interest of finding a *live* target to brighten up their practice exercises.

Gipsy Moth sailed all that day and night and all the next day with a following wind. The naval crew, salts of the old tradition, had never seen self-steering before and were absolutely fascinated. With so many able hands and a following wind, the boat fairly scudded along and she was able to sneak into Plymouth harbour on the Sunday night. No one expected her to arrive so soon and not a soul noticed the famous *Gipsy Moth* quietly picking up a mooring outside Mashford's yard. After a merry supper – Francis always felt in form when in congenial company – they all lay down for a good night's sleep. Commander Martin had agreed to go ashore next day to ask the Admiral for permission for Francis to enter the naval hospital where he had been so contented after his round-the-world voyage.

It was quite late in the morning when the pressmen realized that the boat sitting outside Mashford's actually was *Gipsy Moth*! They gathered in force. Chichester *must* produce drama – the least he could do was to be carried ashore on a stretcher.

Giles gave them a few words, but when Commander Martin returned with permission for hospitalization, Francis climbed unaided into the launch, and the one photographer who risked breaking his neck to reach the likely landing place only got a picture of him *walking* ashore!

Giles saw his father into hospital and a bulletin was issued that he had gone there for 'rest and observation'. This hardly satisfied public curiosity, but although Francis was always ready to give interviews about sailing adventures, he felt his actual skin and bones to be a private matter – the pain of cancer when limbs are knocked about was a subject he did not wish to discuss.

As Sheila arrived Giles departed for London. Not until he reached St James's Place did he remember he'd left his car at Northolt Airport.

Francis settled down tranquilly in the naval hospital, confident that he would get well because he was among people he liked. A few friends visited him. Among them Sir Peter Bristow came to joke about R.A.F. days and he recorded: 'Although he looked desperately ill, all the old fire was there.' The incredible drama was yet to break.

Francis was keeping himself occupied jotting down 'afterthoughts' to help John Anderson compose the most interesting article possible for the *Sunday Times*, who had reaped nothing whatever for their 'exclusive rights' to Chichester's radio reports, when he heard that a Socialist M.P. was asking questions in Parliament concerning the 'cost to the public of the recent air-sea rescue of Sir Francis Chichester'. He had never wanted to be rescued, he had never asked to be rescued, and only his faulty radio had prevented him announcing the fact that (like several other yachts) he was pulling out of the race, and indeed begging *not* to be rescued if such a suggestion was made.

An unfortunate sequence of events had occurred. If the S.S. *Barrister* had never sighted *Gipsy Moth* he would have continued to sail home unobserved. The R.A.F. planes (naturally glad to enliven their regular routine training sorties by searching for a *live* target) would not have obtained his position, and Francis would not have flashed words which had an impact he did not desire. The weather-ship would not have reached him to cause damage. And instead of H.M.S. *Salisbury* being detailed to offer assistance (which had indeed proved extremely welcome after the encounter with the *France II*), *Gipsy Moth*, rigging intact, would have reached the Western Approaches quietly where Giles and John Anderson might have boarded the boat to help for the last lap.

To be accused of costing the nation money because H.M.S. *Salisbury* had found him and sent over a keen volunteer crew of three simply did not make sense. The service aircraft, ships and men had to be kept in trim by constant exercise – why had it cost anything for a naval ship to find him on its way back to Plymouth? Maybe the crew reached port a few hours late – but *they* were not the ones who complained. Certainly the *Sunday Times* would be glad to pay for the fuel of the helicopter which landed Giles and their reporter on board the frigate – that *had* been their idea – 'But I didn't need to be rescued – I didn't ask to be rescued,' Francis reiterated. 'Of course I enjoyed the company and efficiency of those fellows when the rigging was in the hell of a mess but damaged as she was I could have got *Gipsy Moth* home.'

Francis had hardly organized his 'Notes' on the race for John Anderson when a worse, more bewildering, blow fell.

Some twelve hours after leaving *Gipsy Moth V*, the weather-ship *France II* had, soon after midnight, run down and sunk an American yacht, the *Lefteria*.* Of the eleven people aboard, seven were drowned. The four survivors were taken to La Rochelle by *France II*. It was a particularly tragic accident. The first Press communiqué (issued before any of the survivors had had an opportunity to recover from their ordeal) stated that *both* the *France II* and the *Lefteria* had gone to the aid of *Gipsy Moth V*. This was immediately picked up in articles in a number of newspapers, which made out that Francis was responsible for the drowning of seven people. One of the surviving owners of the *Lefteria* later sent a full account to Sheila insisting that his yacht had *not* gone to the aid of *Gipsy Moth*, that the crew had in fact no knowledge of her.

---

* See Appendix, page 243, for a full account of the affair.

The clamour which had arisen continued to prey on Francis's mind. He wrote to George Greenfield:

19.7.72

My dear George – I was most disappointed after John Anderson's visit. I felt pretty ill, could not think or act & I believe that is why the final article was so poor & missed so much stuff which I think was good story matter.

I have had 4 or 5 offensive attacking letters, say 5% of the total fan mail, 2 are probably from a madman, but one today is a special case. It is unsigned but typewritten & noted as being a copy of a letter to the *Observer*. It abuses me thoroughly. I must get a copy sent you, I think. 'Done harm to sailing', 'arrogance', 'loss of life'. He can only hope in the fullness of time I may apologise to the Master of *France II* (For not sinking me outright perhaps!!) . . .

On 3 August Francis published a long letter to *The Times* headed *What Happened on Gipsy Moth*:

Sir, I have been severely criticised for entering the 1972 single-handed race against medical advice, so perhaps the time has come for me to say frankly what has been wrong.

After returning from my round-the-world trip in 1967 an illness developed and in due course it was discovered that I had a malignant growth near the base of my spine. The tumour spread to involve my spine and later other bones. With the help of appropriate treatment I have been fighting this trouble, especially since 1970, and on the whole it has been a successful fight, because it did not prevent me from building a new yacht and improving the single-handed long distance world speed record which I had held since 1967.

Unfortunately it presented two particular problems. It made me become anaemic because the bones which were involved with the tumour could no longer do their normal job of making blood; and secondly, as the bones were increasingly affected it became increasingly painful.

The first could be put right – and was – by blood transfusions, but it was the increasing pain due to my hitting my bones against the side of the bunk when the yacht rolled in the recent race which stopped my latest voyage. I had been given pain-killers to use as necessary and I had to take them at times in order to get some sleep. In spite of their help, continued buffeting during the first part of the race made the pain more and more intense and I feared if I did not get some sleep I would be unable to go on. So I gave myself an injection of one of the emergency pain-killers. It certainly stopped the pain but I soon realised that, under its influence, my mind was no longer functioning normally. I could not think clearly and in particular could not rely on my calculations. There was a danger that my navigation would become inaccurate, and I was heading towards the Azores, a difficult area for currents and variable winds.

It was then that I decided to give up, not because of hazard to myself, but because of the risks to others if I passed out, which seemed probable, so I put about and headed for home. I did not want any help then and I certainly did not ask for any.

Even after *France II* had hit me and damaged *Gipsy Moth V*, I regained control and continued on my way home, and was confident of reaching Plymouth provided the broken mizzen did not carry away and drop through the deck and hull, or cause other damage such as to myself. Although I shall always be grateful for the kindness and skill of the help I received from the Royal Navy in removing the damaged mizzen mast and sailing back, especially as I was so weak and tired, I still believe I would have made it alone.

My treatment has continued in hospital, and although there has been some improvement, it has been very slow. Doctors insist that I must have a long period of complete physical and mental rest, and that there could be no question of even contemplating another single-handed race for at least a year, otherwise it is likely to end in a spinnaker run across the Styx from which there is no return.

Yours sincerely – Francis Chichester

At the Royal Naval Hospital, Plymouth.

On 4 August Francis left the Royal Naval Hospital to spend a week at the Meudon Hotel in Cornwall. The proprietor, Harry Pilgrim, had offered the Chichesters a free week in the best suite and Francis relished such treats like a schoolboy. He got through the eighty-mile drive quite well and was soon walking rather gingerly around the lawns and eyeing the sea longingly. 'I think a swim might do me good . . .' Francis could be a very naughty patient – but who could blame him when the enemy was pain?

The only interview he gave at this time was to his old friend Christopher Brasher – Chris, a sportsman who had known the *effort* of Olympic competition, and of climbing in the Himalayas, remained, with John Anderson, his link with the media. Since the distant excitements of the first Transatlantic Race when Chris had been Sheila's New York companion-in-waiting, Francis had always liked talking to him. It was natural that Chris Brasher should understand that Francis had been using this ocean race to foil death. It was a pity the game had hurt quite so much. On this occasion Chris felt a sadness he tried not to show. The cameramen had been told that shooting time must not exceed ten minutes and the team determined they would not be tiring, but Francis had other views. No, he didn't want to drive in their motor to the sea, he preferred to walk. Yes, he could perfectly explain why he had sailed in the race. He thought it would do him good. Life should be adventure to the end. Of course he knew he was ill, 'after all you *do* have to die somewhere. I'd as soon die at sea'. Giles might have put a word in here. Knowing how much his father cared for beautiful *Gipsy Moth V* he did not believe that he would willingly let himself die on board and allow her to sail on into unknown dangers.

The camera team were astonished by his gaiety. Francis was not even averse to discussing his meeting with *France II* – he joked about the harp-like twanging noises made as the ship's flanges swept through his rigging – a comic episode if not so destructive. The television team were amazed by his resilience and humour. He tried to hand them out a shred of what he'd learnt during long experience. 'Train your will to concentrate on a limited objective. When young you spread your effort over too many things.' 'Life is dull without a challenge, but don't just go pot hunting,' he said. 'If your try fails what does that matter – all life is a failure in the end. The thing is to get sport out of trying.'

32. The End

Francis did not think he was dying. He was used to ups and downs and although he never again wished to endure the pain of being thrown about at sea, he reckoned that for a couple of years he might give Sheila the kind of cruising she had always longed for – the Greek islands – or even the South Seas? 'No, let's settle for Greece,' she murmured.

On 22 August he was not so well and returned to hospital by ambulance. Sister Anne, whom he respected and obeyed, took charge. If nursing could get him well hers would. She had the extra touch. Sheila packed up their belongings in the hotel and followed quietly. A friend put her up near Plymouth. When Sheila telephoned that Francis was weakening Giles arrived and stayed nearby. For the first time he was stricken by the bitter realization that courage cannot sustain the human frame indefinitely. And he was immensely close to his father.

There would be no Greek islands, no South Seas. On 26 August 1972 Francis died quietly. His wife and son were at his side. They wanted to stay with him alone for a bit trying to accept it, trying to banish sorrow. Francis Chichester was cast in the heroic not in the tragic mould. He had fought to the end. Drums not tears should mark his passing.

But tears happen. They dreaded having to open the door which would lead them back into public view. So much to be arranged. Francis would be buried in Shirwell churchyard, but he could not have a private funeral. Thousands of people wanted to pay their tribute. It was glorious sunny weather just like the famous day on which he had sailed in from Australia. Telegrams and telephone calls never ceased. Obituaries blazed blackly in every paper. At the funeral service at St Andrew's Church in Plymouth, the coffin was carried by his son and flag officers of the Royal Western Yacht Club. The church was packed and hundreds of people lined the streets outside just as they had done when he went there in the hour of triumph.

After this Plymouth service the cortège drove through the sunlit countryside of his youth to that little old church where he had been christened, where he had suffered the long sermons of his father, and where both his parents lay under the grass. The Devon folk had turned out *en masse*. Sheila noticed two small boys standing to attention on a bank. They saluted like soldiers as the cortège passed. Francis would have loved that. Among the villagers were some who, looking up at the white Rectory on the hill, remembered the eager face of young Chichester running out to find refuge in the woods.

After the words of committal a joyous peal of bells rang forth – not with slow dolefulness, but in triumphant thanksgiving. Sustained by an absolute sense of continuity Sheila stood in the golden evening light. So much was over for her – the toughness, the tantrums, the tenderness.

After this long day of music and sunshine she and Giles must return to London. It would be strange to enter St James's Place without him. A memorial service at Westminster Abbey was to be organized. Edward Heath, Prime Minister, would honour Francis, giving the address and speaking from the heart of this Englishman's achievements.

The trappings of success had been laid on that thin frame with exceptional glitter. A shy schoolboy would have enjoyed looking forward into the kaleidoscope of his life. But trappings must not be confused with the bone of the matter. What counted were the inner battles and the resolution. The story of Francis Chichester will last because every man who reads it will find that he is touching facets of himself.

Appendix

The Tragedy of the *Lefteria* (see page 237)

The *Lefteria* was a converted Baltic schooner eighty years old, which had been bought by two Americans, Peter Gallagher and Philip Bates, both graduates of Kings Point University, New York, which specialized in merchant marine training. These young men had, with their friends, spent over a year refitting the boat in Denmark. They were sailing her to the Caribbean with the intention of running a charter business. The crew was American except for two Swedes and a Canadian. Mrs Gallagher and Mrs Bates were the only women aboard. Both were drowned when the yacht was cut in two, so were three young American men, the Canadian and one of the Swedes.

When the weather-ship, *France II*, arrived at La Rochelle with the four men who had been picked out of the water, these survivors were naturally in a state of extreme shock, especially Bates and Gallagher who had lost their wives. None of them was up to speaking to the Press. An Associated Press statement dated 3 July read:

An official enquiry was opened today into the collision between the French weather-observation ship *France II* and the Danish yacht *Lefteria* . . . Both ships had gone to the aid of Sir Francis Chichester, the British yachtsman entered in the solo transatlantic race who had been reported ill.

A number of newspapers immediately picked up the Associated Press statement and some vitriolic articles were published accusing Francis of going to sea unfit, rudely refusing assistance, endangering people's lives and finally of being responsible for the drowning of seven people. The articles made it appear that both the weather-ship and the *Lefteria* were hurrying to save him after he had sent out a cry for help. This was a terrible indictment and although Francis maintained that he never asked for either ship, he was cut to the quick by the thought that an ordinary yacht – however unwanted – had tried to come to his aid.

At this moment he was rushed into dictating an article for the *Sunday Times* of 8 July in which he lamented the *Lefteria*'s loss of life, and stated what a shock it had been when he learned that the yacht was proceeding to offer him help. This article was published before any clear statement could be made by Philip Bates. When Bates recovered sufficiently to speak it was to insist that the *Lefteria*'s crew knew nothing of *Gipsy Moth*, and it had never entered their heads to deviate from their course to the West Indies. However, by that time the general public had received the impression that lives had somehow been lost because of Francis. Philip Bates's story was as follows. The *Lefteria* had been sailing along in a southerly direction when around 1 a.m. on Saturday 1 July he had seen the lights of a fairly big ship coming up from astern. This ship, which was *France II*, overtook the *Lefteria*'s starboard side on a parallel course. Bates had exchanged signals by Aldis lamp, mainly to check his position, but he was unable to get a satisfactory reply. He watched the weather-ship go by and when it was ahead, and he thought clear, he went below to the chart table. He reckoned he had not been there for more than two minutes when *Lefteria* heeled violently having been struck amidships. Bates climbed into the cockpit and was washed overboard. The yacht sank almost immediately and only four survivors were pulled out of the water.

No person in his senses could have blamed Francis for the *Lefteria*'s sinking, even if she had been sailing in his direction, but the tragedy had preyed on his mind and he naturally felt relief that this cruel story in no way involved *Gipsy Moth*. Had there been *no* survivors he would have continued to suffer the anguish of believing that seven people had been drowned while coming to his aid. As it was, he had already expressed regret in the *Sunday Times*. Even when completely exonerated from all responsibility he remained downcast at the loss of life, and injured in spirit that anyone could publish false statements deliberately calculated to hurt him. Hundreds of letters poured in from French and English sailors of all kinds which assured Francis that he must not fret because he could not consider himself even indirectly responsible for this tragic sinking. But the headlines given to his vindication were much smaller than those containing the acid accusation, and a number of abusive missives reached the hospital.

So painful was the issue of the weather-ship's responsibility that

Sheila took it to 10 Downing Street. The Foreign Office and the American Embassy in Paris strove to ascertain exact facts. Professor Francis Conant, who had been Mrs Philip Bates's professor at college, saw her bereaved husband in Paris. Bates told him that none of them knew anything about *Gipsy Moth* and that they had never thought of turning to her aid. The Professor came over to London to assure Sheila of this. Later he wrote poignantly from the U.S.A. to say that Philip Bates had had to attend seven funerals and 'explain' to seven families. He was fairly shattered. Sheila felt she could not press for more information.

It was a long time before Philip Bates sent a direct account. He again insisted that his yacht had not been searching for *Gipsy Moth*, and continued:

Almost all the accounts that appeared in the newspapers were erroneous and most were written from pure conjecture while all the survivors of *Lefteria* were still aboard *France II* . . . The newspapers recognized *France II* as the weather ship involved with both sail boats and simply assumed that since *France II* had been searching for Sir Francis we must have been doing the same.

By mid-August Giles was able to close the legal file which for the sake of his father's reputation it had been necessary to open. He sent the following letter:

15 August 1972

Le Capitaine de Vaisseau
Chef du Service des Navires

I feel I should make it quite clear that Sir Francis Chichester at no time asked for assistance or rescue. He was in complete control of the *Gipsy Moth V* and could have reached Plymouth without aid had it not been for the damage caused when the *France II* was in collision with his yacht.

While naturally he would have appreciated the kind intention of the Captain and crew of the *France II* had he asked for their assistance, he did not in fact ask for it, and the result of their intervention was most unfortunate in causing unnecessary and expensive damage to *Gipsy Moth V* which could have been very dangerous indeed to Sir Francis.

From Sir Francis' account of the incident there is no doubt in my mind that had the *France II* understood and respected his signals that he required no assistance and let *Gipsy Moth V* go on her way, the big weathership would not have gone too close to the yacht and run into it.

It seems a pity that having come with the good intention of helping, the *France II* should leave *Gipsy Moth V* in a damaged condition without checking the state of the yacht especially after Sir Francis had invited a member of the crew of *France II* to examine the damage. This could hardly be described as giving assistance and if you had been in Sir Francis' position would you have been grateful?

However, notwithstanding the above and many other points I could make also of this incident, in view of Sir Francis Chichester's long standing affection for France and connections with your country we do not wish to proceed further with this matter of claiming for damages.

Yours sincerely,
Giles Chichester.

Two days later he received this acknowledgement.

17 Août 1972

Ministère des Transports

Francis Chichester Ltd

J'ai l'honneur d'accuser réception de votre lettre du 15 courant par laquelle vous me déclarez aimablement votre désistement de réclamer compensation pour l'avarie soufferte par la *Gipsy Moth V* lors de son abordage avec le N.M.S. *France II*.

Je vous prie de croire que le Commandant du N.M.S. France II et moi-même avons été désolés de cet incident, le Commandant du N.M.S. *France II* ayant fait tout ce qu'il croyait nécessaire pour aider Sir Francis . . .*

---

* 'I have the honour of acknowledging your letter of the 15th instant in which you kindly state that you will refrain from claiming compensation for the damage suffered by *Gipsy Moth V* in the collision with N.M.S. *France II*.

I beg of you to believe that the Commander of N.M.S. *France II* and myself remain desolate at this incident, the Commander having done all he believed necessary to help Sir Francis . . .'

Index

247